3⁰⁰

IMAGES OF WOMAN
ADVERTISING IN WOMEN'S MAGAZINES

Images of Woman

ADVERTISING
IN WOMEN'S MAGAZINES

by

TREVOR MILLUM

1975

CHATTO & WINDUS

LONDON

Published by
Chatto & Windus Ltd
42 William IV Street
London WC2

*

Clarke, Irwin & Co Ltd
Toronto

ISBN 0 7011 2010 X

© Trevor Millum 1975

Printed in Great Britain by
Cox and Wyman Ltd
London, Fakenham and Reading

To
GEORGE CHARLES MILLUM

Contents

Advertisements Reproduced

Colour Plates

Monochrome Plates

between pages 80–81

Foreword

To write about the role of advertising and the role of women is to deal with two areas of continuing controversy. This book considers and connects the two. It is, foremost, a detailed and systematic survey of advertisements. Within the field of advertising the study is narrowed to printed display advertisements, with women's magazines as the central area of research. The focus of the work rests on the visual aspects of the advertisements. It is an attempt to analyse and understand one area of visual communication.

The existing studies of advertising are considered and, largely, rejected. Work on visual communication is also considered, and the most useful approaches are discussed and used as one of the bases for developing a system of analysis applicable to pictures rather than words. The method of classification which is developed is specially suited to advertisements in women's magazines, but should be applicable to the study of most magazine and newspaper advertisements–and useful as a guide in the study of other types of illustrations.

The method of analysis, having been defined, is then applied to a large sample of advertisements. This, and the conclusions and suggestions which follow, comprise the major section of the book.

The sample is taken from magazines during 1969. Changes which have taken place since then seem rather fewer than I would have expected. The magazines under consideration are largely unchanged, and–more important–the advertisements are also much the same. The growing voice of women's liberation seems to have had no effect on the advertisements and very little on the magazines, especially those of the *Woman–Woman's Own* type. Changes in style and presentation have been extremely few, and the content is very familiar. Poses, expressions, relationships, props . . . all recur in much the same way as they did five years ago.

From the vantage point of 1974 it now appears that the period covered by the study (and especially the year from which the sample was taken) was quite a crucial time. It was a time when advertisements were beginning to move in new directions–both in content, and–more markedly–in form. The advertisements of 1969 seem more sophisticated, more 'streamlined', more adventurous in technique than the advertisements of two or three years before. Much of the visual content was

10   IMAGES OF WOMAN

more adventurous, also. The pace of change has not, however, been maintained. It may be, although it is too early to be sure, that the last years of the 1960s was one of the times when visual communication in advertising (and elsewhere) changed gear. A lot more work on advertising before that time, and since, would have to be carried out before this hypothesis could be substantiated and developed. Advertising, perhaps, develops or changes in more or less sudden leaps and bounds, rather than evolving gradually or continuously. This may be true of other media–or indeed of media in general.

This book is based on work carried out at the Centre for Contemporary Cultural Studies, Birmingham University. I want to thank everyone at the Centre for their help and interest, and Dorothy Wright who undertook the typing. Many people have given their time and thought generously–of no one is this more true than Stuart Hall to whom I am especially grateful.

Nchelenge, February 1974

Trevor Millum

Introduction

This work is a study of contemporary advertising, in particular advertising in women's magazines. One of its purposes is to understand the nature of the advertisement as cultural artefact, and to examine how advertising contains cultural meanings above and beyond the sales message. Another equally important purpose is to contribute to the development of methods of analysis in the general area of cultural studies. The task is made more complex by the concentration in this study on visual rather than verbal communication, a mode of communication long recognized as crucial by advertisers yet one largely neglected by those who take upon themselves the critical study of the mass media. The nature of this work is therefore exploratory.

Advertising is a form of social communication. Its manifest purpose is to sell consumer goods to the public. Little advertising–especially of the display kind–is concerned exclusively with the product: display advertisements set the product in a physical and social space, in an environment, and associate with it both actors and actions. In other words, advertisements construct a 'social world' around the product and this is the latent function of the visual and verbal languages of advertisements, which transfer a manifest message in this social meaning. The appeal to the consumer is indirect–mediated through the social connotations. Advertising discourse is social communication in that it draws on an existing stock of images and knowledge and speaks to the consumer about the product by way of social messages which will be readily understood. Thus advertising expresses a wider social and cultural world than can be accounted for in terms of specific messages about specific products.

It, therefore, becomes feasible to study the social meanings in and for themselves. Theoretically, advertisements could make use of any available social meaning, but in practice, this does not happen. Certain meanings tend to recur–certain settings, items, action, actors and so on, appear at any one time to be more powerful carriers of meaning for the purposes of the advertisers than others. The advertisements can then be seen to reflect–selectively–and to mediate and reinforce certain *preferred* meanings taken from the overall cultural knowledge-to-hand. These clusters or patterns of meaning are the heart of the study.

In its execution the emergence of patterns through repetition is of the greatest importance for it provides a more objective and substantial foundation upon which to build our inferences and hypotheses than has hitherto been available. Too much attention has been paid to special cases – at least in advertising – as if meanings of global significance could be read from one illustration. One could easily pick out special advertisements, ones that were felt to be 'significant' – but it is, at least for our purpose, the everyday ones, those that make up the bulk of the advertising published every month, that matter in terms of cultural significance. Lasting impressions are made, and deeply engrained patterns and meanings are carried, by the entire range of communication acting cumulatively and reciprocally, not by half a dozen special cases, or the Creative Circle's choice.

Clearly, one would like to be able to reach one's conclusions by consulting a sample of women about magazine advertising, but the theoretical and practical difficulties are immense. Does one ask about advertisements, about response, or about roles, about life? Or does one hope to derive this sort of information from other, more general questions and conversation? What would be the status of such information – would not that information itself now have to be analysed and indeed interpreted? How is one to discover the cumulative effect of advertising messages which will obviously not be acting on a conscious level, and which will certainly be acting in conjunction with an infinite number of other stimuli?

Bearing these problems in mind, this study restricts itself to the range and the structure of meanings carried by the communication in question. They are likely to be more 'effective' than those meanings which are not present, and should be compared and contrasted with those of other types of advertising and with other sorts of communication directed to the same audience.

The study proceeds by way of a description of the work which has been done on advertising and on visual communication and a discussion of the process of advertising as seen in its social context. Drawing on previous work (pilot studies, etc.) and material from various relevant fields – non-verbal communication and female psychology, for example – a system of classification is developed and then applied to a large sample of advertisements.

The study was carried out in the period 1968–70, the sample being drawn from the year 1969. The findings derive specifically from that year, but have a far wider application both in terms of time and other media.

I

Advertising and Visual Communication

ABOUT ADVERTISING

In 1934 *The Times Literary Supplement* reviewing *The Economics of Advertising* by F. P. Bishop commented: 'That advertising is indispensable, or at least inevitable, in the present organization of industry is a matter of debate. The existing literature on the subject comes for the most part from theoretical economists whose attitude is critical, or enthusiastic advertising men.' The literature on the subject is indeed sharply divided into two opposed and committed camps: literary pundits and liberal academics joining with the 'theoretical economists' on the one side, and businessmen and other economists manning the defences alongside the 'enthusiastic advertising men'. The debate has always been passionate, polemical and acrimonious, and in these circumstances the status of evidence drawn upon by each side is rarely thought about or investigated. Part of the endeavour of this work is to provide a means of learning more deeply about the nature of the medium and understanding the way in which it operates.

Writing, one is clearly not uncommitted and it is as well to declare one's conscious prejudices at an early stage. This study is by its very nature academic, and is written from a standpoint critical of advertising and distrustful of the justifications commonly made for it, but dissatisfied with the level of criticism so far attained. It is realized, however, that advertising is but a single aspect of the culture and a particular way of organizing an advanced industrial economy. In the light of the tendentious nature of the subject it is probably of some use to begin with a survey of the debate so far, to fill out the background to this study and the motivation behind it.

By the 1930s much had already been written about advertising (*Advertising and Psychology* by Scott had been published in 1908!) and criticisms of the business were being expressed vociferously: the debate was perhaps to reach its peak in this decade. This is how A. S. J. Baster in *Advertising Reconsidered* saw the industry in 1935: 'The major part of informative advertising is, and always has been, a campaign of exaggeration, half truths, intended ambiguities, direct lies and general deception ... [Their] chief function is to deceive buyers as to the real merits and demerits of the commodity being sold. Apart from the more obvious results of this from the consumer's point of view, the effect on the character of this constant obligation to deceive others in more and more refined and subtle ways must be far reaching ... Appeals to reason are heavily frowned upon in expert advertising circles as very much out of date, and the modern tendency is to steer clear of the consumer's rational faculty altogether.' *The Times Literary Supplement* when reviewing his work (4 January, 1936) called it 'a total denial of the moral validity of advertising'.

Thompson and Leavis echoed these criticisms in tones of even greater moral outrage and indignation, mixed with substantial sarcasm and ridicule in *Culture and Environment*. They analysed–in a rather flimsy, superficial way–the appeals made by advertisers, and said of advertisements in general: 'All offer satisfaction at the lowest level and inculcate the choosing of the more immediate pleasures, got with the least effort.' They quoted Gilbert Russell's *Advertisement Writing* in support of their views: 'Successful copywriting depends upon insight into people's minds ... Advertising is becoming increasingly exact every day. Where instinct used to be enough, it is being replaced by inquiry. Advertising men nowadays don't say "the public will buy this article from such and such a motive", they employ what is called market research, to find out the buying motives as exactly as time and money and opportunity permit, from the public itself.'

Some of the criticisms seemed to be supported elsewhere, for example an address given to the convention of the Association of Advertising Clubs in 1928 by W. R. Hotchkiss on 'Making advertising appeal to the emotions', and the statement 'Fear is a great salesman' in *Advertising* by Dixon, and also by some of the advertisements:

'a mere scratch ... a tiny trace of dirt ... a festering wound ... THE DREAD OF AMPUTATION ... why risk it?', or
'a mere midge bite ... a trace of unseen dirt ... burning pain ... blood poisoning ... and then the SURGEON'S KNIFE!', both headlines for 'Family Health, the Safety Soap' advertisements in *Picture Post* for 6 May and 27 July, 1939.

Well-known literary figures also viewed advertising with distaste. It is clear that George Orwell in *Keep the Aspidistra Flying* shared his hero, Gordon Comstock's hatred of advertisers and advertisements with their 'goofy optimism' and J. B. Priestley, later to become a strong critic of the 'admass society' described an advertising agency in *They Walk in the City* as 'A small army of extremely clever and quite unscrupulous persons, trained to lie with enthusiasm'.

In the *Illustrated London News* and *Sphere* in 1938 there were several advertisements for the motion of advertising proclaiming that 'Advertised goods are the goods to buy'. For example, a line drawing of a man smoking a cigar on board a ship with below it the caption: '"That's a good cigar mister!" "So it should be, stoker! I saw it advertised." Men of the world who want the best, wherever they find it, know that advertised goods are invariably the best of their kind: for only reliable products can stand up to intensive publicity. The manufacturer who makes a public claim must be able to prove it. So Advertised Goods are the Goods to Buy.'

Advertising was on the defensive even though the majority of the attacks on it were as distorted and ill-judged as the replies. Neither side thought to substantiate its far-reaching claims and assumptions by reference to any evidence beyond the citing of one or two disreputable advertisements or a few production/price figures.

The debate was continued through the next decade in much the same vein – indeed the character of the controversy has changed little to this day. Denys Thompson's *Voice of Civilization* published in 1943 was an all-out attack on advertising and its effects on society: 'Advertising by constant pressure through a hundred different channels, has succeeded in imprinting its own philosophy of life on our minds, [and has caused] The promotion of acquisition to the status of religion.' The philosophies offered by advertising were 'for society, one of progress in the invention and multiplication of material adjuncts to living; and for the individual, the acquisition of as many as possible of these goods'. *The Times Literary Supplement*, reviewing this book on 30 October, 1943 commented: 'It is true that there are wastes in advertising; that serious objection may be taken to the methods employed by some advertisers; that there is danger of misdirection of demand into undesirable channels; and that advertising can, and sometimes does, set up false ideals and appeal to unworthy motives . . . A more balanced view, while not denying the force in these and other criticisms of much current advertising would recognize that there is another side to the picture.'

F. P. Bishop, returning to the debate in *The Ethics of Advertising*, relied heavily on Thompson's book, but was less dramatic or vitriolic. He claimed that in the interests of business, advertisers concentrated attention on developing those desires which respond most quickly and profitably and: 'which are not likely to be those of most value to society'. He mentions appeals to snobbery, greed, vanity, luxury, envy, false sentiment and false ideas of culture, using Thompson's examples. To him, advertising is partial, selective, incomplete and highly coloured. He quotes John Morse, of the US Department of Commerce as saying: 'If we are to cajole the masses to buy the things we advertise, we must talk the language they understand, step down and mingle with the milling throng . . .' According to Bishop, as long ago as 1911 a writer in *The Times* claimed that: 'The distinguishing mark of modern advertising is that it does not merely direct an existing demand, it creates new wants.'

Robert Brandon's book *The Truth About Advertising* was largely a reply to Thompsonite attacks in the style of most advertising apologies (see, for example, Martyn Davis below) and John Gloag took a traditional free enterprise standpoint in his general account of the business, *Advertising in Modern Life*: 'The amenities, the abundance and the freedom that we enjoy come largely from the enterprise of the industrialists who manufacture goods, the distributors who make them accessible, and the advertising that keeps sales going, shops busy and wheels turning in various ways: "Buy! Buy! Buy!" Nobody need pay any attention. Most people do.'

In general, however, the arguments over advertising seem to have died down between the end of the war and the mid-1950s–in Britain at least–due in part to the restrictions both on newsprint and general spending. In 1956 John McEwan gave 'An advertising practitioner's views on the essential nature of his work,' in his *Advertising as a Service to Society* which began on the defensive, and mentioned the critics of advertising on the first page. In dividing advertising virtually into 'educational' (i.e. informative) and 'reminder', he said: 'Typical educational advertising is that which plays upon the emotions and instincts . . . advertisements can, and do, play upon the emotions with tremendous power.' In this he saw psychology as indispensable. He went on to give a list of emotions which could be exploited most profitably, including vanity, laziness, curiosity, the desire for comfort, the love of money and greed. 'It can, and does, appeal in varying degree to other senses as well. And other instincts too! Here are just a few: sexual instincts, paternal and maternal instincts, fear, envy . . .' He apparently saw nothing reprehensible in this, indeed: 'Before the Second World War, there were many examples of advertisements that were not merely misleading, but used crude and even vulgar methods of appeal . . . [Today] it would surprise me if you found any at all.' McEwan's attempts to provide the effective influence of advertisements did in fact substantiate the arguments of many of advertising's critics, particularly those to do with the cumulative effect – 'Advertising is a phenomenon of continuity. Its effect depends upon the cumulative power of constant and consistent recognition.'

The year 1957 saw the publication in Britain and the United States of Vance Packard's *The Hidden Persuaders* which had a great impact then and has had a lasting influence. It was a triumph of sensational journalism, but if nothing else, revived the controversy which had been quiescent. Perhaps more than any other book it has led the public to distrust advertisers in general and led agencies to view Motivation

Research (as distinct from its predecessor, market research) with strong reservations. *The Times Literary Supplement* of 15 May 1959 said: [the book] 'told us something of the new technique of motivational research which aims to discover the "reasons behind the reasons" why people buy (or do not buy) certain consumer goods.' But as Packard pointed out, the technique was neither very new nor unknown, at least in the USA. According to him, two-thirds of America's one hundred largest advertisers had geared their campaigns to this 'depth approach' which had been developing in the late 1940s and early 1950s. Its two greatest protagonists were Ernest Dichter, President of the Institute for Motivational Research Inc., and Louis Chetkin, Director of the Colour Research Institute. The implication to be drawn from Packard was that psychological investigation used in order to overcome conscious sales resistance by subconscious emotional and instinctive means was likely to be in use in Britain in the near future, if not already.

The Institute of Practitioners in Advertising in fact published a booklet called *Motivation Research* in 1957: 'Motivation Research is founded on the assumption that consumer behaviour *may* be influenced by factors, the existence of which the individual may either not suspect or be unwilling to reveal . . . [Motivation Research] seeks to tap a deeper level of human attitudes than has hitherto proved possible by the established methods of market research. In doing so it draws upon conceptions and techniques evolved by the science of psychology.'

Dichter's books make the point again and again, as did Packard's, that man is irrational and his actions are conditioned by innumerable factors. To sell anything to him we must analyse his attitude to that thing and then overcome his innate and probably illogical dislike or increase his equally illogical liking. He maintains that the social scientist does not have the power to create human desires. He can strengthen them, make people aware of them, and suggest how they might be satisfied.

Harry Henry's book on the subject added little to the main points of the discussion. He declared: 'It is the function of advertising to reinforce or to change an existing brand image or to create a new one.'

The late 1950s were also notable for the publication of J. K. Galbraith's *The Affluent Society* and Richard Hoggart's *The Uses of Literacy*, which criticized the nature of society and the part played in it by advertising, one from an economic, the other from a cultural viewpoint. Galbraith questioned the whole notion of affluence and the economic organization of contemporary society, giving special attention to 'private affluence and public squalor' and the promotion of artificial needs in order to boost consumption. Hoggart's critique of advertising, however, was little more than a continuation of the Leavis and Thompson approach. In his article 'The Case Against Advertising' though, he

points out that advertisers cannot both highlight the efficient and
influential role that advertising plays in the economy and also claim that
nobody is really foolish enough to believe all they read in advertisements. Further, 'At bottom the case against advertising is the same as
that against political propaganda, much religious proselytizing and any
other form of emotional blackmail . . . Advertising tries to achieve its
ends by emotionally abusing its audiences. Recognising that we all have
fears, hopes, anxieties, aspirations, insecurities, advertisers seek not to
increase our understanding of them, but to use their existence to increase the sales of whatever product they happen to have been paid to
sell at any particular time.'

Raymond Williams began an original and thoroughgoing critique in
New Left Review in 1960. He maintained, paradoxically, that the crucial,
cultural quality of the modern forms of advertising is that the object
being sold is never enough. 'If we were sensibly materialist, in that
part of our living in which we use things, we should find most of advertising to be of insane irrelevance. Beer would be enough for us, without
the additional promise that in drinking it we show ourselves to be
manly, young at heart, or neighbourly. A washing machine would be a
useful machine to wash clothes, rather than an indication that we are
forward-looking or an object of envy to our neighbours . . . But if these
associations sell beer, washing machines and cars, as some of the evidence suggests, it is clear that we have a cultural pattern in which the
objects are not enough but must be validated, if only in fantasy by association with social and personal meanings which in a different cultural
pattern might be more directly available. The short description of the
pattern we have is magic: a highly organised and professional system of
magical inducements and satisfactions.'

Because many of people's needs are social (e.g. roads, hospitals,
schools) they do not come within the consumer ideal–and are even
denied by it, since consumption tends to be defined as an individual
activity. To satisfy this range of needs involves a criticism of the priorities of the economic system, and advertising exists to preserve the
consumption ideal from this criticism. 'If the consumption of individual goods leaves whole areas of human need unsatisfied, the attempt
is made, by magic, to associate this consumption with human desires to
which it has no real reference.' The magical system can work, to some
extent, on a personal level–but only at the cost of preserving the general
unreality which it obscures: the real failures of the society. It should
not, of course, be assumed that the magicians disbelieve their own
magic.

Subsequent publications have tended to adhere to the defensive–
critical pattern, or to be case histories, handbooks, advice from those in
the business to those in the business. Some examples of the last have

been Rosser Reeves' *Reality in Advertising, Advertising in Action* by Harris and Seldon and, by Pearson and Turner *The Persuasion Industry* which had a sting in its tail, however–'The artificial creation of the advertisers and the media owners, the agency is always in a particularly exposed and vulnerable position. It has maximum visibility with minimum responsibility . . . Existing on sufferance, living always on its wits, it is accountable for the image of companies over whose policies it has no ultimate control . . . The chronic insecurity of the advertising business accounts for many of the examples of silliness, assertiveness and anxiety which we have described . . . The sillier and more out of touch advertising becomes, the more misleading and irresponsible it is likely to be. What would be incorrect, however, would be to suggest . . . that as a nation, our buying preferences, our ideals, even our morals are menaced by a sinister conspiracy of hidden persuaders in the advertising agencies.' In the introduction the authors said of the advertising world: 'We found it crazier, gentler, more varied and yet in a curious way more sinister than either its critics or its defenders had led us to expect. It seemed a lonely, rather ingrown world, strangely cut off from the society it spends so much time and money attempting to reach,' and all in all 'advertising can hardly help but be a fairly cynical business'.

Traditional defences have come from, amongst others, Robert Caplin and Martyn Davis. Caplin sketches the historical evolution of advertising and explains what it is all about: 'The basic purpose of every advertisement is to induce a required response from the person to whom it is addressed.' After an adman's view of modern psychology, Caplin moves on to sociology, and what that means for advertising. He divides society into three–the workers, the bosses and the intellectuals. 'The great mass of people have been conditioned to obey instructions given to them by others in a superior position . . . reaction to an order is instinctive obedience . . . because they are used to being told what to do in this group usually respond well to advertisements.' The advertisements should, therefore, be simple and direct. Bosses, on the other hand, do not like being told what to do, but respond to 'suggestions' supported by good reasons. Finally, there are those who are above it all through their education, who find 'advertising repulsive to their cultural sensitivities and say "I never read advertisements".' To get at this group, advertisements should be witty and whimsical and appear to poke fun at themselves as advertisements–and not suggest that any action is required by the reader: it will be enough merely to make clear the name and image of the product.

The specific defences of advertising by Caplin (and by other similar writers) are both summarized by Martyn Davis in his *Handbook for Media Representatives*. The reasons for advertising, first of all, are the following: reminding customers, countering natural declines in the market, informing the constant flow of desirable potential customers, giving information about new developments, overcoming resistance (especially to unfamiliar products), stabilizing production–evening out troughs and peaks, and maximizing profits through increased sales. The virtues of advertising for the society are that it spreads information, increases the range and variety of goods available, leads to branding and thereby to the maintenance of quality (because of the importance of repeat sales), cuts prices, preserves full employment, subsidizes television, magazines and newspapers and last but not least–brightens everyday life for all of us. To the critics of advertising Davis maintains that the consumer is sovereign with full freedom of choice and under no compulsion to buy. Advertising states the case for the product and it is up to the consumer to decide whether or not to buy it. To the spirit of materialism which advertising is alleged to encourage, he asks, what is wrong with wanting a better home or car, or to provide a better standard of living for one's family? In this respect one's expectation of the quote from John Burns is not disappointed–i.e. 'The tragedy of the working man is the poverty of his desires', but this is backed up by no less an authority than Winston Churchill who maintained that advertising nourished the consuming power of man. It created want for a better standard of living, setting up before a man the goal of a better home, better clothing, better food for himself and his family. It spurred individual effort and greater production. To the criticism that advertisements talk down to people, Davis replies that the world of advertising has a high respect for the general level of intelligence and gives the public what it wants and can understand. Advertising merely reflects society and is only one among many influences–so why blame it for what it reflects? It does not in fact eliminate competition but allows it to prosper, and as far as truth is concerned the voluntary restrictions that advertisers have imposed upon themselves are quite adequate–the public need have no fear.

Two other books represent a similar standpoint but are written from a slightly different viewpoint. Ogilvy in his sock-it-'em get-up-and-go book, *Confessions of an Advertising Man*, is enthusiastically and self-confidently on the side of advertising, against mystification and over-sophistication, and in favour of truthful and factual advertisements because they sell goods more efficiently.

Charles Adams seemed also to be reacting against the Dichter school in his *Common Sense in Advertising*. 'There is too much hocus-pocus, hanky-panky and mumbo-jumbo in advertising today, and not enough common sense. Many essentially simple and basic businesses eventually get cluttered up with needless obfuscations, continued jargon and unnecessary technicalities.' Nevertheless, he remarked subsequently, 'The essence of good advertising is not to inspire hope, but to create greed.'

In view of some of the remarks made by the defenders of advertising, it seems in some ways unnecessary for the opponents to do more than quote them. However, there have been some deviations from the Thompson line in recent years, although that tradition lives on–notably in the section on advertising by Frank Whitehead in a book called *Discrimination and Popular Culture* (the editor being none other than Denys Thompson). In 1966 Henry Wolf delivered a lecture at the International Design Conference where he stressed the technical difficulties of working within the advertising business: 'The problem today is this tremendous pressure for newness. An advertising agency calls you up and they don't say we want you to do something good; they want you to astonish the crowd every time out. You have to be a kind of supersonic clown who invents new tricks as he goes.' Other more detailed and lengthy attacks have come from those with experience of the business. Tunstall in *The Advertising Man* comes to the conclusion that the advertising industry, for all its claims, self-justifications and pretensions is in fact impotent, looked down upon, failing even to promote a pleasant image for itself. The continued ignorance of why and how people buy, and how they react to advertisements make it impossible to judge the success or failure of a campaign except in the most extreme cases. It is a disreputable business which fails even to convince its own protagonists of its worth. Of the Institute of Practitioners in Advertising he says that its by-laws are regularly broken, it has no effective sanctions and has banished only two members in its lifetime. An American book by Samuel S. Baker, *The Permissible Lie*, comprises a detailed indictment of American advertising–its power over the media, especially television, its repetitiveness, its trickery and fraud and its overall uncaring irresponsibility. Baker is an advertising man himself who believes that advertising is necessary but can be honest. The book had considerable difficulty in finding a publisher–bearing out some of the author's allegations regarding the power and influence of the advertising industry.

The Golden Fleece by Robert Millar and *The Affluent Sheep* by Joseph Seldin are set in the mainstream of informed journalism. Robert Millar approaches the subject as a layman and takes some care to be fair in his criticisms. He traces a trend towards a greater desire for material possessions and explains that consumers' choices are not founded on knowledge, even when it is available. Tradition, chance, habit and emotions play a greater part. Regarding the 'New Techniques of Seduction' he remarks that: 'All the advertising experts do not go all the way with Dr Dichter, but though there may be some differences of appearance and emphasis, few large advertising agencies in America or Britain do not use Motivation Research to some extent or other. The concept has been accepted as valid in principle.' Joseph Seldin's book-sub-titled 'Selling the Good Life to Americans'-is, like Millar's, a critique of all aspects of American marketing techniques-not just the advertisements themselves but also packaging, obsolescence, give-aways and image building. These books, more restrained than Packard's, make some use of evidence-and give instances of the things they object to-but never attempt to discover how widespread is the recurrence of these factors. The reader is left to wonder whether the examples are the one or two advertisements and campaigns that caught the writer's eye or whether they are typical of the whole mass of advertising.

A rather different attack is to be found in the essay by Mason Griff 'Advertising: the central institution of mass society', where advertising is described as an institution of social control. 'By central institution, we mean an institution which makes a crucial difference in men's relationships to one another. It has the connotations of omnipotence and omnipresence in a sense comparable to the church in the Middle Ages or industry during the nineteenth century. It is central in containing greater social power over the institutional arrangement than any other of the basic institutions of a society.' Institutions of social control guide the life of an individual by creating a new idea of him-and encouraging him to conform as far as possible to that concept. In contrast to previous such institutions (e.g. religion, which sought to instill virtue and ideas of social morality) advertising has nothing within its institutional structure which seeks to improve the individual or impart values of social importance. In fact, it can, and does, impart values-such as irrationality-which are directly disadvantageous to society's well being. '... Advertising has as its goal the deliberate breaking down of the rational process both directly through persuasion and indirectly through the use of techniques to circumvent the conscious rational processes.'

Advertising fares as badly with contemporary writers as it did in the 1930s. 'Talk of pornography ought to begin at the modern root: advertising ... One can of course not be certain it is necessarily bad to live in a country where almost every commodity is festooned with sexual symbol ... There is no one of power who has a tongue to say that sex has become the centre of our economy, and so the commodities which wall the years of our lives are not going to be presented to us for what they are: machine made sacraments closer to the consumer than the bread and wine of the Host', writes Norman Mailer in a chapter of *Advertisements for Myself*: 'A note of comparative pornography'. Bob Dylan expresses his view more succinctly:

> *'Advertising signs: they con*
> *you into thinking you're the one*
> *that can do what's never been done*

that can win what's never been won
meantime life outside goes on
all around you . . .'[1]

In the attacks on advertising and the defences made, a change in emphasis can be discerned over the years. The criticisms of writers like Baster were directed mainly against the deception of advertisements, and to a lesser extent against their repetitiveness, anti-rationality and appeal to emotion. The defenders replied either that people did not believe all they read, or that anyway advertisers were–for the most part–honest, and could not afford to be anything else. The most common defence was that products needed to be good in order to sell again and to stand up to continuous publicity. Separate criticisms were that advertisers influenced the press, and added to the cost of the product. On the other hand, advertising was said to enable choice, more goods to be produced more cheaply, and was anyway an indispensable part of the economy. With modifications in the law (such as the Pharmacy and Medicines Act 1941, The Food and Drugs Act 1955 and the Merchandise Marks Act 1953), and the development of accepted standards within the advertising industry (the British Code of Advertising Practice), advertising men were able more easily to rebut charges of deception or offensiveness. In the 1950s and 1960s, although the old criticisms and defences continued, it was the use of motivational research and psychological techniques, the creation of wants and the stimulation of people to buy what they did not want which provoked most criticism. Developing from the views of the past thirty years, criticisms were tending to be of the general and cumulative effects of advertising rather than of specific advertisements or deceptions. These cumulative effects were held to lie in the area of materialism, trivialization and the debasement of culture and values . . . which lay not in the messages or appeals of certain advertisements, but in the whole aura and *raison d'être* of mass advertising. Many of the more recent critics have specified advertising as an outstanding culprit, but have stated, with differing emphasis, that it is only indicative of a wider cultural (and political) malaise typical of a society dominated by 'mass-entertainment' or 'mass media'. The attack on the cult of materialism and triviality allegedly fostered by advertising is one to which its defenders have only been able to reply by denigrating their critics as illiberal, puritans or academics, or by quoting Burn's statement about the poverty of the working man's desires.

Criticisms of advertising have tended to be the work of individuals responding to an aspect of the culture that they do not like, and have more in common with sermons than the presentation of an ordered and analytical case. The existing approaches have almost all concentrated

on both (a) language, and (b) manipulative appeals. Observations on
the latter have tended to be dogmatic, indiscriminate and written in a
highly moral tone. The prime examples of this are Leavis and Thompson's *Culture and Environment* and Thompson's *Voice of Civilization*.
This approach–whatever its value in the past–is invalid now, at least
for the purpose of an organized investigation. Furthermore, it is becoming increasingly clear that the most crucial part of the advertisement is
not the linguistic but the visual. The stress on language and the explicit
'appeals' contained in it has led critics to pass blindly by that aspect
which is most readily noticed, consciously remembered and which
carries subconscious messages most effectively, namely the picture.
With technical advances in both photography and printing, the picture
–in most cases a photograph–has become the central dominating feature
of most display advertising, not to mention the more complex television commercials. This is immediately apparent to anyone opening
almost any large-circulation newspaper or magazine. The indications
are that the advertisers have realized the potency of visual communication (with varying degrees of intellectual comprehension) but the
watching world has not. Advertising, says McLuhan in *Understanding
Media* got into high gear only at the end of the last century, with the
invention of photo-engraving, which made it easy to illustrate the text
with pictures. 'Today it is inconceivable that any publication . . . could
hold more than a few thousand readers without pictures. For both the
pictorial advertisement and the picture story provide large quantities of
instant information . . . The young should be trained in graphic and
photographic perception as much as in typographic . . . in fact they
need more training in graphics, because the art of casting and arranging
actors in advertisements is both complex and forcefully insidious.'
People trained in a book-orientated society can evaluate and therefore
choose to reject a verbal claim but 'they do not have the art to argue
with pictures'.

The advertising world has produced its own summary of McLuhan's
ideas on the subject and the implications for agencies. Barry Day of
Lintas has put together a booklet called *The Message of Marshall Mc-
Luhan* which explains clearly the ways advertisement creators ought to
be thinking:

> 'A picture is a subtle creation and almost always what emerges
> turns out to be more complex than what the creator thought he
> was putting in. Quite often it is capable of being interpreted in a
> series of ways, according to the personality of the individual look-
> ing at it. Knowing this to be true, the picture is thus potentially a
> much more important weapon in terms of advertising than the
> printed or spoken word since some of these non-verbal meanings

strike deeper without leaving a scar. McLuhan goes as far as to say that since the advent of pictures the copy in an advertisement is quite incidental and often a deliberate red herring to distract the recipient into logical analysis of an "issue" while the visual image, with its appealing overtones of things perhaps too snobbish or self-seeking ever to be overtly stated, is soaking into the mind ... Make sure the picture tells the "real" story: words get you into arguments because everyone is to some degree trained to cope with them and question them. Few people can cope with pictures or even be entirely sure what the pictures have said to them on other than a superficial level. We should pay meticulous attention to details of decor, location, models to everything which can convey the "hidden depth messages" of an advertisement. To say *quality* a picture of a man getting into a Rolls is more than a mite too obvious, whereas the right kind of cuff-links could well have done the trick.'

Advertising man Stephen Baker in *Visual Persuasion* takes up the same theme: 'In the art of visual persuasion, the understanding of associations that every picture, without exception brings forth, is essential ... Businessmen usually judge the effectiveness of visual devices on a purely rational basis, forgetting that people react to images as automatically (and unanalytically) as a small child to a piece of candy. Of course, it is easier to pass judgement on the more obvious, explainable aspects of an illustration (perspective, accuracy in rendering) than on such intangible factors as "mood", psychological effect of colours, and the implication of deliberate distortions.' The realization of the importance of the visual image in the advertisement is not a new thing. In 1932 C. Knight wrote: 'With the masses, showing is infinitely to be preferred to telling. In what may be loosely termed "popular advertising", pictures reinforced by words may be used to sell at least as often as words reinforced by pictures.' And in 1956 Ernest Briggs wrote: 'Relatively few advertisements get to work at once on the upper levels of our consciousness. Most of them are fleeting visual impressions, not consciously remembered, but working overtime on our subconscious minds. In the advertising of a wide range of products, the importance of words is overestimated.'

Though Barry Day might be overstating his case, and overestimating the ability of the advertisement *creators* to cope with pictures at the production end of the process the basic premise regarding the importance of pictures in advertising communication, is valid. McLuhan is right, we know very little (and seem to care very little) about dealing with visual images—yet advertising depends upon them and relishes them. It is the picture which sets the tone, attracts attention, gains interest, arouses curiosity and attempts to lead us into the text. The picture can say things which stated verbally would sound pretentious, shocking, banal, silly or impossible. The picture is easier to take in, quicker to be perceived, offers greater opportunity for excitement, admiration, wonder, emulation and most important of all, imagination. During the last thirty years the text has been getting smaller and the picture larger. In many cases the copy disappears completely. Advertising has become a predominantly visual phenomenon. A detailed comparison recently carried out of advertisements in four magazines in 1938/9 and 1957/8 showed a substantial increase in the average amount of space given to illustration.[2] This trend has continued and, if anything, accelerated. One factor to be considered about the picture in an advertisement is that it is frequently used to draw the reader's attention to the copy and to the brand name or slogan – and it is this part which, finally, sells the product. This may be so, but the central concern of any analysis is not necessarily what sells the product but the messages which the advertisements are communicating to the readers. A full colour picture of a naked red Indian may sell no packets of chewing gum – but that does not mean that the picture has communicated no messages. Advertisement after advertisement offers a host of meanings and values and assumptions in its pictures, and for every ten people who see the picture, perhaps one or two will bother to read a bit of the copy. This can be verified by watching anyone leafing through a magazine or colour supplement. This study is not concerned with which pictures are effective in the sense of achieving direct sales (for even the advertisers are unsure of this) but which pictures – and what sort of pictures – are there, on the page, the seemingly passive recipients of a glance. The central problem for this study, then, is how to come to terms with advertising visuals. The question of the copy can be left to one side for a while: it has received a lot of attention with rather too few results. When more is known about the pictures we can look again at the words.

ABOUT VISUAL COMMUNICATION

The next stage is to investigate existing approaches to visual material and see how far it can assist. One cannot be expert in all fields from semiology (the science of signs) to the psychology of visual perception, but one can try to understand enough to indicate what various approaches are capable of and how well suited they are to the analysis of mass-produced photographs in large-circulation press publications functioning for a specifically commercial purpose.

The psychology of visual perception is tackled most comprehensively by Arnheim, but always with the emphasis on the drawn or painted image, or the perception of objects in life. He explains how one perceives, how the mind deals with concepts such as balance, shape, form and space. He describes how the mind tries to establish balance in visual images and how 'a visual perception of balance or imbalance comes before intellectual measurement'. This leads on to one of the central concepts of perception: that vision consists of an active exploration. Our vision is unlike the camera–it is highly selective and only grasps essentials. 'Seeing' is not a passive process–by which meaningless impressions are stored up for the use of an organizing mind which construes forms out of the amorphous data to suit its own purposes; seeing is itself a process of formulation, and our understanding of the visual world begins not in the mind but in the eye. Further, the look of an object is never determined only by the image that strikes the eye. (For example, when we see a ball, we do not see a partial, but a complete, sphere–even though the partial sphere is all that is strictly visible to us.) Knowledge is wedded intimately to observation. As he writes in *Art and Visual Perception*, 'The mind contains a huge stock of images which tie with the image seen–what is seen will depend on the relative strength of the visual stimulus, and the strength of traces in the memory.' Underlying all this is the mind's attempt to establish balance and simplicity and to eliminate ambiguity. Arnheim is however most concerned with understanding visual art–the way in which life is drawn (coded) to simulate reality, and the way in which the viewer decodes the drawn picture. There is little, unfortunately, to indicate how one might proceed to analyse and understand–not a painting or drawing, but a piece of sophisticated photography. Perhaps more relevant is Arnheim's consideration of expression, and his theory that expression is embedded in structure. A weeping willow, he says, does not look sad because it looks like a sad person, but because the shape, direction and flexibility of willow branches convey a sort of passive hanging, a comparison with the structurally similar state of mind and body which we call sadness.

Much of Langer's discussion of visual perception is bound up with a debate about the meaning of art and the importance of symbolization as a basic human need. In *Philosophy in a New Key* he writes: 'Many symbols–not only words, but other forms–may be said to be "charged" with meanings. They have many symbolic and signific functions, and these functions have been integrated into a complex so that they are all apt to be sympathetically invoked with any chosen one'; and in *Problems of Art*: 'A symbol is any occurrence, usually linguistic in status, which is taken to signify something else by way of tacit or explicit conventions or rules of language. In this way a word conveys a concept, and refers to, or denotes, whatever exemplifies that concept ... Words are usually used in complexes which constitute discourse ... The second office of symbols is not to refer to things and communicate facts but to express ideas.' Is this expression of ideas by symbols other than words systematic in any way? The symbolism furnished by purely sensory appreciation of form is peculiarly well suited to the expression of ideas that defy linguistic 'projection' (for example, our understanding of space, which we owe to sight and touch, could never be developed by a discursive knowledge of geometry) but although visual forms–lines, colours, proportions, etc.–are just as capable of articulation, of complex combination, as words, visual forms are not discursive and the laws governing this sort of articulation are very different from the laws governing language. The salient features of language or discourse, says Langer, are (a) that every language has a vocabulary and syntax, its elements are words with fixed meanings out of which one can construct–according to rules of syntax–composite symbols with resultant new meanings; (b) some words are whole combinations of others, therefore meaning may be expressed in different ways–i.e. it is possible to construct a dictionary; and (c) there may be alternative words for the same meaning. A picture, on the other hand, is composed of elements that represent various respective constituents in the object portrayed (as does language) but these elements are *not units with individual meanings*, areas of light and shade, for example, have no significance by themselves. They represent the visual elements of the object but do not represent, item for item, those elements which have names–e.g. not one blotch for nose, one for eye, etc., they are many times more numerous. A symbolism with so many units, such myriad relationships, cannot be broken up into units: there is therefore no visual vocabulary. Nor can visual symbols be defined in terms of others as words or numbers can. If this is so, it ends any search for a system on which to base an analysis at least on one, fundamental, level.

Turning to another authority in the field, Gyorgy Kepes, we find some interesting general comments but he gives little indication of any ways in which a method might be derived. He states very clearly in *The Language of Vision* the importance and complexity of the visual experience (of McLuhan, etc. above) and makes a similar point to Arnheim and Langer on the interdependence of visual sensations and knowledge/memory. 'Visual experience is more than the experience of pure sensory qualities. Visual sensations are interwoven with memory overlays. Each visual configuration contains a meaningful text, evokes associations of things, events, creates emotional and conscious responses ... The visual language is capable of disseminating knowledge more effectively than almost any other vehicle of communication. With it, man can express and relay his experience in object form ... Visual language can convey facts and ideas in a wider and deeper range than almost any other means of communication. It can reinforce the static verbal concept with the sensory vitality of dynamic imagery.'

Kepes has some interesting comments to make on the development of a visual language to suit the development of a modern mass-communication society. 'Easel-painting . . . was the historical manifestation in the pictorial art of the spirit of individualism. But the historical background is changed . . . Social interdependence brought up a new meaning of the individual, the social individual. To speak to this new man a different language was required, a language that must penetrate in depth individual regions but at the same time speak to the largest possible group . . . The mass spectator demands the amplification of optical intensity and a levelling down of the visual language towards common idioms. Such idioms demand simplicity, force, and precision.' An example of this visual simplicity and intensity is traffic signs. 'There is no time now for the perception of too many details. The duration of the visual impacts is too short. To attract the eye and convey the full meaning in this visual turmoil of events, the image must possess, like the traffic sign, simplicity of elements and lucid forcefulness.' Advertising art has been able to make use of these new possibilities because it was not handicapped by conventions and traditional forms in the same way that other art forms were.

Kepes explains how a picture can convey more complex messages by the use of contradiction and opposition. 'We look at a photograph of two men sitting on a bench and each unit of the picture brings up associations. One man is better dressed than the other. They are sitting back to back. Their bodies, their postures, are full of associative suggestions. We compare them and contrast them, discovering differences and similarities. The image becomes a dynamic experience. It has a self-movement because of the discovered opposition. The experience attains a unity as we fill out, with a living story, the latent human background of the visible situation. We do not see things, fixed static units, but perceive instead living relationships.' The contradiction inherent in the associations of certain elements keeps our mind moving until the contradiction is resolved in a meaning. 'Contradiction is then the basis of dynamic organization of the associative qualities of the image. When representational units within the same picture contain statements which seem counter to the accepted logic of events, the spectators' attention is forced to seek out the possible relationships until a central idea is found which weaves the meaningful signs together in a meaningful whole.' This, in language, is the basis of metaphor, a device which can be used equally powerfully visually as the mind attempts to 'eliminate ambiguity'. The concept of metaphor is one which might prove to be useful, and about which more is said later. But what constitutes a 'representational unit' which Kepes mentions?–is it one particular object, as from life, or the parts which constitute an object?–why would the metaphor be unlikely to work if the two objects comprising it were left together on a table rather than in a picture? This clearly has something to do with the singling out, framing and *presenting* quality of photography. Presented with the picture we are forced to try to make sense of it because we know that it has been produced by human intellect and therefore 'means' something. Even absurd objects photographed together would still (if nothing else) connote 'absurdity' while the same objects together on the floor might mean nothing more to an observer than 'some objects left on the floor'. Photographing an object adds a particular quality to that object; a cat is not a cat, it is a picture of a cat.

In *Art and Illusion* E. Gombrich writes: 'The very reason why the representation of nature can now be looked upon as something commonplace should be of the greatest interest to the historian. Never before has there been an age like ours when the visual image was so cheap in every sense of the word. We are surrounded and assailed by posters and advertisements, by comics and magazine illustrations. We see aspects of reality represented on the television screen and in the movies, on postage stamps and on food packages.'

Gombrich deals with symbols and metaphor in his *Visual Metaphors of Value in Art* although as the title suggests his main concern, too, is with visual *art*, in the sense of fine art. He first disposes of the difference which exists in language between metaphor and simile and which cannot exist visually. Symbols and metaphors are closely linked–something is only a symbol until it is placed in relation to something else when it can function metaphorically. The lion, to take Gombrich's example, may symbolize bravery, and placed alongside soldiers in a memorial it acts as a metaphor, saying 'these soldiers were brave in the way that lions were brave'. In contrast to the use of images as labels, like the attributes of divinities, the symbol in this sense is not a code-sign, for the image of a lion can be used in different contexts to convey different ideas. The only thing these ideas have in common is that they are derived–in the example of the lion–'from such traditional lore about the lion as is crystallized in bestiaries and fable. It is this lore which defines what may be called the area of metaphor'. Which of the qualities we use depends on our aim–we may want to convey the idea of nobility, ferocity, bravery or even some ludicrous aspect as in the story of the lion fearing the crowing of the cock. 'Each of these qualities ... can be "isolated" and "transferred" to another object ... this is not a code-symbol of the type "the lion in art means courage". Rather should we say, because of its alleged courage the lion lends itself to being used as a symbol (or metaphor) for heroes.' Symbols or images cannot then be said to 'have' a meaning–though that belief is widespread–'Its latest version is to be found in writings of C. G. Jung, where it is often implied that certain images are endowed with an intrinsic and constant significance.' This absoluteness Gombrich rejects.

Panofsky is another scholar from the world of art and art appreciation, and his work on iconography is of relevance to this study. Iconography is concerned with the subject matter or meaning, as opposed to the form of an image. 'Formal perception' consists of light, colour, shapes and movement. 'Factual meaning' involves elementary understanding of such perception and 'Expressional meaning' is apprehended not by simple identification but by 'empathy'—to understand one needs a certain sensitivity to appreciate nuances and variations. All these are part of everyday familiar practical experience, they are 'Primary or Natural Meanings'. Beyond this level is that of 'Secondary or Conventional Meanings' which involve familiarity with the more-than-practical world of 'customs and cultural traditions peculiar to certain civilizations'. This sort of meaning underlies the connexion between, for example, the raising of a hat and giving of a greeting. This 'Conventional Meaning' has been consciously imported to the practical action by which it is conveyed. Finally, according to Panofsky, the action of a friend in removing his hat, can reveal to an experienced observer all that goes to make up his 'personality'. This personality is conditioned by his being a man of the twentieth century, by national, social and educational background, by the previous history of his life and his present surroundings, but it is also distinguished by an individual manner of viewing things and reacting to the world—which if rationalized would have to be called a philosophy ... The hat raising action is symptomatic ... The qualities shown by a mental portrait of the friend are implicitly inherent in every single action. This meaning is the 'Intrinsic Meaning or Content'.

Thus there are three levels of meaning:

(i) Primary or Natural Subject Matter—forms lines and colours which make up representations of objects and men; their interrelations which comprise events; and their gestures and poses which are expressional qualities.

(ii) Secondary or Conventional Subject Matter is concerned with the wider culture and the connexion of motifs and combinations of motifs (i.e. compositions) with *themes* and *concepts*. Certain motifs recognized as carrying such secondary meanings may be called images, and combinations of images called stories or allegories. It is not clear whether Panofsky is implying the sort of one-to-one relationship between image and meaning which Gombrich rejects. The identification of images, stories and allegories is the domain of iconography in the narrow sense. This is the area referred to when one talks of subject matter as opposed to form in artistic criticism.

(iii) Intrinsic Meaning or Content is apprehended by 'ascertaining those underlying principles which reveal the basic attitude of a nation, a period, a class, a religious or philosophic persuasion—unconsciously qualified by one personality and condensed into one work'. This breakdown of levels of meaning has a similarity both to Barthes' semiological approach to pictures and to the cultural studies' approach to cultural artefacts. One can identify the constituents of a pictorial representation, and fairly readily though not with absolute certainty interpret the meanings, themes and concepts they carry, but how one goes about ascertaining the underlying principles condensed into that picture is far from apparent.

This is a problem with which cultural studies, since their inception, have been concerned.* As far as the analysis of material, of cultural artefacts, is concerned, the assistance given by cultural studies in concrete terms is limited.

'Cultural reading' has been used to describe the process of understanding a work and of bringing out its 'cultural significance' – isolating the underlying attitudes, assumptions and values as they are expressed in the material. This latter is what Panofsky is concerned with at his level of intrinsic meaning. How 'cultural reading' is practically performed is largely up to the individual and the material itself. One of the main tenets of cultural studies has been that the material studied should be allowed to speak for itself, should be understood and experienced as a 'thing in itself' *before* any attempt is made to trace larger connexions. This understanding is to be accomplished by intimate acquaintance with the material, including where possible, an involvement with it, an appreciation and feeling for it (be it a television programme, a comic or a novel). The 'reading' of the material, as the term implies, frequently involves the use of the tools and insights employed in literary criticism. Much of the interpretation, then will be subjective and affected by the values of the interpreter, as well as by his skill. The task of cultural studies, as much as anything else, has been to discover how far this factor of subjectivity and value-judgement, can be overcome or taken into account in analyses of this type. The movement from the material 'in itself' to its relation to society and culture remains problematic. The preoccupation of cultural studies with this relationship implies sometimes that the question of the rigorous analysis of the material in the beginning has been solved.

The methodical analysis of film or photographs has been an area of investigation in which not a great deal of academic work has been accomplished, except on the level of technical aspects of items like camera angle, lighting and close-up.

Those studies concerned with the science of photography rarely pay

* See Hoggart, Richard, *Contemporary Cultural Studies;* Centre for C.C.S. Occasional Paper No. 6, 1969. And Hall, Stuart, *Cultural Analysis;* in *Cambridge Review*, January 1967.

much attention to the nature of the finished print, beyond considerations of suitable papers and emulsions. Photography manuals make attempts at defining rules for good pictures – to do with techniques (filters, lighting, focus, etc.) as well as composition (centres of interest, tone values, proportion, etc.) but the remarks are more in the way of advice from experience than a carefully thought out approach to visual communication. Generally, the photographer is not concerned with interpreting or analysing his picture – he is interested in taking it and in processing it – and in arriving at a technically perfect print, according to his taste.

There have been attempts to construct a grammar of film, notably by Spottiswoode and by Eisenstein but the obstacle has always been the difficulty of pinning down any specific *unit* in the way that one can isolate a sentence, a phrase, a word or a phoneme. This has made the derivation of a syntax of the relationships *between* units impossible. Semiology has attempted to approach the area once again with some – but not complete – success. Wollen spends a chapter of his book *Signs and Meaning in the Cinema* discussing the possible avenues opened up by semiological studies, which is useful if only as an introduction to the material. Which of the various types of signs is the photographic print? he asks. Taking Pierce's definition, an icon is a sign which represents the object mainly by similarity to it – for example, a portrait; an index is a sign by virtue of an existential bond between itself and its object (e.g. a pulse rate, a barometer level); and a symbol is a sign by virtue of a 'contract' demanding neither resemblances nor an existential bond, for example a No Speed Limit sign. Photographs, especially instantaneous photographs are, according to Pierce, very instructive, because we know that in certain respects they are exactly like the objects they represent. But this resemblance is due to the photographs having been produced under such circumstances that they were physically forced to correspond point by point to nature. In that aspect, then, they belong to the second class of signs, those by physical connexion. Barthes however sees the photographic print as simply iconic – the photographic icon represents 'a kind of natural being-there of the object'. There is no human intervention, no transformation, no code, between the object and the sign – hence the paradox that a photograph is a message without a code. As Metz says 'a close-up of a revolver does not signify "revolver" but signifies as a minimum "Here is a revolver". It carries with it its own actualization, a kind of "Here is (*Voici!*)".'

Barthes remains the central figure in this debate. The work of most relevance here is, clearly, 'Rhetorique de l'Image' in which he explains the uses of semiological procedure, using as an example an advertisement picture. 'How does meaning come into the picture? Where does meaning end? – and if it ends, what is there beyond? These are the

questions one would ask in subjecting the image to a spectral analysis
of the message that it can contain. We can make it considerably easier
at the start: we will study only the advertising image. Why? Because in
advertising the signification of the image is assuredly intentional . . .'
Barthes here is surely overstating, for even in the advertising picture
one would expect there to be a range of significance of which even the
creators were not fully aware. Indeed, one would expect the explicit
meaning to be stated clearly, but that is not the limit of the meanings in
a picture for an advertisement. However, this is not crucial to Barthes'
analysis with which he proceeds as follows: 'The analysed photograph
suggests three messages to us, a linguistic message, a coded iconic
message, an uncoded iconic message.' The linguistic message can be
easily separated from the others, but since these two messages have the
same substance it is more difficult to distinguish between them. These
messages can be considered one by one, nevertheless. Barthes maintains
that the linguistic message is present in all visual forms–as the caption
to the photograph, the bubble to the strip cartoon and the dialogue to
the film–though there may be disagreement about this, and there
have been instances, admittedly rare, of poster advertisements devoid
of linguistic message. The function of this linguistic message in the case
of the fixed image is usually that of anchorage. The other function,
relay, is common in film but occurs rarely with stills (except perhaps in
cartoon strips) where the words stand in a complementary relationship
to the picture and the unity of the message occurs at a superior level,
that of story or anecdote. Anchorage, on the other hand, functions by
selecting a message from the mass of messages available in the image and
presenting it as The Message.

The second message is the *literal* message, the denoted image. The
level of denotation is that of identification–objects or beings without
their connotations. As it is impossible ever to experience a picture
without experiencing its connotations, this level is theoretical, or as
Barthes puts it 'utopian'. The third level of meaning is that of the
connoted 'symbolic' message, and is the level of interpretation. The
'signs' are drawn from a cultural code–but the number of readings of
the same lexical item (i.e. of the same image) varies according to individuals. Although the variation of the readings is not completely arbitrary and chaotic, the image can be read in different ways by different
individuals–each sign corresponds to a body of 'attitudes' of which a
certain number may be lacking at the level of an individual. Another
difficulty attached to the analysis of connotation is that 'there is no particular analytic language corresponding to the particularity of the
signifieds of the connotation'. Is it possible, then, to classify in any
ordered but still meaningful way, these signs of connotation? In doing so
would one be doing anything different from making a list of symbols and

their assumed meanings in particular contexts? Can this be considered a code in any real sense? Furthermore, is it any more accurate to describe the denotive message as uncoded – does not the camera in fact act as a sophisticated codifying mechanism – does the spectator not in fact decode from the artificial flat two-dimensional little print an impression of a real life-size three-dimensional world? Umberto Eco has since made the same point in *Articulations of Cinematic Code*; and his breakdown of the image into figures, signs and senses is similar to those already considered.

There are one or two tangential strands to be considered before making any attempt at a summary. First, the psycho-analytical approach. This is based on an interpretation of symbols in a Jungian sense and has been put into practice by Giancarlo Marmori in his book *Senso e Anagramma*. He is concerned predominantly with women in advertisements and the images of femininity offered to the readers. According to Marmori, advertising possesses a complete range of stereotypes (from 'Wanda the abuser' to 'Justine the abused') from which it selects according to the exigencies of the advertisement's product and emphasis and the creator's whim. Each advertisement contains a collection of symbols which are interpreted in psycho-analytical terms and to conclusions of this order: 'On account of the reversal of the meaning of the situation, though Temptation and Fall remain the main themes of the two rhetorics, it turns out that the industrial Eve (and Adam eventually) does not foster fears or prophetic feelings. She is pervaded, on the contrary, by a serene, even blessed, mood. Likewise the commercial Fall is never followed by an expulsion from the Garden, but on the contrary, by admission into the Eden of the consumers of the product advertised by the advertising Serpent and also into the most orthodox phallus-centred eroticism (erotismo fallo-centrico ortodosso).' Another interesting example is his interpretation of an advertisement for '*Fems* Feminine Napkins'. 'Eve, in an emergency state, but still radiant, is finishing crossing a country bridge; she holds a few apples in one of her arms. The apples are brightly red: they are in fact metaphors for the physiological state of the bearer – and the chromatic allusion is emphasized by the red colour of the cardigan she wears on her shoulders while she steps along at a brisk pace. The arm holding the apples is a metaphor for Fems as it shows the qualities of protection and support in a nice efficient manner. A complementary metaphor is the phallic bridge that the consumer has just crossed. In other words Eve – being in an emergency – carries away the contaminated apple, having interrupted any intercourse with the bridge, and without any sense of frustration being caused by the interruption. As a consequence she remains agreeable and desirable. Thanks to the napkin she is still full of sex appeal.' The limitations of this sort of interpretation are that the sample

is simply those advertisements which have been selected as amenable
to the analysis–most advertisements are not like these–and that the
interpretation offered of the 'meanings' is idiosyncratic and rather
forced at many points. Further, the usefulness to anyone unfamiliar with
psycho-analytic interpretation is exceedingly limited. Marmori's analyses constantly turn on and emphasize sexual themes and ideas which
are often obviously present, but rarely comprise the *sole* meaning
contained in the picture. One should also bear in mind Arnheim's warn-
ing from *Art and Visual Perception*: 'The psycho-analytic theory
describes the visible facts of the work of art as a representation of other,
equally concrete and individual facts. If, after penetrating the work of
a master, we are left with nothing but references to organs and functions of the human body or to some close relative, we wonder what
makes art such a universal and supposedly important creation of the
human mind. Its message seems pitifully obvious. A little thought
shows that sex is no more final and no less symbolic than other human
experiences ... For our purpose it is especially significant that sex
stands often for a highly abstract power.'

In explaining his interpretations Marmori makes frequent use of rhetorical terms derived from language like metaphor and metonymy,
which have also been touched on above. Mention should be made of the
contribution made by Gui Bonsiepe in *Persuasive Communication: Towards a Visual Rhetoric*. 'If you examine when verbal figures have
analogues in the visual field, you can straightaway exclude grammatical
figures as typical language phenomena. On the other hand some figures
of speech and thought can be transferred to the field of visual signs ...
In verbal rhetoric the metaphor takes a prominent position ... A
metaphor is a transfer of a word from one range of meaning to another,
where there exists, or should exist, some similarity between the ranges
thus put in relation with each other.' Bonsiepe concludes, however,
that 'there are visual metaphors; but they don't have autonomous
character. They only illustrate already verbally formulated metaphors'.
There are also analogies in the visual field to other rhetorical figures
such as condensation and exaggeration. It is not clear why it should be
impossible for there to be autonomous visual metaphors unless it is to
be inferred that the mind works linguistically in making sense of the
variously juxtaposed referents, in eliminating ambiguity. The garden
pea peeping out of the shell of an oyster says quite clearly that this
pea is as fine and precious as a pearl; and the scales which have gold
bars on one tray and fish fingers weighing heavier on the other is making
an obvious statement about the worth of those fish fingers. Some
metaphors and other rhetorical devices will need verbal explanation
or perhaps linguistic anchorage in order to make the meaning clear, but
the view that autonomous visual metaphors are impossible seems un-

tenable. As Gombrich states in *Visual Metaphors of Value in Art :* 'The possibility of metaphor springs from the infinite elasticity of the human mind; it testifies to its capacity to perceive and assimilate new experiences as modifications of earlier ones, of finding equivalences in the most disparate phenomena and of substituting one for another. Without this constant process of substitution neither language nor art, nor indeed civilized life would be possible.'

Leaving aside for the time all the insights and warnings, amplifications and hesitations of the writers that have fleetingly been considered, the two most usefully systematic approaches seem to be those of Panofsky and Barthes. Barthes proposes a linguistic level which relates to the picture through the function (usually) of anchorage. His level of the denotive message is similar to Panofsky's 'primary subject matter', and his level of the connotive message to Panofsky's 'secondary or conventional subject matter'. Panofsky goes on then to establish a further level–that of the 'intrinsic subject matter', with which Barthes is not necessarily concerned. The concept of the linguistic message and the function it has may be of use in the analysis of the advertisements, and it is as well at least to be aware of it. The level of the denotive is the level of identification and enumeration, and this, over a certain amount of material might provide valuable evidence in terms of repetitions and patterns. The level of the connotive message is the most important and unclear. How is one to decide the connotations, to interpret the symbols or the metaphors? The use of metaphor and similar devices offers a possible way of understanding how the connexion between the denotive and connotive level functions–at least in *some* advertisements. But the central problem remains that of an adequate, sensitive, yet not idiosyncratic interpretation of the 'symbols'–being aware that the possibility of building systematically a sort of dictionary and grammar for visual language is (cf. Langer and others) not very strong. One has to proceed by the use of at least some intuition and general cultural knowledge (as finely tuned as one can get it) while organizing the study in an ordered and logical fashion with as much room for substantiation and evidence as possible. In other words, because there is no fully defined quasi-scientific and tested procedure, there is nevertheless no excuse for indulging in a completely personal and subjective account based on examples chosen for reasons of individual whim. One must state exactly what is under scrutiny at any point, and why (and what precedes and what follows), what deductions are being made *from* and *to* what (and where possible for which reasons) and the conclusions that might be arrived at, taking into account and giving acknowledgement to the individual's limitations and personal *Weltanschauung*. Only then can any attempt be made to tackle the 'intrinsic subject matter'. Only then can any more wide-ranging connexions be made and hypotheses suggested, any links with' those underlying principles which reveal the basic attitude of a nation . . .', with the pulse of society's life, be established. In most cases conclusions at this level must of necessity be questions.

References

[1] From 'It's All Right Ma–I'm Only Bleeding' on CBS 62515 'Bringing It All Back Home'.

[2] Millum, T., B.A. Dissertation (Birmingham University, 1967). *Modes and Techniques in Magazine Advertising,* 1938–58.

2

Who Makes Advertisements?

The process by which advertisements are produced will in some way affect the final artefact. Some consideration should be given to the way an advertisement is evolved, if only to make one aware of the mechanical and technical intervening variables. This is not a sociological study, but the advertisements must be placed in context and the skeleton of their relationships traced, if what is to be investigated subsequently is to be read from the correct perspective.

Advertising is a distinctive form of communication in that it exists to communicate a message the sole purpose of which, however many stages removed, is to convert potential consumers into actual consumers. The pressures within the business are such that more research, planning and thought go into the production of each advertising message than into any other comparable form of communication. The result is that the advertisement is a very conscious and deliberate construction of messages. Nevertheless, every aspect of the advertising communication cannot be consciously constructed–there will be a residue which is not thought out, that which is taken for granted, which is a part of all communication. To understand the way in which the advertisement functions, it is necessary to describe the particular view of society held, and the way in which it affects the communication process.

Society comprises both human relationships–personal relations, political institutions, social institutions and so on–and objects, for example, books, tools, buildings. These latter form part of the former and in many cases are the channels through which the former function. They have a dual role: a simple functional one in which tools are used to grow food, and roofs to keep out the rain, and a more complex, but still functional role. This is the way objects express the human values and meanings of the society, of the institutions, and in this respect these concrete objects or artefacts constitute the very fabric of the society. In the course of constructing and organizing their world, men communicate with things as well as with words–sometimes with ostensibly very 'non-articulate' things.

Society is not only the product of man, but man is also the product of society. Society takes on a sort of objective existence–sometimes apparently existing in its own right 'out there'. This is partly due to the attitude of man towards it, and partly because of the existence of concrete artefacts which are its own expressions. The relationship between man and society is thus a dialectical one, and involves three activities: externalization, objectivation, and internalization.[1] These activities (which include socialization) are ongoing processes which are continuously taking place in society. Externalization is the creation by man (collectively) of his own culture (being the totality of man's products, material and non-material), and objectivation is the attainment by these products of a reality, an existence, external to their creators. Both the material (a tool, a plough, a letter) and the non-material (social institutions, values, etc.) acquire this objectivity and this existence separate from their creators. As P. Berger neatly puts it in *The Social Reality of Religion*, although man is not consciously aware of what he is doing, and the process does not happen overnight: 'Man invents a language and then finds both his speaking and his thinking are dominated by its grammar. Man produces values and discovers that he feels guilt when he contravenes them.' Internalization is the reabsorption into man's own consciousness of the objectivated world in such a way that the structures of this world come to determine the structures of consciousness itself. Man reclaims the objectivated world as his own. The culture which is thus internalized by the individual includes not only for example, kinship patterns and ideas of respect, but also the meanings and values contained in mainstream literature on the one hand and in the advertisements in magazines on the other. Through internalization man comes to make the norms and values of the society a part of himself, to accept them unthinkingly as if there were no possible alternatives, and to believe that things are as they are because that is what is 'right' or 'natural' in some absolute way. However, no person takes the complete culture to himself, and the individual's subjective world differs from the objective world of society. Nevertheless, to be a member of a society there must be a large degree of affinity between the two worlds. The transmission of society's objectivated meanings from one generation to the next is achieved by socialization – through which a new generation is taught to live in accordance with the established social rules and values. This socialization continues throughout life and formal schooling comprises only a part of it.

The advertisements with which we are concerned are part of those objectivations which loom so large over us, but are no more than the creations of man and as subject to the pressures of the communally created culture as everyone else. A model, much simplified, of the processes in which we are interested might be posed as follows. Within the culture and part of the culture are particular groups which have a special function – namely *professional* communicators. One of these groups is concerned with a very special type of communication in that it is an instrumental kind of communication, directly linked to the economics of selling. The communications which this group (advertisers, agencies, etc.) produce are as much the product of the culture as are the communicators; and the people to whom the communications are addressed are equally as much of that same culture, and are receiving and interacting with many other stimuli besides these advertisements. The images and language used are drawn from the culture, and the communications produced are a contributory factor to the body of the culture. The audience understands because it is part of the culture, and shares its meanings. The whole process is a complex all-embracing dialectic–but one of the important aspects is that the communications from the 'advertisers' to the 'audience' are stimuli with extra power and deliberation behind them, and may function as transformations and/or reinforcements of particular aspects. In one sense everybody belongs to the culture and is part of its reproducing itself, but in another sense the group of advertisers has much greater power (in terms of thought, money, time, skill–it is after all its job), and although it is *part* of the culture it is one of the groups which helps to give particular meanings a specific emphasis or concretism (e.g. by selection and association), the effect of which is to reinforce certain clusters of meanings and to ignore others.

Our concern is with the agency and the advertisements for two reasons: the information the process yields about advertising (as an important moulder and modifier of the culture) and the information or insight it yields about the culture and the prevailing cultural values.

The basic questions one feels bound to ask are these. Who is it who directs and decides what the advertisement communication should be like, and then who actually carries it out? How do these people accumulate their ideas about the culture, and their information about what life 'outside' is like–and what is its status; are these communicators ill-informed, dwellers in fools' paradises, or well-versed, in touch and informed? Each of these questions needs to be considered in greater depth.

The process of the creation of an advertisement is detailed, 'professional', expensive and mysterious. In terms of the operative mechanics the process is roughly that simplified in diagrammatic form. Some parts will differ in particular cases or with particular agencies, some will vary according to the type of product in question and the sort of advertising which is decided upon. The concern here is to explain the emergence of the magazine display advertisement; other types of advertising–filmed commercials especially–will be created in slightly different and more complex ways.

Diagram I Agency Relationships: How the ad is made.

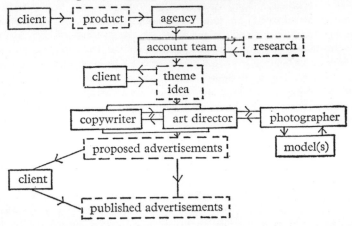

It will be clear that the finished advertisement is the product of many minds and many men, but that nevertheless, some of these are more crucial than others. Certain parts of the process can be seen as crucial pivots. From the point of view of the illustration, these are (a) the account team's relationship with the client, their brief and their decision as to the campaign's 'idea', theme and content; (b) the art director's relationship with his colleagues and his setting up of the 'idea', etc. in visual terms; (c) the photographer's relationship with the art-director and his contribution to the theme or content in the actualization of the illustration. A subsidiary pivot is the photographer's relationship with the model or models who may form part of the illustration.

More research may be undertaken when the rough forms of the advertisements have been decided, to see the kind of reactions they elicit on a trial run; and there may be follow-up research on the effectiveness of the campaign–though this may often consist of no more than an analysis of sales. According to 'professional' critics whose views can often be found in the pages of advertising periodicals, the man in the agency is out of touch with the people with whom he wants to communicate. John Doe wrote in *Advertiser's Weekly* of 13 October 1967: 'Advertising is first and foremost communication, and in a country which stratifies its society as rigidly as Britain, almost all communication is horizontal, rather than vertical. Since advertising directed at the mass market in Britain involves an A+ creative man who wouldn't be seen dead in Golders Green, Shepherd's Bush or Bermondsey trying to communicate meaningfully with every stratum of society–all the way down–the end result is only too often a complete breakdown in

Diagram II Agency Relationships:
How the ideas, themes and messages build up.

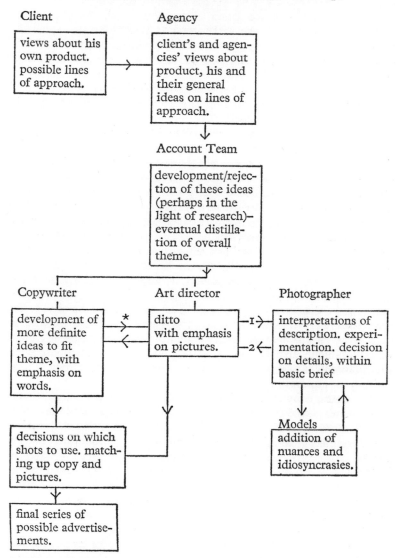

Client

| views about his own product. possible lines of approach. |

Agency

| client's and agencies' views about product, his and their general ideas on lines of approach. |

Account Team

| development/rejection of these ideas (perhaps in the light of research)– eventual distillation of overall theme. |

Copywriter

| development of more definite ideas to fit theme, with emphasis on words. |

Art director

| ditto with emphasis on pictures. |

Photographer

| interpretations of description. experimentation. decision on details, within basic brief |

| decisions on which shots to use. matching up copy and pictures. |

Models

| addition of nuances and idiosyncrasies. |

| final series of possible advertisements. |

* agreement on how ideas/theme to be concretized in terms of actual content.
1 instructions to photographer
2 series of shots selected by photographer

communication.' McLuhan in *Understanding Media* takes the opposite
view: 'Far more thought and care go into the composition of any prominent advertisement in a newspaper than go into the writing of their
features and editorials. No group of sociologists can approximate the
advertisement teams in the gathering and processing of exploitable
social data. The advertisement teams have billions to spend annually
on research and testing of reactions and their products are magnificent
accumulations of material about the shared experience and feelings of
an entire community. Of course, if advertisements were to depart from
the centre of this shared experience, they would collapse at once, by
losing all hold on our feelings.'

It is obvious, though, that advertisements do not reflect reality in
any simple way. If they did then there would be far more pictures of
tenement and council houses than of town-houses and sleek semi-
detacheds. To take the example of hair-styles, a large number of
advertisements seem to feature girls with long fair hair, whereas the
majority of girls has neither: there is no direct proportional relationship
to the 'facts' of society. In this particular case long hair is fashionable,
it has some kind of status (which might disappear if it becomes the
property of the majority) and as such it represents an abstraction (it is
a symbol of what is desirable) and an aspiration. In the same way,
beauty as a particular interpretation of appearance has a status, is
an aspiration: it is widely used in advertisement pictures, while not
being the property of the majority. The same might be said of the
semi-detached house. Nevertheless the aspiration would have to be
held by a substantial part of the audience for there to be any point
in exploiting it. In this way advertising would be seen to portray an
interpretation of reality which reinforces or transforms certain aspects
of it.

The transmission of common aspirations (and together with aspirations, values and cultural assumptions) current in the society as assumed
by the producers of advertisements does not presume a conscious
understanding of the process on the part of these producers. To take
the case of items in an illustration used symbolically, they may be
included not because, for example, research has shown that a poodle
means class or chic, or because anyone has articulated this connexion,
but simply because it 'looks right' and there is no deliberate or conscious
symbolic intention. It may be, to take another possibility, that there is
self-consciousness about the iconography, but no awareness of the
reasons why a certain appeal or reference seems to work for this product
at this time, and perhaps no real interest.

The status of the information drawn upon by the producers of the
advertisements varies between ostensibly objective research material,
both generally available and specially commissioned, and intuition,

'feel', common sense and so on. Between the two extremes there is perhaps the area of information disseminated by the mass media, by social observers and commentators. All of these go to make up the complex of what one feels society to be like. Following from this, the ideas transmitted by advertisements are certainly current in the society to a greater or lesser degree. Some parts may be new or have some aspect of originality in them, but the percentage of true invention in any human creation–even the greatest of art–is likely to be fairly small. One might further hypothesize that the more basic the ideas in question, the less altered or transformed by the advertising man's intervention they are likely to be, for they will be that much further below the threshold of consciousness.

The ideas, the values, the meanings, however, are selective, and are transformed by the process, and overlaid with the producers' view of the world. The ideas transmitted may be transformations, they may be reinforcements–but however different from 'reality' they are paradoxically part of reality, part of the mass of cultural stimuli in which all people are immersed.

Whatever effects advertisements have on tastes and values 'acting in a cumulative way) they are clearly not acting alone. Nevertheless, advertisements are, currently, one of the most universal and pervasive channels of communication. The world of the advertisement producers is smaller in every way than the society in which it exists, and only if it were extremely perceptive, thorough, creative and intelligent–yet also possessed of some sort of mystical power–would it be able to present a picture of the whole society, and the whole culture. The spokesmen of the culture always tend to relay the version most familiar to them, and the more so the more restricted–socially, commercially, intellectually–their own world is. Hence one would expect advertising to function as a reinforcement of certain areas of the culture, with the corollary that other areas get neglected. Few of the critics of advertising have claimed that it changes human nature or society. It is, however, difficult to understand how societies do change unless it is by a gradual process of intensification of certain parts and the atrophication of others. J. T. Klapper writes about this in his chapter of *Public Opinion and Communication*: 'The Effects of Mass Communication', and Raymond Williams in *Communications* writes: 'It seems to be generally agreed that in the movement of public taste and opinion you cannot start a trend but you can accentuate one that exists. In the process, of course, you may be distorting the balance of interests and limiting the range of original potential response.'

Thus, one might say, first, advertisements reveal some of the major preoccupations and cultural values of a society, simply by existing and functioning as retransmission. (One of the points of taking a fairly large sample is to neutralize the individual idiosyncrasies and arbitrarinesses of agencies, art directors and photographers.) Second, advertisements purvey cultural values as interpreted by a certain section of society whose views and tastes issue as (often unintentional and unconscious) propaganda.

The next step one might take in order to gain insight into this process of production, and to understand more clearly the reasons why the advertisement appears as it does, would be to talk to those involved in the process themselves. The interviews from which the following material is taken were conducted with the primary aim of discovering the relationships between the parts of the machinery which produces the advertisement, and the relationships of that machinery to the world it was addressing. Those interviewed were copy-writers, art directors and account executives in advertising agencies, and photographers who were experienced in advertising work. The interviews were conducted during a two-week period and were tape-recorded.

'How much freedom is the agency given by the client?'

It became clear that the client has an idea of the qualities of his product which he wants to stress, but the business of finding a theme or an idea is the job of the agency. It is also the job of the agency to suggest which, if any, of the product's qualities is most exploitable at that time.

'Who makes the running in the agency–the verbal men or the visual men?'

Once the account team has decided which is the exploitable quality, it rather depends on the relative talents of the copy-writer and art director, but in the main the team works to a verbal brief, notwithstanding the fact that, for certain products, such as cosmetics, the illustration is often the principal factor.

'Where does the idea for the advertisement come from–that is, the theme rather than the specific content?'

It appeared that where there was no obviously exploitable theme, the account team, perhaps with the assistance of the client, usually invented a gimmick or selling point, either to overcome prejudices or develop preferences. The team usually tried to make the product personal in some way.

'Given the overall theme, how much freedom does the art director have?'

Within the given brief it transpired that it was up to the art director, or even the photographer concerned, to decide, for example, whether the advertisement should be set in a country cottage or a town flat, and to decide whether it should be sexy, demure or bizarre. There was a feeling among the art directors and photographers that the verbal men did not fully appreciate the importance of the visual side nor fully understand all its connotations.

'What, then, is the nature of the relationship between the art director and the photographer?'

The main reaction from account directors was that the photographer was virtually another tool or piece of possibly temperamental equipment for the art director to use. Yet the art directors perceived a greater degree of team work and would expect the photographers to try many shots with them and many models before selecting the final one. It was generally agreed that the photographer largely determined the colour scheme, if not the lay-out.

As far as one can tell, the photographers see themselves sometimes as 'doing a job', acting as a piece of machinery (although this may be a defence mechanism), and sometimes as artists who care very little about what sells the product or whether the product sells at all. They like taking beautiful pictures and are not necessarily interested in selling anything. Sometimes they may convince the art director into this attitude as well, in a conspiracy against the advertisement's singleness of purpose. Many seem to have a rather dim view of advertising agencies and their abilities.

'How is something like "mood" decided upon? Can it be planned or does it have to be left to the skill and intuition of the art director and photographer?'

Interestingly, a photographer felt that the art director usually knew what he wanted, whereas a director saw mood as a clever substitute for specific selling points–an elusive quality, not found until the right combination of light and mystery and suggestion is arrived at–a process requiring hundreds of shots.

'How is the model chosen, and what sort of factors influence the choice?'

She is chosen by the art director and the photographer, and the choice, of course, is limited by, on the one hand, the availability of models, and on the other, the magazine in which the advertisement is to appear–with-it in *Nova*, more staid in *Woman*. But once that was said there were differences in opinion. It was felt that the models should look a cut above the average woman, yet sufficiently true to life to appear plausible. Some felt the women should always be beautiful, but the men could be ordinary, others thought that where a woman was virtually a prop for a gas stove, she should be just that. For jewellery and cosmetics, a photographer who otherwise favoured the non-model girl, felt it was important that the woman should be aloof. When asked why, he thought it was probably the old 'dream world touch', the idea of a special separateness, something slightly unobtainable. The stimulus for that sort of choice often does come from the agency.

'How does one get the right expression from the model–is it specified, or a matter of chance?'

Photographers here expressed varying degrees of faith in the competence of the models to produce a variety of suitable poses which can be modified by lighting. Given the copy line and the lay-out some felt the mood created itself. Others felt it was the photographer's skill which generated the mood, and that often one did not know what one wanted until one had the right shot. Fashion had to be borne in mind for many aspects, the type of girl, the type of hair, the camera angle used. The straight, cool, self-confident look caught on and became fashionable due to copying by photographers and models, and being liked by agencies and clients. But these sorts of expressions would be shot as one of the whole series of shots, and would have to be selected afterwards–unless specifically asked for.

'How are props and background decided upon, and in whose hands do these decisions lie?'

These are sometimes specified, whereas sometimes there is a general description and it is up to the photographer to use his own experience. There is a variety of sources from which all sorts of props can be hired, and there is increasingly less distinction between what used to be called working-class and middle-class photographic backgrounds. Almost everyone now wants props to be tasteful without being more specific. Being London-based the whole of the advertisement industry reflects little more than the sort of outlook that you would get in London and the Home Counties. According to one photographer the general appearance of the houses in the Midlands is something that would never be used in a photo. Especially on TV, advertisements have to present a life style and a sort of setting and a house, that is (a) identifiable–so that the consumer can say: 'That is not my house but I can see how it might be', and (b) 'one stage up'–to which the consumer is assumed to be aspiring. Advertisements never present a total reality, but a one-stage-up reality, taking care that the props are never too expensive and thus take the whole picture too far away from the consumer's experience. Of course if there is to be a towel, it is nice to have a towel the same colour as the wallpaper and so it goes for all the other props–chosen on the basis of experience ('what fits'), good taste and simplicity. Once one starts showing real homes one has to be careful, which is why all TV commercials look the same: all treading the same thin dividing line; all sticking to safe semi-detacheds.

However, according to another photographer, advertisements frequently influence taste not through their explicit selling propaganda, but through the incidental items that are included by photographers because they like them. For example, to take pictures of food it was necessary to raise some of the dishes above the others, and because cake-stands were no longer available, plates balanced on upturned cups and similar devices were used. Subsequently (these devices having been in use over a period of time perhaps amounting to a year) public demand for cake-stands reached the stage where manufacturers began to make them again. At no stage had they been advertised. A similar effect has occurred with other items, such as Georgian style wrought-iron tables. These claims are not substantiable, of course. Nevertheless the hypothesis is a useful corrective to the idea that advertisements sell only the product.

In the area of models and props the art director and photographer have a considerable amount of freedom within the overall brief. Many of the last minute touches–which may have an important influence on the appearance of the illustration as a whole–are left in the hands of the photographer. The more complex the illustration, the more difficult it is for the agency to spell out exactly the picture it wants, especially where expression and atmosphere are involved.

'What is the nature of the relationship between the advertisement producers and the world they both attempt to portray and to communicate with? What sort of information do they find useful?

According to some of the workers in agencies research is a bugbear and a problem. There are group discussions for housewife information, with resident psychologists who take group discussions, but what the women actually say is not necessarily what they are feeling, and all agencies are suspicious of such techniques whilst agreeing that they give clues. Most direct changes in advertisement themes or campaigns arise from research. However, being an art director in London trying to picture a suburban housewife was seen as a major problem although there is some help from research: things that most housewives react to, certain types of situation, shopping habits, what they give their kids for tea, what they feel about vitamins, etc. In a national campaign one has to compromise to produce the epitome of a housewife. The 'ideal housewife' is constantly changing, and influenced very much by fashion, fashion in literature, social fashion, the world of pop, etc. Advertisements reflect trends, popular types, the social scene, for otherwise they would fail. All in all the account directors felt they were very much in touch with the consumers and any changes in the markets.

Leaving the words of the advertising men and the photographers, let us try to sum up. Each part of the machinery that produces the advertisement has a similar idea about the scope available: that the brief is very tight, the amount of freedom small. On closer analysis however, it appears that anything less than a complete *carte blanche* with the campaign is interpreted as no scope at all. It is the job of the agency to decide upon the theme of the campaign, a task carried out by a group of people more often than not led by the writers rather than by the illustrators. Once this has been decided there is not much likelihood of the art director or photographer changing it substantially. However, because the brief is verbal, a large amount of the visual side of the advertisement is left unspecified. This is perhaps one of the most overlooked but crucial factors in the putting together of the advertisement. However much is specified, the degree of interpretation available to those responsible for producing the picture must remain large because of this discrepancy. This is the advantage the art director reaps from the fact of the copy-writer's taking the lead, and it enables him to exercise a fair amount of freedom in important areas. For similar reasons the photographer also has room to manoeuvre—although less than the art director. Props, models, expressions, poses, mood—all these are very dependent on the art director and the photographer. Their respective power will depend to a large extent on the personalities involved.

The advertising world is overflowing with serious 'creative' people who are individually and collectively certain that they know 'what's right', what 'fits', what 'feels right'. 'Maybe you don't know it's right until you've got it, but when you've got it you know you've got it.' These tautologies sound like a definition of rhythm, or of how to find salvation. The general acceptance of criteria such as what 'fits' or what is 'tasteful' shows the lack of any real intention of matching advertisements to reality, or perhaps of any ability to do so. It is an uneasy union of 'creativeness' and 'business' which is revealed here—after all, the writers and designers and photographers do consider themselves (albeit vaguely) as artists—and since when has the artist had to bother about the correspondence of his work to objective data? The main concern is whether the end product looks nice or is tasteful (according to the artist's own concepts of taste) rather than with the varieties of taste and discrimination amongst consumers at large.

The interviews lead one to suppose that such props, backgrounds, and models as are used in advertisement illustrations are chosen on a basis of personal preference and of what is fashionable in certain metropolitan circles at the time. 'Tasteful props' ... 'Doesn't reflect more than the sort of outlook you would mainly get in London and the Home Counties' ... 'Experience, good taste, simplicity ...' and so on. Further, 'We don't present a total reality, but a one-stage-up reality.' What sort of reality is this one-stage-up reality? Given the difficulties involved in trying to represent the real tastes and styles of a particular class or group—what sort of a mutated specimen of existence is a one-stage-up reality going to be?

The information on which all of these people draw is a mixed bag of intuition, personal knowledge and research. The greatest stress and reliance is placed upon the first two, however much lip service (and money) is paid to research and concrete data. There is, not surprisingly, a professionally *shared* idea of what is good (or right, or tasteful)—a consensus, and of course, the consensus changes. There is, further, an assertion that, 'when it comes down to it, we in the agencies are just like everyone else, and we know what life is like'. The impression received, however, is that the producers of advertisements (and especially of the illustrations) have only a sketchy idea of what reality is like for the rest of society, and make little use of what they do know, because it mightn't look nice. Ogilvy's advice to agencies is significant: 'The consumer is not a moron. She is *your* wife.' (It's interesting that the worker should be assumed to be male and the consumer to be female.) Indeed, she may not be a moron, but the consumer is not likely either, generally speaking, to be the wife of the ad agency man, or anything like her. Unconsciously everyone is assumed to be roughly the same, basically middle class, basically tasteful. We can agree with McLuhan that ads are composed with an inordinate amount of care, but we would have to deny that there is necessarily any corresponding high degree of accuracy.

Media practitioners, spokesmen for the culture, tend to relay that version of the world which is most familiar to them; the more so the more restricted is their own world. The world of the advertising man is bound to be a restricted one – restricted geographically to the metropolis, and socially to a particular sub-group.

It is a world full of vogues and trends, full of pressures to create something new, original, unique – or something which gives the impression of being new, original and unique. The world is inward-looking. A great deal of attention is paid to other agencies' advertisements, other magazines, especially colour supplements, and other media. This means that certain trends, styles, or ideas can receive a greatly increased intensity of exposure than they might otherwise have merited. If something catches on in the media world, a snowball effect can develop – an idea, or a trend, or a style may receive coverage which has no relation at all to its hold, relevance or popularity at large. In this connexion, as indeed in others, it would be illuminating to study advertisement illustrations alongside editorial illustrations in a variety of magazines (including colour supplements), for it seems that the same sort of people are responsible for the creation of both.

The need to represent 'typical' people and 'typical' situations leads to the production of compromises, of composites, or of stereotypes. The account executives and the copy-writers may decide that what is wanted in a given campaign is a typical housewife – but it is those on the visual side who will decide on what she will look like, how she dresses, how she smiles, who she is. It is their taste, their choice, which is crucial – and what they prefer are nice-looking objects, or things which photograph well, which look 'right'. Further, when the team decides on a typical housewife they *mean* an ordinarily middle-class housewife. She is presented, nevertheless, as the *genus* housewife, not as one particular *species*, middle-class housewife. Hence what is in general terms middle class becomes the norm, that standard against which we measure ourselves, that which we must desire if we wish to be normal. A particular reality is presented as if it were the only reality. A particular idea of what life is like is presented as if it were the only, or at least the best, way of life. The composite, synthesized, drawing-board middle-class woman, and all her accoutrements, marches on.

Regardless of the accuracy of the presentation, it is the unspoken message of the majority of advertisement illustrations that *this is how things are*, which is quickly transformed in to *this is how things should be*. Advertisements become the (often unconscious) unofficial arbiters and judges of canons of taste. What they do is *not* to present styles of life as suggestions or possibilities, but as *faits accomplis*-'these styles are already accepted' is the implicit message of the advertising photograph, though they may be at that point accepted only in a photographer's studio.

As the good taste of the middle class (and not just of the middle class, but a certain special sub-group within that class, perhaps considering themselves to be the permanently one-stage-up people posited by their persuasive strategy) becomes the taste or aspiration of the rest of the country, socially and geographically, what can be said of the values, ideals and priorities of that same group? There is no need to suppose the existence of a conspiracy, but there seems a very real possibility that the tastes and values of a fairly small and inward-looking group (or even those tastes and values which they *presume* some real or supposed group outside of their own to appreciate or want) are being relayed and reinforced via the mass media to the rest of the population. Individual, regional, social and ethnic divergencies from these universally purveyed images of what is acceptable and desirable become, in this situation, even more tenuous pockets of resistance.

References

[1] For further exposition see Berger, P., *The Social Reality of Religion*; Faber & Faber, 1969, and Berger, Shuckman *The Social Construction of Reality*; Alan Lane, The Penguin Press, 1967.

3

Physical Appearance
and Concepts of Femininity

This chapter deals with the preparation for a detailed and systematic survey of such artefacts as advertisements, and reviews some of the problems likely to be encountered and some of the areas of interest upon which light might be thrown. Within the field of advertising the study is further defined by its concern with the printed advertisements: the problems would be of much greater magnitude were the subject television commercials, which open up a whole new range of debate as to possible procedure. Some of what follows might have some relevance to a study of television advertisements, but the area of film is even more a frontier of research than is the static advertising visual. The advantage to the analyst in the case of newspaper and magazine advertisements is that the image is there, static and available for scrutiny and rescrutiny at any time–though this should not lead one to a misplaced sense of the simplicity of the investigation. The field is further delimited by the selection of women's magazines as the specific area of research. The greater part of the approach underlying this study should however be as applicable to the study of any magazine advertisements–especially for example to the study of colour supplement advertisements–and of some relevance to the study of newspaper advertisements.

The problem that faces one at the outset is where and how to begin: whether to jump hopefully straight in, or to reconnoitre the area in order to get some idea of how the land lies. The latter approach was adopted, because in such a study as this no leads can be passed up, and the very essence of the work depends on its openness and flexibility. It should not be pretended that one is dealing with an area about which nothing is known or about which there are no preconceptions. With regard to some of the prime interests–appearance as meaning, the use of hair, cosmetics and the concept of 'femininity' for example–there is a body of thought and opinion already in existence, mixed though it is. Hence, before beginning to devise a specific system of analysis and classification, it may be that one can gain, apart from a general insight, ideas on how to construct the analysis, which factors to look out for, which to be more inclined to disregard, and so on. The material comes from many different sources, both academic and non-academic (neither proved more intrinsically valuable) and the approach to it is eclectic and selective. Those spheres of interest which seem the most illuminating and perspicacious are investigated most thoroughly, for example, the debate centering around the idea of the 'feminine mystique'. Following this review of the landscape an attempt will be made to synthesize insights and information gained from it with insights and information that has been gained from the experience of previous investigations (pilot studies of the actual advertisements), in order to produce a series of practical classifications on which an analysis can be firmly based.

THE SIGNIFICANCE OF PHYSICAL APPEARANCE

One's attention is drawn first of all to the human aspect of the advertisements: the actors. In every picture one's eyes go first of all to the men or women portrayed, and this in itself presents great difficulties. For each person is so complex, and the picture conjures up so many associations, feelings and meanings for the reader that it is hard to begin any sort of systematic analysis. The expression and pose of the actor will convey one level of meanings, and almost as important will be the hair, the clothes and accessories (like jewellery, spectacles, etc.). Before all this there is, surely, a level which has to do with overall appearance, total impression, and is connected with age and context, and beyond this one would want to consider the relationship of one actor to another.

Some work has been carried out by sociologists and anthropologists who are concerned to discover how expression and gesture carry meanings, and whether these meanings are inherent or culturally learned. There seems to be a general agreement that some basic expressive movements of the face and body have physiological connexions with the emotions and that therefore to a certain degree meanings may be inherently understood by anyone from any culture. Beyond this point there is some disagreement, which need not necessarily concern us as the advertisements being studied are the products of one culture and are read and understood within that culture. Whether there is a universal grammar of expression which is opposed to a culturally imposed grammar of expression, or whether cultures select from the available universal grammar, and in certain instances modify it, is a problem which remains unsolved, although the evidence to date suggests the latter to be more likely. This question is discussed in greater detail by E. Hall in *The Silent Language*. It is quite clear that expressive movements do convey quite detailed information to the on-looker even if it is not completely understood how the code underlying these meanings has been established. According to Paul Ekman in *The Recognition and Display of Facial Behaviour in Literate and Non-Literate Cultures*: 'Most affective displays are informative (that is, they can provide consistent information to observers), particularly if they are of sufficient duration to be easily observed ... Many affective displays can be cross-culturally understood, and within cultures they act as very efficient carriers of meaning.' He is here referring primarily to facial expression and gesture, when considering the advertisement, however, we are confronted with one frozen moment in time, and see only one part of the movement of a gesture of the expression on the face. In recognition of this the actor and photographer tend to concentrate on static poses and expressions – and this increases any tendency there might be already towards stereotyping.

The development of the science of kinesics, mainly by Birdwhistell points to a gradually greater understanding of the way in which 'visual aspects of non-verbal interpersonal communication' function. For the present purpose it is sufficient to note that pose and expression do convey meanings, and in many cases, very specific meanings. Stone sketches in a great deal of the background to the discussion on what one might call 'appearance as communication' and establishes the importance of clothes, especially as symbols capable of carrying vital meanings for the wearer and the onlooker. This is, of course, spelled out in a rather different way by Barthes in 'Système de la Mode' and in a short section in 'Elements of Semiology' (1.2.2.) where clothes are seen as comprising a complex language of their own. In this system the 'speech' comprises the individual ways of wearing the various garments (size of garment, degree of cleanliness, personal quirks, combinations of garments, etc.). Both the social-psychological and the semiological approach agree that personal appearance is a system of signification although they might differ when it came to deciding what – in a given case – was being signified.

Stone draws the distinction between appearance and discourse: ordinary appearance is communicated by 'such non-verbal symbols as gestures, grooming, clothing, location and the like'; discourse by verbal symbolism. 'Appearance and discourse are in fact dialectic processes going on whenever people converse or correspond. They work back and forth on one another, at times shifting, at other times maintaining the direction of the transaction.' One's appearance establishes one's identity, and to have an identity is 'to join with some and depart from others, to enter and leave social relations at once'. Stone goes on to say that a 'person's clothing often served to establish a mood for himself capable of eliciting validation in the reviews aroused by others'.

This is of interest for the light it throws not only on attempts to understand the meanings conveyed in visual advertising material, but also on the nature of clothes as products in the advertisements, and indeed all products connected with appearance.

Goffman has some interesting things to say in *The Presentation of Self in Everyday Life*, connecting the actors with the setting in which they figure, a primary concern of any analysis of advertisements. 'If we take the term "setting" to refer to the scenic parts of expressive equipment, we may take the term "personal front" to refer to the other items of expressive equipment, the items we most intimately identify with the performer himself and that we naturally expect will follow the performer wherever he goes. As part of personal front we may include: insignia of office or rank; clothing; sex, age and racial characteristics; size and looks; posture, speech patterns; facial expressions; bodily gestures and the like.' Some of these vehicles for conveying signs, as Goffman calls them, are relatively fixed over a period of time, but others are relatively mobile or transitory–like facial expression–and are adapted from 'performance' to 'performance'. The former might be termed 'Appearance', having to do with social status and activity and being fairly constant over time, and the latter 'Manner', having to do with the indication of behaviour at any one time. One expects some coherence and consistency between setting, appearance and manner. Here we approach again the area of stereotype, general type, ideal type touched on above. Significantly Goffman maintains that the 'Mass Media confirm general conventions of ideal type'–'while also searching out the exceptions to it. Finally, with advertisements in mind we should note this statement as in some ways a summary: 'Whether an honest performer wishes to convey the truth or whether a dishonest performer wishes to convey a falsehood, both must take care to enliven their performance with appropriate expressions, exclude from the performance expressions that might discredit the impression being fostered and take care lest the audience impute unintended meanings.'

Bearing all the above in mind, what practical implications does this have for a system of classification? First, that there should be a fairly detailed inventory concerning the characteristics of the actor(s). These characteristics can be subdivided into Appearance, Manner and Activity. Appearance would include age, sex, racial characteristics, size and looks; manner would include expression, pose and clothing; and activity simply what the actor is doing. A final area of interest would clearly be the relationship of actors to each other. At this stage of an analysis there would ideally be no attempt to 'decode' the expressions, gestures, etc. but merely to record, as any effort at uncovering the meanings expressed in this way forms a subsequent stage of investigation.

Before leaving the area of appearance it seems appropriate to consider in slightly greater detail the two major expressors of meaning: the face and the body. The overall survey being especially concerned with magazines for women, *most attention will be focused on the female aspects of each.* Where sex is not specified in the work which follows, it should be assumed that it is the female side which is under discussion.

The Face

In a way the importance of the face goes without saying. It is the part of the body which houses all five senses, from which we also speak, cry, laugh and kiss. It is the last part of the body to be covered, in Western society at least, remaining naked in almost all conditions except the most unusual or extreme. The face is used as a symbol of the whole person: people, convicts and celebrities, are recognized not by their whole physical selves, but by one small part of their bodies. There is here more detail and variation within a small space than in any other area of the person, and it is here, behind the face, that we imagine ourselves to exist. Hence the impossibility of regarding our faces with the same calm objectivity with which we can view our stomachs, knees and toes. Because the face is taken as a representation of the whole person and because it is the conveyor of messages to the outside world, the importance of its appearance can assume enormous proportions, especially when the additional persuasions of fashion and conventions of beauty are brought to bear. John Brophy from the stance of an art critic, states that 'From the sameness of our faces we obtain a feeling of security as an accepted member of a herd: from the tiny points of variation we draw the satisfaction and pride of being, after all, not quite like all the rest. This minuscule difference in the face becomes for us the outward sign of the subjective difference within, the difference which makes us, in varying ways and to varying degrees, individuals. Because of this the face is universally treated as an index to personality, and it is by their faces, far more than by their bodies (which are usually clothed), their voices (which cannot always be heard) or their fingerprints (which are rarely available) that we identify people ... It is the face and not any other part of the body upon which, love, passions, infatuation, any form of sexual drive–except that which is desire and nothing else–fixes itself.

The face may be the representative of the body, but the eyes are the representatives of the face, 'mirrors of the soul' and so on. 'The meeting of two pairs of eyes is one of the closest possible relations, whether this meeting expresses love, hatred, or the hundreds of variations between these two emotions,' as writes Feldman in *Mannerisms of Speech and Gesture in Everyday Life,* and E. Goffman reinforces this in *Behaviour in Public Places:* 'Eye to eye looks, then, play a special role in the communicated life of the community ... In Simmel's words [*Soziologie*] "of the special sense-organs, the eye has a uniquely sociological function. The union and interaction of individuals is based upon mutual glances. This is perhaps the most directly and purest reciprocity which exists anywhere."' Brophy speaks with greater lyricism: 'The eyes are the quickest and most vivid of all means of question and answer, that is to say, of intercommunication. They make nothing of nominally prohibitive barriers such as difference of race, class and language. What the *eyes* have to say has little to do with intellect or morality and may be communicated in a fraction of a second and involuntarily: its import is nevertheless unmistakable ... To give and receive signals, the eyes must seek out and hold, however briefly, the attention of another pair of eyes.' The face is frequently equated with the eyes, whether consciously or unconsciously. There is interesting linguistic evidence for this in the form of the French *visage* and German *Gesicht*. Even deeper significance has been found in the eye of psychiatrists. It is variously thought to be symbolic of the male or female sexual organs, according to circumstances and the anthropological and mythical background knowledge of the psycho-analyst.

If the eyes are of such importance, then the covering or shading of them must also assume considerable significance. This point is put by Feldman: 'Blinking with only one eye is used by women, usually of ill-repute, for seduction and invitation to further sexual action. If this is the purpose, it must be done with only one eye. The same meaning may be conveyed by another phenomenon, a feminine hair-do that covers one eye. Such a hair-do intends to create the desire in man to uncover and to see the eye, again a displacement from below upwards. For the same reason women like to wear dark glasses. It is true that the glasses may protect the eyes from the sun (but not always); but wearing them provides a secondary gain. The dark glasses tempt man to uncover the eyes and create in him a desire to get closer to the wearer.' Presumably hats with wide, floppy brims would be adequate substitute for the hair styles mentioned. Spectacles–whether darkened or plain– clearly have significance other than the psycho-sexual, that is, in the domain of fashion, image-creation and status. As accessories they became increasingly fashionable in the late 1960s. Most of the large annual sale of sunglasses is to 'A pure fashion market, putting increasingly expensive gear to increasingly frivolous use. And granny specs are the epitome of that frivolity, worn simply for show,' wrote Reyner Banham in *New Society* 29 June 1967, concluding 'It's another way of manipulating your image, and quicker than having a body like Charles Atlas in ten days.'

The world of fashion exerts its weight and influence on all aspects of the appearance, the face itself no less than the dispensable glasses. Whole facial styles become fashionable, designated the 'Twenties Look' or the 'Forties Look' and so on. These different styles are arrived at through hair-dos and the use of cosmetics, and to a lesser extent, clothes; they are therefore part of manner rather than appearance. A given style, however, seems often to become so established over a fairly long period of time, and so unexceptional, that it seems almost to attain the status of appearance, minor modifications within the style comprising the manner. The fashionable style (or 'Sixties Look'?) during the period of research can be briefly described as: long hair, preferably blonde, unpermed, hanging straight or with a slight wave, or surrounding the face in a great mass of luxuriant and chaotic growth; a light brown tinted skin relieved by pale lipstick and the use of dark eye-liners and generally fairly heavy eye make-up, including often the use of false eye-lashes. Examples of the style are ubiquitous: almost any photograph of the 1960s 'top model' Jean Shrimpton. The original exponent of the style may be said to be Brigitte Bardot, who also originated (if any person can be said to do such a thing) the characteristic accompanying expression: the wide coolly appraising eyes and the pout. Brophy's description of women's faces as depicted by Romantic artists in the first half of the nineteenth century is very close to this: 'Topped or framed with windblown hair, the lips parted and lax, the eyes enlarged to show more of the white than one would expect, appear to indicate a satisfying emotional experience, probably sexual, just brought to a climax. Women's facial make-up in the late 1950s and early 1960s, in particular the use of mascara on the upper lashes only, together with a pallid lipstick, seems to aim at a similar effect.'

The world of facial fashion is closely allied to the world of cosmetics and, of course, to advertising and promotion. The question of make-up is one on which there is very little objective information except for a few scholarly footnotes mainly deriving a connexion from anthropological sources from warpaint and the rituals associated with puberty. 'Themes in Cosmetics and Growing' by Murray Wax is about the only useful paper available on the subject where he begins: 'This paper deals with some practices concerning highly conscious social aspects of physical appearance, in particular, the appearance of women. These go under the names of "grooming" and "cosmetics" and they involve the manipulation of one's superficial structure so as to make a desired impression upon others. The manipulations include bathing, anointing and colouring the skin; cutting, shaving, plucking, braiding, waving and setting the hair; deodorizing and scenting the body; colouring or marking the lips, nails, hands, eyes, face or other exposed regions; cleansing, colouring or filling the teeth; moulding, restraining and concealing various parts of the body, and so on.' Wax notes, in common with some anthropologists and sociologists, the close association of patterns of dress and grooming with social status, but he does not explain how these associations work.

He also has several interesting ideas about cosmetics and grooming which might be noted at this point. One is his comparison of the average American woman to an artist or craftsman, who 'Tends to view her body as a craftsman or artist views his raw material. This is the matter which she can shape, colour and arrange to produce an object which, hopefully, will be at once attractive, fashionable, and expressive of her own individuality'. Another is the connexion of cosmetics and role adoption. According to Wax, women–especially the girl in adolescence–are continually experimenting with new styles which amount to trying on 'this or that personality'. An older woman, he maintains, knows herself and her role far better and can view fad and fashion from a distance. Finally, Wax asks–for whom does a woman dress? He answers that 'a woman dresses and grooms herself in anticipation of a social situation . . . the function of grooming in our society is understandable from the perspective of sociability, not of sexuality'. This provides a useful counter to the Freudian interpretation which would see the function from the sexual angle. Yet Wax himself admits that his explanation does not fit, for example, the suburban housewife who is always made-up but not in any anticipation of confrontations with peers or superiors. This seems an important problem upon which the advertisements themselves might shed some light.

Regardless of the changes of fashion, real and imagined innovations, real and imagined effects, cosmetics–including slimming and hair preparations–are a basic part of women's lives. The effects–as far as the consumer is concerned–may be intangible, but they are certainly not imaginary. The need felt by women to improve their looks seems to be extremely widespread in as far as it recurs through most societies. Nevertheless, the specific use of cosmetics and the feelings women have about not being caught 'without their face on' seems to be something that is culturally learned in a Western society. The fact that women feel they need make-up and that men feel that men do not is indicative of the obviously very basic connexion with female sexuality. The woman expects to be looked at in a way that the man does not, she is the passive 'looked-at' rather than the active 'looker'. It may also compensate for feelings of inferiority. Maureen Green in 'What Makes a Woman Pay £50 for a Pot of Face Cream' (*Observer* Colour Magazine, 13 April 1969) wrote: 'Cosmetics to most women are a way of emphasizing themselves, both in appearance but also in some subtler way. It seems to reinforce our identity, more firmly outline our own and everyone's view of us. It is narcissistic . . . but when it fails it seems to mean that the woman is ill.' One should also note Flügel's comment on cosmetics and narcissism in *Psychology of Clothes*: 'Another way in which painting may be said to contradict the reality principle is that it leads to narcissism rather than to love of others or interest in the outside world.'

Make-up is concerned with the making of impressions–on others or on oneself, and not just on men but on other women. It is also connected with special occasions–there are many women who wear little or no make-up most of the time and yet wear a great deal at a family or neighbourly gathering where they are meeting only the people they meet every day.

Another function of make-up may be–explicitly–the masking effect (bearing in mind the way some women refer to cosmetics as 'something to hide behind'). Flügel explains the use of masks drawing on anthropology and psychology, and suggests the contemporary anology of spectacles. There seems no reason to exclude facial make-up, 'When we wear a mask, we cease, to some extent, to be ourselves; we conceal from others both our identity and the natural expression of our emotions, and, in consequence we do not feel the same responsibility as when our faces are uncovered . . . The masked person is apt to be freer and less inhibited, both in feeling and in action, and can do things from which he might otherwise be impeded by fear or shame . . . If we ourselves are unmasked, we feel at a distinct disadvantage in talking to a masked person. To some extent the same effect may be produced by any garment (such as the veil) that tends to conceal the face, or even by spectacles or eyeglasses, since these make it more difficult to note the direction and movement of the gaze.'

Social pressures, role emphasis, special occasions, sexuality–and morale: all these are reasons, hypothetical explanations, some of which may hold true for some women, and some for others. It will be interesting to see on which aspects the advertisements tend to concentrate.

Hair

Hair is perhaps neither face nor body, yet the eye cannot consider the face without also taking in the hair–its colour, length, style and texture. Hair can in fact be used as much as cosmetics to alter the contours of the face, reshape the outline. Hair is not merely an accessory to the face but a most important and integral part of the facial image. Hair is a very potent symbol, and as such is more amenable to alteration and adaptation than is the face: for it can be dyed different colours, made to stand on end or hand down, cut into shapes or removed altogether–none of which can be done to the face beneath it. As a useful signifier it is an element to which close attention should be paid in the advertisements.

Hair, both male and female, has long been imbued with great symbolic significance. Charles Berg, a psychiatrist, interprets hair in Freudian terms and says that 'short hair is in the nature of castration', applicable to male *and* female. Hair is in fact the battleground where the conflict between the libido and repressing forces is fought; this conflict is manifested in the form of exhibitionism versus castration anxiety. Hair is the only phallus permitted to males by society. This leads to anxiety about its appearance: desiring approval (exhibitionism) yet fearing disapproval (castration) expressed by brushing it flat, keeping it tidy, shaving, etc.: socializing (castrating) oneself to prevent more serious socialization (castration) at the hands of society. Connected with this are all the concerns regarding hair thinning, falling out or going grey.

The anthropologist, Edmund Leach, tells us that in ritual situations, long hair = unrestrained sexuality; short hair, a partially shaved head, tightly bound head = restricted sexuality, and a closely shaven head =celibacy. His finding is that 'Head hair is widely used as a ritual symbol with genital and anal connotations.' It is used because the genital organs themselves have been made invisible by taboo. It is only the prudery of clothing which makes haircutting a more obvious symbolic act than circumcision. Head hair, according to Leach, is 'a symbolic displacement of the invisible genitals. It is precisely because hair behaviour embraces a widely understood set of conscious sexual symbolization that it plays such an important part in rituals of a *rites de passage* type which involve the formal transfer of an individual from one socio-sexual status to another.' In conventional English society male adulthood is still manifested in the clean shave and the short back and sides.

Women, brimming over with penis-envy (see p. 68), are allowed by society to grow their hair rather longer than men, 'Implying possibly a compensatory indulgence, compensatory for the phantasied genital castration' according to Berg, and also Simmel. There is also a religious factor. Women have biblical backing for their longer hair–but that support itself rests on what is presumed to be natural.

> 'Doth not even nature itself teach you, that, if a man have long hair, it is a shame unto him? But if a woman have long hair, it is a glory to her: for her hair is given her for a covering.'[1]

In the same way it is presumed that it is unnatural (in the way that homosexuality is 'unnatural') for men to have long hair, and this therefore suffers biblical proscription. Whether men are prohibited from having long hair *per se* or because it makes them look like women, is unclear. The latter seems more likely.

Hair is the most generally noted part of the feminine body after the eyes according to Havelock Ellis who establishes a connexion between the qualities of the hair and the potency or sexual virility of the individual. Roheim puts that connexion thus: 'Stags and lions grow antlers and manes (hair) in the rutting period because the surplus of libidinal energy recedes back from the genital organ to the whole body.'

Be that as it may, hair is none the less a loaded sexual symbol for both male and female—whatever the causes, hair is an obvious and deep-seated sexual symbol. A full head of hair, grown long, speaks of freedom: virility unrestrained by orthodox morality, even though paradoxically, long male hair diminishes the ostensible differences between male and female. Apart from its symbolic quality it has sensual and tactile qualities of its own. It is both aesthetically satisfying to look at and a pleasure to touch.

Long male hair is an affront not just because it upsets ideas of normality, sociability or tidiness, but because it jars on the sensitive nerve of sexual repression. Long free-flowing female hair is less of an affront, although the sexual and social connotations still apply, and there are specific hair taboos. Axillary hair is, according to Berg, commonly shaved off by women if it is liable to exposure for no other reason that it is liable to arouse effects associated with pubic hair.

To Berg, fair hair means passivity and purity: 'It may be that the frequent preference for fair hair in women . . . may be in keeping with an ideal of their passive role in the sexual situation . . . I consider that another element here is a preference for "cleanliness". The fair person, or the fair hair, seems cleaner, and does not so strongly disturb or mobilize anal-erotic reaction formations.' Fair hair has a vast number of mythical/romantic associations. Whiteness equals purity, and more than purity: innocence. Could Lolita, Candy, etc. have been portrayed with anything other than blonde hair? Fair hair, being a cool shade, assists the coolness of that level cat-like style of appearance affected by sophisticated womanhood (see above). The fashion for very short hair on women did not persist for long, and was restricted mainly to pop-oriented young teenagers. It appears that women look more to the worlds of cinema, modelling and advertising for their styles.

Paragons of Hollywood glamour had worn hair that was short and curled (Clara Bow) or bobbed, or post-war, hair that was curled, waved and ringletted—long, but elaborately and precisely arranged (Betty Grable), becoming a little freer as time went on, but still with lots of curls and close-waves (Marilyn Monroe). Alongside the decline of Hollywood as an influence and an institution, and the passing of the initiative to Europe, Brigitte Bardot presented an opposing image: blonde hair that was long, but tousled, free and natural. Jean Shrimpton popularized the style in England and it was continued by other models, for instance Maudie James.

Female hair can be both seductive and narcissistic. Long hair, suggestive of sensuality and sexual opulence is the most effective weapon of sirens and Loreleis in luring males to ruin, and an item of continual praise by writers and poets. One particular use of the hair in the seductive situation has already been noted: the covering or shading

of one eye. It is true also in this respect that it acts as a mask, in the way which Flügel suggests. But the alluring mermaidens with their flowing tresses have other interests: they sit with hand-mirrors, engrossed in themselves. For the narcissistic in women, what better object of admiration and pride, than the fruit of labour, care and expense, recipient of conditioners, sprays, rinses and colourants: her long voluptuous streams of (preferably blond) hair. For it is not only a question of hair, nor of hair which is long, but of hair which is long, loose and free–not set and curled in dainty waves and elegant ringlets.

The Body

The body can be either clothed or naked. If it is clothed it is clothed in a particular way. Items of clothing carry meanings as much as facial expression–on the other hand the naked body is not value free: it has certain meanings with reference to a particular society's norms and values. Regardless of the way the body is clothed or unclothed, the pose it adopts also conveys meaning. We learn to recognize certain expressive poses in the same way that we interpret facial movements. There are aggressive poses, compliant poses, aloof, seductive and narcissistic poses, lazy, active, and functional poses; the number and variation is infinite. Some are quite rigidly codified–for example, the soldier standing to attention–and others may depend on context and individual interpretations–the worker with his feet on the boss's desk. We may be less aware of this form of expressive activity than we are of our own and other people's facial expressions, but it is just as significant a part of our whole act of communication.

Much recent discussion about the body has concentrated on the increasing frequency of the phenomenon of nakedness–in theatres, film, books, advertisements, record covers, and presumably, in life. Nakedness has become impossible to detach from the concept of permissiveness and the weakening of moral restrictions and taboos. Almost every magazine or journal of general distribution has carried an article on the phenomenon. One section of society seems to see the naked body as signifying immorality, sexual licence and decadence while another views it as symbolizing freedom, self-knowledge and progress. In between one suspects the existence of a large group of people who enjoy the thrill of visions of nakedness but regard it as rather risqué or bad taste and regret the way that it is becoming so commonplace.

Advertising has not been averse to the opportunity of gaining extra attention in an easy way. An increasing amount of flesh of both sexes–but mainly female–has been exposed since the Breeze soap campaign in 1959. 'Views change, and you've got a permissive society today which accepts things it wouldn't have done twenty years ago' as John Braun, a secretary of the Advertising Standards Authority, expressed the con-

ventional advertising wisdom in the *Sunday Times* of 10 December
1967. Advertisements using nude or semi-nude models were initially
confined to the more fashion-oriented glossy magazines, but had spread
across the majority of the woman's magazine field by 1968–69. The
Enkasheeer tights advertisement was one of the first to risk naked
nipples (in magazines like *Honey* and *Nova*) but magazines like *Woman*
seemed reluctant to allow their advertising managers to go that far. Regarding advertisements directed at women, the theory currently expressed is that women should identify with the naked model, not that
it should appeal to men. Commenting on this sort of advertisement in
New Society on 15 May 1969, Charles Rycroft, a psycho-analyst, said:
'This is the most interesting part . . . it seems to involve this tendency
of women to conceive of themselves as objects . . . and also the idea
a woman may have that if she's not being looked at, she's not real.' To
Bob Wright, who created the advertisement of the nude-in-boots for
Elliotts, the appeal is exhibitionism as he explained in the *Sunday Times*
on 10 December 1967. Exhibitionism, narcissism, woman as object,
are the appeals suggested; there may be other simpler ones: aesthetic
pleasure, excitement, incongruity, daring.

In his work *The Psychology of Clothes*, Flügel states three reasons for
the wearing of clothes: Protection, Modesty and Decoration. Protection
he dismisses as a reason for lack of evidence, pointing to unclothed
tribes in inclement climates (e.g. Tierra del Fuego). He likewise dismisses Modesty, although both may be reasons for the continued wearing
of clothes. The *initial* impetus he maintains lay in the instinct for
Decoration, to which we will return.

According to Flügel, pleasures derived from the body stem from two
main sources, one source is primarily narcissistic, the other primarily
auto-erotic. 'The narcissistic element consists in the tendency to
admire one's own body and display it to others, so that these others can
share in the admiration . . . Some of the original interest in the naked
body becomes displaced onto the clothing or ornaments that appear to
augment the aesthetic effect of the body . . . There now exists an interest
in clothing which is relatively distinct from the interest in the body that
is clothed; the original crude exhibitionistic tendency has been to some
extent sublimated on to clothes.' Furthermore, Flügel says, 'The execu-
sive social idealisation of the female body exposes women to enormous
temptation in the direction of an exaggerated indulgence in narcissism.'
Auto-eroticism, on the other hand, is not displaced on to clothes. It is
connected with the pleasures of natural skin stimulation, air, wind and
sun on the body, and hence with bathing and with sunbathing–and at
one stage further, with the feel of clothes against the skin, especially
satins, silks and similar materials. The narcissistic and auto-erotic
elements are not unconnected of course.

According to Flügel women make use of decoration *and* exposure in the way they treat themselves in relation to their clothing. 'The female sexual libido is diffused over the woman's body. The male sexual libido is concentrated in the genital zone. Hence the exposure of *any* part of the female body is more erotic than the corresponding exposure of the male body–save only the genitals themselves.' Hence, according to this view, women are both more modest and more exhibitionistic than men: both shame and attractiveness relate to the whole body, though obviously some areas are more erotic than others. The exposure of the female body is more erotic to men *and* women than the exposure of the male body.

To return to the decorative aspect of clothing, Flügel enumerates the six formal aspects as he sees them, thus:

Vertical–to increase the apparent height;
Dimensional–to increase apparent size;
Directional–emphasizing the movements of the body;
Circular–drawing attention to the body's roundness;
Local–emphasizing a particular part of the body;
Sartorial–the embellishment of existing garments.

Some aspects seem more relevant than others in the contemporary situation, although all are present–the vertical for example in the use of high-heeled shoes, (and some hair styles). The dimensional aspect needs expanding to include garments which attempt to decrease the apparent size, such as girdles and corsets. Items such as brassières seem to fall into both this and the local category.

Clothes, as decoration, are concerned with making impressions, and are thus socially oriented. Angela Carter described them so in 'Notes for a Theory of Sixties Style' in *New Society* 14 December 1967: 'Clothes are our weapons, our challenges, our visible insults. And more. For we think our dress expresses ourselves but in fact it expresses our environment, and like advertising, pop music, pulp fiction and second-feature films, it does so almost at a subliminal, emotionally charged, instinctual, non-intellectual level.' She is here referring to a very particular area of society–the youthful, rebellious, trend-setting sector. Her underlying point holds true for all parts of society, as Stone recognizes. 'The meaning of appearance, therefore, can be studied by examining the responses mobilized by clothes. Such responses take on at least four forms: identities are placed, values appraised, moods appreciated, and attitudes anticipated. Appearance provides the identities, values, moods and attitudes of the person-in-communication, since it arouses in others the assignment of words embodying these dimensions to the one who appears ... In a variety of ways, as a matter of fact, reviews of a person's appearance are intricately linked with the responses he makes to his own appearance.' Clothes not only carry meaning in a very significant way, they are also closely connected to the self. '"I had to feel right . . . when I get the dress I feel right in, I feel like a million dollars. It makes an altogether different person out of me. That's an awful thing to say, but that's true for me." Similar but less dramatic remarks abound in our interview materials. All point to the undeniable and intimate linkage of self and appearance.'

There is a body of opinion which is concerned with the extent to which the identity of the female is bound up with her 'social front'. Is woman becoming alienated from herself? 'If our social front helps us to sustain a worthy social note', we must, as Simone de Beauvoir says, in *The Second Sex*, live up to the fixed character of our inanimate sign equipment: 'Even if each woman dresses in conformity with her status a game is still being played: artifice, like art, belongs to the realm of the imaginary. It is not only that girdle, brassière, hair dye, make-up disguise body and face; but that the least sophisticated of women, once she is "dressed" does not present *herself* to observation; she is, like the picture or the statue, or the actor on the stage, an agent through whom someone is suggested who is not there–that is, the character she represents, but is not.'

An echo to these views is found from a very different source, namely McLuhan in *The Mechanical Bride*. 'Held within a single filmy frame, these figures are a dream, secure in its irresistability. The resemblance to "the line" of a beauty chorus is a factor of some interest. The trade motto "Bodies by Fisher" is relevant to the present discussion because it insists on the close relation of motorcar glamour to sex, just as the feminine glamour advertisements and the modern beauty chorus insist on their relation to the machine. These two advertisements help us to see one of the most peculiar features of our world–the interfusion of sex and technology. It is not a feature created by the advertisement men, but it seems rather to be born of a hungry curiosity to explore and enlarge the domain of sex by mechanical technique on the one hand, and on the other, to possess machines in a sexually gratifying way.' This is a very useful and suggestive analogy which we would do well to bear in mind throughout the following chapters. In this respect the treatment of the body runs exactly counter to the treatment of the body in, for example, some sections of the *avant-garde* theatre, which abhor man's alienation from anything human, especially his own body, and seeks to achieve a reintegration of man, mind and body, with nature. The body, therefore, and in this sense including the face, can be experienced in two ways, alienated/object and integrated/subject.

CONCEPTS OF FEMININITY

It seems clear from the foregoing that in many different ways the actor can communicate to an audience, even in a silent and still representation

such as makes up the magazine advertisement. Some of this communication will be explicit and conscious, some implicit and unconscious
and some implicit and conscious: in the advertisement photograph a far
smaller part will be unconscious than in everyday interaction, for the
situation is artificial and the event is being staged for very *particular*
reasons. Apart from this, however, the areas that have been considered
raise other questions unconnected with symbolization and the communication of meanings, which are relevant to the subject of study. These
questions concern, basically and broadly, the nature of woman. How
seriously should the suggestions and assertions of narcissism, passivity,
insecure identity, etc. that have been made, be taken?

The classical Freudian interpretation of female psychology is, briefly,
as follows. A boy's mother is his first love-object, the Oedipal phase
develops and he perceives his father as a rival for his mother's affection.
Subsequently through knowledge that there exist people without
penises, the boy develops castration fears which lead to the repression
of the Oedipus complex and the formation of the super-ego. 'It is the
discovery of the possibility of castration, as proved by the sight of the
female genitals, which forces on him the transformation of his Oedipus
complex, and which leads to the creation of his super-ego and thus
initiates all the processes that are designed to make the individual find
a place in the cultural community.' In girls there is a pre-Oedipal phase
during which they are attached to the mother, but which, through the
realization of castration, the missing penis, is transformed into love of
the father. According to Freud the Oedipus complex therefore remains
and there is no creation of the super-ego, and hence women have less
ability in cultural and creative activities with which the super-ego is
concerned. Furthermore, the difficulties involved in the transfer of love
from the mother to the father, and in the change from clitoral to vaginal
sexuality, mean that women have less energy and ability to develop other
aspects of their characters. 'The small girl's first object, too, was her
mother. How then does she find her way to her father? How, when and
why does she detach herself from her mother? We have long understood that the development of female sexuality is complicated by the
fact that the girl has the task of giving up what was originally her leading genital zone–the clitoris–in favour of a new zone–the vagina. But
it now seems to us that there is a second change of the same sort which
is no less characteristic and important for the development of the female;
the exchange of her original object–her mother–for her father.' The
Freudian interpretation leads to a theory of female sexual inferiority
which is manifested in their notorious 'penis-envy'. 'The effect of
penis-envy has a share in the physical vanity of women, since they are
bound to value their charms more highly as a late compensation for
their original sexual inferiority.' According to Harnik, female beauty,

especially that of a woman's face, is a substitute to her for her loss of a penis. This interpretation of women's lot has been fiercely contested, but before considering other interpretations it is opportune at this point to consider in greater depth a phenomenon which has recurred throughout the areas that have been covered so far, and a phenomenon of which Freud is still a recognized authority, namely narcissism.

According to Freud, the human being has originally two sexual objects, him/herself and the mother figure. Both types of object choice, the narcissistic or the anaclitic, are open to each individual and either in the long run many manifest itself as dominating his object-choice. Object love of the anaclitic type is characteristic of the man. 'It displays the sexual over-valuation which is doubtless derived from the child's original narcissism and thus corresponds to a transference of that narcissism to the sexual object.' Object-love of the narcissistic type is characteristic of the woman. 'Women develop a certain self-contentment which compensates them for the social restrictions that are imposed upon them for their choice of object. It is only themselves that such women love with an intensity comparable to that of the man's love for them.' Freud suggests that the charm of such women lies, like that of cats, in their lack of concern about others.

Even for the woman who is narcissistic there is a path to complete object-love, through childbirth: 'In the child which they bear, a part of their own body confronts them like an extraneous object, to which, starting out from their narcissism, they can then give complete object love.'

Flügel agrees with Freud's description and draws out some of the social and commercial implications. 'The exclusive social idealization of the female body exposes women to enormous temptation in the direction of an exaggerated indulgence in narcissism. As we have more than once pointed out, our whole social attitude expects women to exhibit a greater narcissism than men. Some difference of this kind may not be harmful; at present, however, it is really difficult for a beautiful woman to develop to the full of her capacities as a lover or a citizen (as a mother it is often easier), her narcissism being so fostered by the admiration she receives as to impede the growth of object-love.' Furthermore, 'Women's greater participation in social life and undoubted greater sense of social values has not led to any great reduction in their narcissism. At any rate, our traditions still sanction and indeed approve a much greater and more open manifestation of narcissism among women than among men. Now it is true that narcissism need not necessarily find expression in fashion (since it is only indirectly connected with competition) but, given the present conditions, it is comparatively easy for the commercial influence to exploit narcissism in the interests of fashion.' Or in the interests of any other commodity, one might suppose.

There seems to be a difference of emphasis between Freud and Flügel which is symptomatic of a division throughout the whole area of female psychology and behaviour. The difference is between the emphasis on the psychologically-biologically innate and the socially constructed. Mention should be made here of the interpretation afforded by Karen Horney. She contests Freudian penis-envy theory and claims women are dominated by anxiety–especially sexual anxiety of being hurt/penetrated/destroyed. She deals at some length with female masochism and concludes that in Western culture it is hard to see how any woman can escape becoming masochistic to some degree, from the effects of the culture alone. Deutsch, on the other hand in *Psychology of Women*, takes a more innately psychological view: 'In many myths and fantasy formations, brutal possession is interpreted as a kindly act of rescue. In young girls' dreams the mighty hairy human-animal figure often appears not as a seducer but as a saviour and reveals the wish-fulfilling character of the girls' dreams and her masochistic longings.'

The school of thought which sees women as characterized by passivity, narcissism, masochism and so on which are all 'natural', innate and determined by the fact of being female, has been forcefully attacked by psychologists, sociologists and propagandists. These writers tend to emphasize the importance of social and cultural factors, while in the main not denying the prevalence of such traits as narcissism, etc.

Clara Thompson, a psychiatrist, points out that it is possible to explain every single trait attributed by Freud to a biologically determined development of the libido–such as all the implications of penis-envy, the repression of aggressiveness, passivity, masochism, the narcissistic need to be loved, the prematurely arrested character development of women, the weaker super-ego and so on–by the 'influence of "cultural pressures", that is, by the impact of a concrete historical situation on character structures.' Helen B. Thompson supports this view, although her methodology has been criticized by Viola Klein. Klein in *The Feminine Character* observes that '. . . the psychological differences between the sexes seem to be largely due, not to difference of average capacity, nor to difference in type of mental activity, but to differences in the social influences brought to bear on the developing individual from early infancy to adult years. The question of the future development of the intellectual life of woman is one of social necessities and ideals, rather than of the inborn psychological characteristics of sex'. She goes on to discuss Terman and Miles' investigation of sex and personality which concludes as follows: '. . . singularly powerful in shaping our development are other people's expectations of us, past and present, as shown by their practice and their precepts . . . At any rate, society in the shape of parents, teachers, and one's own fellows of whichever sex, expects these differences between the sexes, and literature reflects them. Irresistibly each sex plays the role assigned, even in spite of its own protests.'

Klein's own conclusions are that feminine characteristics are almost completely relative to the society, history, culture and very little can be said to be 'innately masculine or feminine'. 'All we can say is that in Western civilization today, because of our heritage and culture, it seems that women exhibit certain traits and men exhibit others, and these are . . . But, in the last resort, to equate narcissism, introversion, exhibitionism, emotionalism, etc., with femininity in any absolute sense is completely erroneous. But it does seem to me that in our present culture women do exhibit those traits because of the conditioning and expectations of the society in which they live: in other words, here and now, women are narcissistic, emotional, introverted, and so on–and any change in that pattern has to fight very powerful and quite successful reaction to it from women themselves–who believe that women are meant "naturally" to be all these things.' This is probably one of the clearest statements of the position, backed up as it is by an impressive weight of psychological, sociological and anthropological evidence. The anthropological evidence comes from Margaret Mead, who concludes that the biological facts of sex difference are irrelevant to the social characters of men and women, and that these are merely arbitrary constructs. The means by which a society enforces the acceptance of a selected pattern are manifold. She maintains that this choice is embodied in every thread of the social fabric–in the care of the young child, the games the children play, the songs the people sing, the structure of the political organization, the religious observance, the art, and the philosophy. Culture creates a coherent background, a mould into which characters grow and by which they are shaped. Part of that mould, of that coherent background, is of course advertising and the world of the woman's magazine.

The reason why the discussion of the femininity is so difficult, and the reason why it should be a topic at all, is that the standards by which mankind in general and societies and individuals in particular have estimated the values of male and female are not neutral, but, as Simmel puts it, 'in themselves essentially masculine'. To be male is to be in some way normal, to be female is to be different, to depart from the norm, to be abnormal. Therefore woman is more conscious of being a woman than a man is of being a man, hence also the endless debate on what it means to be a woman, woman's role, the place of woman in today's world, and so on. 'It cannot be overlooked that woman forgets far less often the fact of being a woman than the man of being a man.'

The consequences, in social terms, of society's view of woman and of woman's view of herself, are far-reaching. Historical and social pressures have been directed towards the identifying of the woman with the home and family. 'Emancipation' has not relieved woman of this, but has instead produced an almost irresolvable conflict between the old-established domain of domesticity and the new world beginning to be accessible to her. Women have acquired many new functions but have lost few of their old ones. This differentiation is not confined to the sphere of work. There are, as Viola Klein points out, two ideologies existing side by side – one stressing the equality of rights and abilities, the other emphasizing the contrasting interests of women. 'While woman appears as citizen and worker on the front pages of our daily press, its advertisement columns appeal to her specifically "feminine" emotions: her desire to please men by her looks and charms, and her longing for romance. Whereas the bulk of papers and books is addressed to all citizens without regard to their sex, there is a flourishing department exclusively for women, assuming, as of old, that they are interested chiefly or only in clothes, make-up, needlework, cookery, and romantic love.'

The struggle for the right to work is no longer directed against external obstacles, and there is no longer the same hostile public opinion to overcome which existed sixty years ago. The conflict, instead, has become internalized and continues as a psychological problem which may assume many different variations and shades. The central figure in the conflict is neither the career woman nor the single girl, but the housewife. It is the dilemma of the housewife which is explored most sensitively in a work by Myrdal and Klein, *Women's Two Roles*. '[The housewife's] status is, as always, derived from her husband as a kind of reflected glory, not from the quality of her own work. To counteract this state of affairs, which many women find depressing, a cult of Home-making and Motherhood is fostered by press and propaganda ... Sometimes this glorification has a suspicious air of persuasion: as if women needed convincing that their lot is better than they thought. Whether this impression is true or not, the sentimental cult of domestic virtues is the cheapest method at society's disposal of keeping women quiet without seriously considering their grievances or improving their position. It has been successfully used to this day, and has helped to perpetuate some dilemmas of home-making women by telling them, on the one hand, that they are devoted to the most sacred duty, while on the other hand keeping them on a level of unpaid drudgery.' The authors go on to place by the side of this image of the housewife another feminine ideal: the lady of leisure.

'This ideal ... put parasitism of women at a premium. The task of an upper middle-class wife was chiefly to be an ornament to her husband's home and a living testimony to his wealth. Her idleness was one of the prerequisites. Up to this day the two contrary ideals vie with each other in the columns of every woman's journal. There are on the one hand the domestic virtues with the fragrance of freshly made bread every day, together with the statistics showing a 14 to 16 hour working day. But there are also the costly cults of the lily-white hands, of lavish entertaining, and of changing one's highly fashionable clothes oftener and oftener ... While on the one hand more and more gadgets are offered to save time and labour, more and more time-consuming beauty treatments are recommended to keep in control a feminine figure which shows the effects of too little exercise and too much leisure.

'There is no use denying that, even today, the twin ideals of the hard-working housewife and of the leisured lady exist in an unholy (and as a rule unrecognized) alliance, jointly circumscribing woman's role as one to be acted out within the home. The worst of this ideology is not that it is irrational and out of harmony with the facts of contemporary life, but that it presents our young girls with a strongly false picture of the practical choice they have to make for their lives. An honest scrutiny should be made to differentiate between productive and necessary work in the house and what is only a time-consuming pretext; a distinction must also be made between well-earned leisure and sheer waste of time.'

The situation here stated clearly may be a one-sided view, but it is an interpretation the main lines of which make sense in conjunction with and as a summary to the psychological and sociological work which has preceded it and on which it is largely based. Before proceeding to see how factual data from English sources squares with the various theories, there are two works which deserve a special consideration at this point. They also take an aggressive and polemical stand on the subject of woman's position in contemporary society. One is *The Feminine Mystique* by Betty Friedan, and the other is *The Second Sex* by Simone de Beauvoir. They differ in that they are not written by anthropologists, sociologists nor psychiatrists nor specialists of that nature, but by writers, journalists – or perhaps more simply, thinking women.

Friedan is concerned with the identity crisis of the American woman as manifested most tangibly in the trend away from the career to the home. This trend is deduced from statistics on the one hand and interview material on the other. The treatment is journalistic and sources are not always accredited, but in less explicitly academic spheres, her style is more convincing. According to her own survey, magazine stories in the 1920s and 1930s depicted career women, with ideas and plans, becoming free, confident, assertive, self-reliant. Then, after the war, the picture is reversed, there is a reaction in the stories against 'masculinization', 'dangerous consequences to the home' and similar themes. This leads to what Friedan calls the feminine mystique, which holds that the highest value and the only real commitment for women lies in the ful- filment of their own femininity. The highest good is keeping house and raising children. In 1958–59 she failed to find a single heroine (in a woman's magazine) who had a career, a commitment to any work, art, profession or mission in the world. According to Friedan, contemporary American education for women places the emphasis on training for the sexual role, for marrying and for motherhood. Girls are directed to- wards the sexual function much too early and their other abilities go unrecognized and undeveloped. Brought up to concentrate on their future as wives, girls marry early, have children quickly and subse- quently discover their lives to be empty and unfulfilled. The conse- quences of this include neurotic fatigue, alcoholism, obesity and nervous disorders. Sex is then the only frontier open to women, hence its un- remitting pursuit and the need to 'search for their sole fulfilment through their sexual role in the home ... There is ... an air of exag- gerated unreality about sex today, whether it is pictured in the frankly lascivious pages of a popular novel or in the curious almost asexual bodies of the women who pose for fashion photographs. According to Kinsey, there has been no increase in sexual "outlet" in recent decades. But in the past decade there has been an enormous increase in the American preoccupation with sex and sexual fantasy.' It is possible that Friedan's description of the social consequences are exaggerated, but her general argument is more credible. In an uncertain situation, unsure of themselves, what they should do and what they really want to do, women are exposed to manipulation and easy prey to persuaders of all sorts, but especially those who stand to gain from the continuation of this particular interpretation of woman's function. 'The public image, in the magazines and TV commercials, is designed to sell washing machines, cake mixes, deodorants, detergents, rejuvenating face creams and hair tints. But the power of that image, on which companies spend millions of dollars for TV time and ad space, comes from this: American women no longer know who they are. They are sorely in need of a new image to help them find their identity. As the Motivation Researchers keep telling the advertisers, American women are so unsure of who they should be that they look to this glossy public image to decide every detail of their lives.' Dichter is quoted as saying: 'In a free enterprise economy, we have to develop the need for new products. We help them rediscover that homemaking is more creative than to compete with men. This can be manipulated. We sell them what they ought to want, speed up the unconscious, move it along ... If he tells her that all she can be is a wife and a mother, she will spit in his face. But we show him how to tell her that it's creative to be in the kitchen.' Friedan sees these manipulators and salesmen as the most powerful perpetrators of the mystique, who 'Blanket the land with persuasive images, flattering the American housewife, diverting her guilt and disguising her growing sense of emptiness'.

It is revealing to notice just how far in fact the American description of 1960 is in agreement with the French description of 1948. In de Beauvoir's France women were still immersed in Victorian social constraints, in the USA of Friedan, things have come full circle and the reaction against career and the outside world has led to a semi-voluntary enslavement encouraged by producers and advertisers.

It is de Beauvoir's central contention that women have been and are forced to occupy second place in the world, like some radical minorities, and that this position is nothing to do with 'natural' feminine characteristics but is due to the strong environmental forces of education and social tradition. This has meant perpetual inequality in all fields and has led to numerous social evils, the majority of them going unremarked because they are hidden behind the walls of domesticity. The ills this phenomenon has caused are not restricted to the concrete or physical sphere but are to be found throughout the whole spectrum of psychological disorder, for example, frigidity, nervous depression, kleptomania.

In childhood and early adolescence girls are brought up to feel inferior to boys and to acknowledge male dominance in all spheres of action. It is made quite unambiguous that decision and authority in the home and in the world lie firmly in male hands. The girl's upbringing stresses always that the male is the subject and the female is but the object; he is the One and she is the Other. Throughout all their formative years they are trained to see their destiny to lie in catching a man and in serving him – in other words, in existing through someone else, without having any individual identity and purpose. The young girl's first contacts with men are unreal. Her adoration of men is mixed with fear, and to solve this conflict 'She will dissociate the male in him that frightens her and the bright divinity whom she piously adores. Abrupt and shy with her male comrades, she idolizes some distant Prince Charming, a movie actor whose portrait she hangs up over her bed, a hero, dead or still living, but always inaccessible, an unknown noticed by chance whom she knows she will never see again. Such amours raise no problems ... In this way the adolescent girl, avoiding real experiences, often develops an intense imaginative life, sometimes indeed, confusing her phantasies with reality.' However, 'It is one thing to kneel before one's personally constructed god who remains afar off, and quite another to yield oneself to a male of flesh and blood.'

Throughout her life, and especially after the onset of menstruation, the girl has experienced feelings of shame and repulsion towards her body, its development, its feelings, and its potential. She fears her body

as she fears sex and men. In spite of these strong feelings she is forced
into a gradual acceptance of femininity and of the destiny imposed
upon women by society. To get a man, in some permanent form, becomes a more and more urgent business. Best friends fade as they are
seen more and more in the guise of rivals, and the world narrows even
further. She feels that if she devotes herself completely to some enterprise or career, she will miss her womanly destiny. The pursuit of man
takes first place–the girl becomes even more an object; she becomes
the prey in order to gain her end. Subsequently, even given her acceptance of the female role, the transition from ideal love to sexual love is
not easy or simple. The idealized man becomes all too real and human
in his sudden physical manifestation. De Beauvoir's view of sexual
initiation involves a very pessimistic outlook towards men–especially
in their roles as the brutal and careless deflowerers of naïve virgins.

In marriage, de Beauvoir sees things in terms of subject and object
once again: the girl being married and the man taking a wife, an old-
fashioned concept wherein the girl has little or no choice as to her husband. There is perhaps more relevance in what she says about the
unenviable position of women who remain unmarried, especially concerning society's disapproval of free love and unmarried motherhood.
But the plight of woman is little better within marriage, for she remains
constrained while the man has the field of action open to him; she is
shut up within the circle of herself. 'Woman is confined within the
conjugal sphere; it is for her to change that prison into a realm.' Hence
the bric-à-brac of the home, which represents the flora and fauna of the
world, the husband who is society, and the baby which is the entire
future in portable form. Home is the centre of the world–or its only
reality, and its decorations provide the expression of the woman's personality; because she does nothing, she seeks self-realization in what she
has. Yet her housework–the mere keeping of things clean and tidy–is
negative and repetitive, and likely to lead to disappointment and boredom. For marriage is the final state, beyond which there is no other
future. She is first and foremost a wife, but her husband is a citizen and
a producer before he is a husband. And as husband his dominance and
superior knowledge of events and of culture make her feel incompetent,
and fill her with a desire to humiliate the man and resist his domination. The wife begins to understand that the man could get along without her, that her children are found to grow away from her and to be
ungrateful. Home no longer saves her from empty liberty–she is alone,
forlorn and melancholy.

Simone de Beauvoir does not see the wife as being employed outside
the home or having any outside interests. How much difference does
having a job make? It brings a certain amount of financial independence,
but as de Beauvoir sees it, it only increases the chores a woman has to

get through, induces guilty feelings about the home and family, and does not provide any real outlet. Certainly the jobs most married women undertake are as boring and repetitious as housework, but they do provide a focus outside the home and an opportunity for meeting other women, and other men. Furthermore, these jobs are hardly more uninteresting than the work many of their husbands will be doing. The more satisfying alternatives seem to be a 'career' or 'outside interests', though the former is not available just for the asking and the latter would presumably have to be something more than the Parent Teacher Association and charity work described and dismissed by Betty Friedan.

Neither Friedan nor de Beauvoir sees the answer to the forlorn and frustrated wife in motherhood. As de Beauvoir sees it the mother obtains in her child what man seeks in woman: another, to whom she is delighted to be necessary. But she is liable to have an ambiguous attitude towards her children, loving them and yet resenting them, wanting her son to be successful and powerful and yet under her control, wanting her daughter to be perfection yet resenting her rivalry. The mother will also feel resentment and jealousy towards her children's friends (both young and adult), and their ideas and independence. Further, 'the amorous type of woman feels resentment towards the children who ruin her seductiveness and deprive her of her husband's attentions. If, on the other hand, she is of the deeply maternal type, she is made jealous by her husband's claim to own the children along with everything else.' Maternity is not enough in itself to crown a woman's life. In this context one might make note of the conclusions reached by Ann Oakley in her article on 'The Myth of Motherhood' in which she uses anthropological and biological evidence to dispute that there is, in fact, anything inherently feminine about motherhood (as distinct from childbirth') She says that the concept of the 'maternal instinct' takes its place as one of the myths according to which social arrangements are conveniently established and constantly reinforced.

So woman moves through life into middle age. According to Simone de Beauvoir: 'Each period in the life of a woman is uniform and monotonous; but the transitions from one stage to another are dangerously abrupt; they are manifested in crises–puberty, sexual initiation, the menopause–which are much more decisive than in the male.' The menopause is accompanied by disappointment and regret; exaltation mingled with depression, the reliving of the past and the desire to prove oneself still youthful. She must eventually make up her mind to grow old. She may, if she identifies with her daughter, take pleasure in her grandchildren, experiencing again the joys of possession and maternity; but only in the role of assistant. To forestall loneliness, regret and boredom, the woman may seek relief in social life or in charitable organizations.

There is, in contrast to some of the assertions that have been considered, a body of factual data concerning women which may throw some light on the problem. Women suffer from discrimination in employment, especially in terms of promotion and pay, and there remain many legal discriminations and fiscal anomalies: for example, the difference in allowances available to widows as against widowers, and the difficulties encountered by women in the fields of hire purchase and mortgages. An example which is typical of legal disabilities is the fact that in the event of a divorce the woman is entitled to only half of the savings she may have accumulated from her housekeeping allowance. In the sphere of work and careers the picture is mixed. The proportion of women going to university has remained at about one-quarter for the last forty years, although the number of girls in 'full-time further education' has increased and is greater than the number of boys.[2] However, once at work, differences are immediately visible–there are four times as many boys as girls on day-release courses or on apprenticeships. Although the number and proportion of women in the labour force has increased (from 42 per 100 working men in 1921 to 52 per 100 working men in 1961) and the proportion of married women working has also increased (from 13·7 per cent in 1921 to 51·5 per cent in 1961), the jobs they carry out tend to be at the lower end of the professional-skilled-unskilled scale. Furthermore there is a decreasing proportion of women in the managerial, professional and skilled manual classes and an increasing proportion in the clerical, semi-skilled and unskilled classes of employment.[3]

At school 'Domestic Science' is in most cases taught to girls only, and as Berger and Maizel put it in *Woman: Fancy or Free?* 'Domestic science would hardly have been chosen if it were not that girls are conditioned to accept marriage and motherhood as their pre-arranged destiny.' The assumption is that home-making is a skilled and complicated job requiring extensive training. Because of the shortage of science staff at many girls' schools the pupils are encouraged to choose arts subjects and to leave science 'for the men' emerged from *The Second Sex* on BBC Radio 4 on 4 June 1968. Other childhood and adolescent influences range from the provision of toys (dolls and dolls' houses for girls) and the assistance expected from daughters in the home to the sentiments and themes of girls magazines and popular records, where the dominant themes are love and securing a man. The overriding desire to marry has been documented by many observers–notably Pearl Jephcott, and Berger and Maizels. Jephcott, in her studies of factory girls, found that employment was considered by these girls as an unavoidable but temporary phase in their lives and the sooner it came to an end the better. Berger and Maizels describe the survey in which 600 girls in secondary schools were asked to give accounts of their lives as they imagined they might be in the future: 90 per cent talked about their marriage.

It would seem from the foregoing that–even allowing for exaggeration–the everyday woman and the model in the advertisement are not as carefree and untroubled as they might appear. The specific nature of the trouble remains incompletely defined but the general lines seem clear enough. Of the greatest importance for this study is the frequently expressed view that the world of the mass media–and most especially advertising–is the major cause and encouragement, acting indeed as a social regulator. The purpose of this regulator is both economic and political: economic in the commercial sense of turning women into reliable consumers of feminine and domestic goods, and in the wider sense of maintaining an unpaid work force in the home and a low paid one in the factory; and political in the sense that by these means men are able to dominate every major sector of society. Since this research was carried out, an increasing amount of information has been brought to light and a great deal of attention focused on these problems, through the activity of the Women's Liberation Movement, and its offshoots. Overall, the result has been to lend support to the arguments of this chapter and to emphasize even more the role of culture in determining how we interpret being 'woman' or being 'man'.

Having investigated some of the complexities with which one is immediately involved when considering the actor in the advertisement, it must not be forgotten that the illustration contains other elements besides. There are four different constituent parts in the advertisement illustration, although not all would be present in each and they would occur in differing combinations. These four are the actor or actors, the product being advertised, the setting and the stage properties or props. Dealing with the inanimate, one is perhaps on easier ground, although this is partly due to the lack of any psychology or sociology of settings and props. These then, will be considered in the following chapter when we are dealing with the problem of developing particular classifications.

References

[1] I Corinthians xi.

[2] DES and DEP figures 1966–67.

[3] Census material/Manpower Research Unit quoted in *New Society*, 26 February 1970.

[4] See especially Germaine Greer's *The Female Eunuch* (Paladin, 1971); also 'Myths about Women' in *Voices from Women's Liberation*, ed. L. B. Tanner (Signet, 1970); 'Psychological and Sexual Repression' in *Sisterhood is Powerful*, ed. R. Morgan (Vintage, 1970); *The Body Politic* (Section III), ed. M. Wandor (Stage I, 1972).

4

Advertisement Illustrations:
A System of Classification

The problem now is to devise a system of classification which will grasp the crucial part of as many of the concerns discussed in the preceding chapter as possible, while still remaining a feasible system. In any synthesis of this sort, some aspects are bound to be left out or paid less attention than others, but is important that the categories that are in fact derived, stem directly from what have already been seen to be central concerns and should not be derived from some theoretical, superimposed structure. *The categories and classifications should emerge from the material rather than be imposed upon it.* Each classification should be the result of previous thought and investigation, and tailored to bring out those aspects felt to be the most significant. In this way categories may be less hard and fast, but the reader can reconstruct their development and can bear in mind the merits and deficiencies attached to each.[1]

Classifications of illustrations are neither 'hard' nor 'soft', completely intuitive nor completely objective–apart from a few classifications based on a distinction such as male/female, indoor/outdoor. Many classifications are a matter of degree, delineations along a spectrum. Although some parts may appear intuitive, or the lines between categories arbitrary, it is still important nevertheless to try to make the distinctions. It may be difficult to say exactly where red becomes mauve, mauve becomes purple, and purple becomes blue, but there is no disputing that blue is very different from red, or that purple and mauve are different from both. Categories and classifications are fairly simple tools to enable the establishment of some sort of order in a seemingly unordered situation: if they are too rigid they become useless, if they are too loose they are equally useless. Somewhere in between one finds the most efficient and fruitful way of bringing out the essence of the material without destroying it. Of course, where the material does not fit the classification it needs to be examined especially, the irregularities being as important as the regularities.

In evolving a system of classification, one is also involved in creating something of a new vocabulary–if only in order to give names to categories. The classification becomes a simple skeleton of basic terms for

CHILDREN'S FAVOURITES WITH LONG GRAIN RICE

1(a). Part of an advertisement for American rice from *Woman*. See particularly the section on lighting and focus (p. 83).

(b). Part of an advertisement for Number Seven moisture cream from *Woman*, illustrating the mirror image special effect. (Notice also the moulded hair style.)

Sulky hair silky!

New Vaseline Beauty Shampoo is so rich it pours out in slow motion. Vaseline Beauty Shampoo is richer, thicker, better for your hair. You can actually feel the rich lather of Vaseline Beauty Shampoo getting right down to the very roots of your hair. Feel the way it penetrates, deep down with its conditioning goodness. See the way your hair comes up bouncing, full of healthy, shining life. Obedient, ready to be styled in the way you want. Vaseline Beauty conditions the sulkiest hair to new bouncing, shining silkiness.

New, enriched Vaseline Beauty Shampoo ...beauty pure and simple.

A Chesebrough–Pond's Beauty Product

2(a). Advertisement for Vaseline shampoo from *Woman*, illustrating particularly the effectiveness of cropping. Notice also the fairness of the model's hair, and the focus of her eye.

New Cheeseland Zedl

that's the feeling you get from
New Zealand Cheddar

New Zealand Cheddar fills 'em up in the best possible way. It's all goodness however you serve it. It gives them go. It gives them that lovely lively feeling that extra something that's really good and really satisfying. Whether it's snacks or meals, you know you're giving them the protein goodness they need. And you feel even better about it when you see the bargain price.
Look for New Zealand Cheddar and give them and yourself that NEW CHEESELAND ZEAL.

2(b). Advertisement for New Zealand cheese from *Woman*, illustrating the special use of camera angle, and the connotations of childhood.

3(a). Advertisement for New
Zealand lamb from *Woman* in the
full immediacy of close-up. Consider
the illustration without the glacé
cherries and frills.

3(b). Advertisement for bread from
Woman's Own in close-up, and with
purely functional props. (Detailed
analysis in Appendix I.)

4(a). Cluttered advertisement for Embassy cigarettes from *Woman.*

4(b). Advertisement for Tampax from *Woman's Own,* showing the full active life.

5(a). Advertisement for Cookeen from *Woman*, showing the Cookeen Pastrycook of the month – an example of testament. (Note also the kitchen-oriented mum, the setting and the props.)

5(b). Advertisement for Belle Color shampoo hair colouring from *Woman*, an example of a celebrity's testament, and with the props of luxury and status.

6(a). Advertisement for Maxwell House instant coffee from *Woman*, uncluttered yet with both functional and metaphorical props.

6(b). Euphemistic advertisement for Noble Lowndes Annuities from *Woman*, with feminine connotations in the jewellery representing the adult child.

6(c). Advertisement for Morny soaps from *Woman's Own*. The setting is romantic and feminine, and the boat laden with flowers is an example of hyperbole.

7(a). Part of an advertisement for Sunsilk hair spray from *Honey*, with barbed wire showing the untouchability of the wrong kind of hair spray.

We move fast with the times. Some of us drive. Some type. Others pack parachutes, help to control aircraft, or handle supplies. Some of us work abroad, others at home. Wherever the R.A.F. operates — we're with it! If you'd like to know how to get with it too, fill in and post the coupon today. Learn how you can move around, meet people and enjoy your work as well. You'll get good pay, comfortable accommodation and 30 days holiday each year. Entry at any age between 17 and 39. Applicants resident in U.K. only.

WOMEN'S ROYAL AIR FORCE

What's so with-it about the W.R.A.F ?
the people in it!

7(b). Advertisement for a career in the Women's Royal Air Force from *Honey*. The women have moulded hair styles and the focus of attention is diversified.

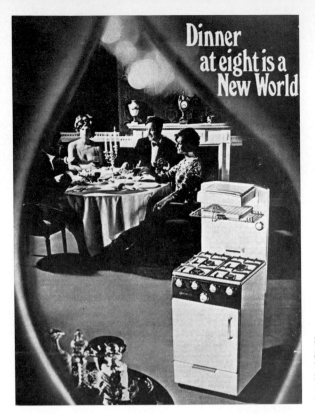

8(a). Advertisement for New World gas stoves from *Honey*, seen through the special lighting effect of a candle flame. The picture is full of connotations of luxury, projecting the hostess image of woman.

8(b). Advertisement for an electric cooker from *Woman's Own*, in direct contrast with that for the gas stove. (The kitchen-centred wife.)

A LIPSTICK IT ISN'T!

It's the first coloured lip gloss — and it comes from Cutex!

You've never seen a lipstick so sheer and shiny. But then it's not a lipstick at all, it's a lip gloss—with just enough colour added to warm your lips and glow through the shine. Colour Gloss — in Sheer Apricot, Lilac, Orange and Damask.

Colour Gloss by

CUTEX

9(a). Advertisement for Cutex lipstick from *Woman's Own*, showing the use of lighting and close-up.

Women have an all-day reason for using a very special kind of deodorant.

Bidex is the first to last all day.

Bidex is the intimate deodorant with the most reassuring advantage a girl could have. All-day action.
Other vaginal deodorants wear off long before Bidex stops working. The secret of Bidex Spray Mist's all-day action is protected by the Swiss gynaecologists who developed it. So only Bidex has the potent all-day comfort and confidence.
Bidex doesn't just cover up odour, it prevents it. Do first thing every morning, use Bidex—to see you confidently through the day.

Bidex
the first all-day intimate protection.

9(b). Advertisement for Bidex deodorant, an extreme example of introverted self-tactility, and the use of metaphor.

COME JOIN THE FREEDOM-LOVERS

Jump into a Shape-Suit* – feel freer, shapelier
than ever before. Step in, pull on, no zip. Just a
shapemaking second skin.

Berlei 'Mardi Gras' Shape-Suit in Crème de Menthe and
Champagne Amber. 32-36A, 32-38B, 34-38C, 59/11.

In the beautiful world of

Berlei

*with LYCRA
Lycra is Du Pont's registered
trademark for its elastomeric fibre.

Berlei (UK) Limited, Slough, Buckinghamshire

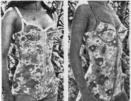

10(a). Advertisement for Berlei
shape-suits from *Woman's Own*:
the setting exotic, the pose artificial
the models ignoring each other and
the reader. (Detailed analysis in
Appendix I.)

10(b). Advertisement for Laird
Portch from *Honey*, portraying an
outdoor world of excitement, the
women active, the man a prop.

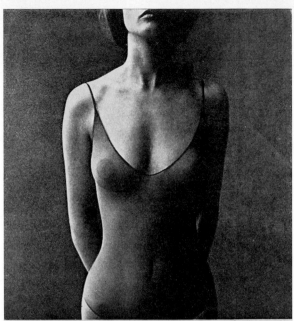

Once again we have nothing to announce.

We are the stocking company who brought you no suspenders.

We also didn't bring you the wrinkled stocking. And later we were the first without bags in tights.

But this time we've really come up with nothing. No bra.

No lumps and bumps to show through your dress. No buttons and bows.

No straps and bones. No pushing and pulling. The little thing we've got is called a Pretty Polly Body Stocking.

It comes in five flesh tones so it looks like nothing. And it costs 9/-. Which is like getting nothing for nothing.

PP
PRETTY POLLY

11(a). Advertisement for Pretty Polly body stocking from *Woman*, an example of cropping and the reified body. (Notice also the logotype.)

We started from scratch

We started from scratch. Softly but softly. Fit by fit. So now you can feel a new sensation. Enkasheerness. That smooth, you scarcely feel it. And so stretchy you'll want to jump for joy. So go ahead and jump.

Because, when you come down to earth you'll realise something else. Stockings and tights in Enkasheer always stay in great shape. And feel more comfortable than any before. Which makes Enkasheer quite a sensational new sensation.

Enkasheer a new sensation from British Enkalon.

11(b). Advertisement for Enkasheer tights from *Woman's Own* showing a fair-haired introverted, self-touching model in the midst of the feminine luxury of fur. (Detailed analysis in Appendix I.)

Félice ...is running barefoot
through the heart of summer
...never seeing
summer's end.

Félice — a summer affair that will last forever.

A NEW PERFUME BY ATKINSONS. Perfume. Parfum de Toilette. Spray Mist. Talc. Soap.

12(a). Advertisement for Félice perfume from *Honey*. Note the setting and the relationship between the man and the woman.

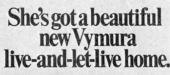

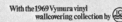

She's got a beautiful
new Vymura
live-and-let-live home.

With the 1969 Vymura vinyl
wallcovering collection by

The new Vymura Collection is a collection of beautifully designed wallcoverings that can make your home more beautiful than ever. With a whole new variety of patterns. Richer, warmer colours. And textures ranging from hessian to silk.

Vymura keeps your home beautiful, because it's vinyl. It's the easiest thing in the world to clean. Fingermarks, jam, coffee, grease and things like that, come off with a wipe. With Vymura on the walls you can let the family carry on living without worrying. And Vymura goes on as easily as wallpaper. And it's easier to strip.

So you too can enjoy the best of both worlds with the beautiful new Vymura live-and-let-live home.

The new 1969 Vymura collection strikes home beautifully.

VYMURA

12(b). Advertisement for Vymura wallpaper from *Woman and Home*, cluttered with the props of childhood and family.

Meet the beautiful ones from Kleenex

new Kleenex Boutique tissues Sizzling colours like Hot Pink, Bold Gold, Peacock Blue and White, packed in show-off boxes! Tall, slim boxes specially made to look gorgeous in any bedroom or bathroom. Full size Silk-Soft tissues inside, so pretty and so useful.

Unwrap to leave a 'no name' box too beautiful for words —a pretty slim box at a pretty slim price!

13(a). Advertisement for Kleenex tissues from *Woman's Own* with the props of femininity and luxury metaphorically eloquent.

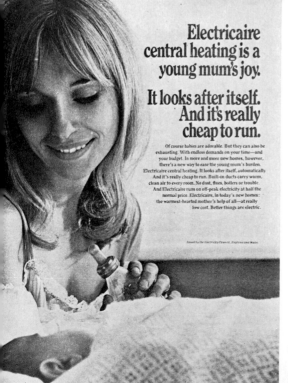

Electricaire central heating is a young mum's joy.

It looks after itself. And it's really cheap to run.

Of course babies are adorable. But they can also be exhausting. With endless demands on your time—and your budget. In more and more new homes, however, there's a new way to ease the young mum's burden. Electricaire central heating. It looks after itself, automatically. And it's really cheap to run. Built-in ducts carry warm, clean air to every room. No dust, flues, boilers or trouble. And Electricaire runs on off-peak electricity at half the normal price. Electricaire, in today's new homes: the warmest-hearted mother's help of all—at really low cost. Better things are electric.

Issued by the Electricity Council, England and Wales

13(b). Streamlined advertisement for electric central heating from *Woman*, showing the young, baby-centred mum and overlaid with further connotations of childhood.

You, too, can rediscover the natural beauty of your hair with the essence of eleven beneficial herbs in new Polyherb shampoo

Only new Polyherb shampoo with 11 beneficial herbs can make your hair so beautiful. 11 time-honoured herbs fill this new conditioning shampoo with natural goodness. Precious essences put gloss, gleam and glow into tired hair, fill it with fragrance and freshness. Herbs and beauty have always gone together. Try new Polyherb and you'll soon see

A traditional use for Arnica, Nettle and Cinchona was to tone and stimulate the scalp. Nettle was also combed through the hair to make it soft and glossy.

Herbalists recommend Birch, Speedwell, Mare's Tail and Coltsfoot for their soothing, curative properties. Yarrow has always been famous as an aromatic hair wash and tonic.

Women have used Camomile for centuries to brighten their hair; sweet-smelling Rosemary and Clover to make it fragrantly beautiful.

POLY means everything for your hair

The bottle, 4/11
The sachet, 1/-

Available at chemists and other good stores

new **Polyherb** shampoo

14. Advertisement for Polyherb shampoo from *Petticoat*. Significant are model's expression and the naturalness of her surroundings. (Detailed analysis in Appendix I.)

rt on Dr. White's

"...every day is much the same"

Dashing about, trying to get Lucy to walk so I can put the shopping bags in the push chair. The days all drift into one another -except the days when I have my period. They're not difficult days though, not now that I use Dr. White's. Dr. White's make you feel so comfortable and safe that you sometimes forget you've got your period. They're soft and reassuring. I always feel I can cope with things. Just as well since I'm going to have to carry Lucy home!

15. Advertisement for Dr White's sanitary towels from *Woman's Own*, set in familiar outdoor surroundings. (Detailed analysis in Appendix I.)

**Ideal discerning country lovers,
these three Norvic properties of
superior design, convenient shops,
schools and station.**
Attractive suede/leather construction
on hard-wearing gristle sole foundation.
Luxurious wall-to-wall foam-back carpeting.
Choice of front elevations and this

year's top decorator colours including:
Kano tan, Mulberry leaf and red.
Left: Dunnock. Below: Whinchat.
And top: Redshank. All about 89/11
freehold. Early inspection advised.
Your nearest Norvic
stockist will gladly
show you round.

NORVIC
Alfresco

For nearest stockist, write Norvic Shoe Co. Ltd.,
Norwich. NOR 32A.

Norvic invite you to step inside
and make your feet at home.

16. Advertisement for Norvic shoes from *Woman*, set with the props of luxury and outdoor
life. (Detailed analysis in Appendix I.)

use in the analysis and ordering of a large number of varied advertisements in order to uncover the meanings and messages of the illustrations
and to discover the most prevalent and recurrent, to note the methods
by which they are communicated, in terms of technique and rhetoric,
and to classify the contents of the illustrations in order to correlate and
compare across the field, discovering recurrencies and patterns.

It is the illustration that one is trying to understand–but an understanding of the elements in the advertisement is necessary where they
affect the illustration. Some account is taken of these other elements
in the question of the overall style of the advertisement. It is impossible
to read the illustration without noticing the copy and headline and any
other verbal elements on the page, and the information or tone of the
verbal content affects the reading of the illustration. It may therefore
affect certain parts of the classificatory system, for example, the decision on the difference between one sort of expression and another.
Since this verbal overlap is inevitable it should be acknowledged, but
this analysis is not a linguistic one and cannot attempt to cover that
field as well as the already complex one of the illustration, any more
than it can cover the rest of the magazine in which the advertisement
appears and which also affects our reading of it.

The first requisite breakdown is into form and content; the form
aspect being twofold: (i) the overall impression and style of the advertisement which is a visual rather than a verbal experience, a complete
impact rather than a linear reading, and (ii) the techniques involved in
the actual illustration, which–as the vast majority is photographs–will
mean photographic techniques. Before considering content pure and
simple, there is an area to which one gives the heading 'rhetoric' and
which concerns the way in which the illustration works, including the
interplay of form and content. Rhetorical devices are methods of persuasion, the means by which the illustration produces its effect.

Moving on to the content, there is firstly the enumerative (what
Barthes would call the denotive) level–the constituents of the picture
regardless of their accompanying meanings and associations. On this
level one can initially note the presence or absence of the four elements
of the advertising image: the product, props, setting and actor(s) and
then enumerate them–what sort of product, which props, what setting,
how many actors of which sex–in terms as clinically neutral as is possible within the confines of language. Simple enumerative lists can be
useful over a series of examples for they provide the basis for unearth-
ing repetitions and patterns. Further, one can note types of setting,
expressions, poses, directions of attention and other details–which although requiring a certain amount of interpretation (e.g. to interpret
'carefree' from a face) do not fall within the sphere of connotation
proper. Obviously this only serves to emphasize the impossibility of

laying down a hard and fast line between the denotive and the connotive, either theoretically or practically. There is then the connotive level, which is more difficult because the connotations, meanings or significations of most items are neither precise nor limited. All the meanings carried by the poses, expressions, props and settings talked about above, must at last be interpreted and expressed. In addition, one must decide the meaning(s) expressed by the image as a whole–which is even more complex as it involves the connotations of all the items as well as their relationships to each other. (Finally, one might wish to pin down which of all these messages are anchored by the accompanying linguistic message.) These levels must now be examined severally, not in terms of theoretical concepts but in terms of practicalities.

FORM

Overall Impression and Style of the Advertisement

This is concerned with the design of the advertisement, its immediate appearance and effect, and involves considerations of impact, neatness, homogeneity, size and the use of colour, amongst other variables. The four basic constituents of the magazine advertisement are the headline, copy, illustration and a miscellaneous group including the logotype[2], slogan and coupon. The general lay-out and appearance of an advertisement depend to a large extent on the arrangement, number and size of these elements. The advertisements can be viewed in this context along a spectrum from crowded and clumsy at one end to streamlined at the other. The greater the number of each of the four elements in an advertisement, the greater its tendency to crowdedness and loss of impact.

The incidence of the various elements affects the appearance in different ways. An increase in headline, copy or logotype (&c) is directly proportional to an increase in crowdedness, and inversely proportional to increase in impact and streamlinedness. However, more (as distinct from larger) illustrations or the use of insets, tends towards crowdedness. In a similar way, a larger headline (in size of type) tends towards greater impact, but more headlines tend towards less impact.

The size of the advertisement is also a contributory factor; there is geometrically more likelihood of crowding in one-eighth of a page than in a full page and correspondingly more opportunity for greater streamlining and high impact in a two-page spread than in one page.

The inclusion of one element within another: e.g. copy within illustration, illustration within copy alters the appearance of the lay-out. The inclusion of any of the other elements within the illustration reduces the number of separate elements and hence is a streamlining factor. The more unobtrusively and homogenously the other elements fit into the illustration the more simple and streamlined it appears. On the other hand, the illustration included within the copy–like the little line drawings in nineteenth-century dictionaries–can have the opposite effect.

As lay-outs have tended increasingly towards streamlining, homo-geneity and simplicity in design, there is also therefore a time/historical element involved, which brings in the concepts of modernity and 'old-fashionedness'. Crowded advertisements look old-fashioned and stream-lined advertisements look modern. Somewhere in between falls perhaps the majority of advertisements with lay-outs which follow a pattern which includes one each of the four elements, usually in the order (vertically) of headline (H), illustration (I), copy (C) and logotype/slo-gan/coupon, etc. (L) or alternatively $IHCL$ or $HCIL$. This type of lay-out and general style could be termed basic.

There are other variables influencing the appearance of the advertise-ment–illustrations of a line-drawing type appear old-fashioned when compared with photographs, as do black and white illustrations when compared with colour. Some of the most important oppositions be-tween factors tending towards a crowded appearance and factors tending towards a streamlined appearance are set out below.

tends towards crowdedness	tends towards streamlinedness
complicated	simple
low impact	high impact
clumsy	smooth
black and white	colour
dark	light
small size advertisement	large size advertisement
drawing	photograph
smaller illustration	larger illustration
many illustrations	one illustration
more copy	less copy, no copy
two or more headlines	one headline, no headlines
separate elements	illustration embracing other elements

Illustration Techniques

The six photographic techniques considered were focus, close-up (distance), colour, cropping, lighting and angle. Focus, including depth of vision, may be used to emphasize certain parts of the picture and fade others, it may be used to give an overall impression of clearness and crisp outlines or on the other hand an impression of vague and ethereal mistiness. Close-up can be used simply to show an object or objects in greater detail but also to show these objects larger than life, not just close-ups but blow-ups. Colour in photographs is familiar enough–but can be used in a non-naturalistic way, for example, with the addition of special filters. The same is true of lighting, frequently inconspicuous but sometimes used in a particular, and often dramatic, way–for example, to draw attention to a certain part of the picture, or to create a mood of mystery through shadow and darkness. Cropping is the cutting of the picture to suit the needs of the advertisement: the model without forehead and hair, the legs without body; cropping is used to draw attention to certain parts of the photograph, to place them centrally, or to exclude distractions. The camera angle is inconspicuous when the photograph is shot horizontally at about eye-level, but variations from this norm become noticeable because of their dramatic and unusual quality. Most of these techniques are part of the taking and presentation of any photograph–every photograph, for example, makes use of focus by its very nature. Therefore, for a classification to be of any significance, it is necessary only to note departures from the norm, techniques which are used in a special, extreme or unusual way, techniques, in fact, which are used for *emphasis*, for controlling the focus of attention. As well as these basic techniques there is an area which comes under the general heading 'special effects' and includes superimposition and montage.

Under the heading of illustration techniques there are two rather different aspects which should be borne in mind in any classification: one is the use of several separate pictures instead of one major picture, the other is the use of drawings, diagrams or paintings instead of photographs.

Some examples will clarify the nature and effect of the techniques mentioned above. Close-up, cropping and differential focus are used in the American Rice advertisement (plate 1a) but much of the mood depends on the lighting, which is subdued, warm and cosy. The advertisement for Number Seven cream (plate 1b) is an example of the use of special effects, in this case a mirror image; the special effect in the Valspar advertisement (colour plate 1) is very clearly the use of a single colour. The Vaseline shampoo advertisement (plate 2a) is an example of the extreme use of cropping, which in this case removes the major part of the model's face, but emphasizes the hair and the action of combing it. Both focus and camera angle are used to great effect in the New Zealand Cheddar advertisement (plate 2b). Together they give the impression of the movement of the swing in an arresting way, while maintaining the central attention on the face of the boy. The use of close-up in the advertisements for New Zealand Lamb and Bread (plates 3a and 3b) gives a larger than life effect. The Embassy advertisement (plate 4a) shows how the illustration can be split into several separate parts, as does the Tampax one (plate 4b) in another way. Almost any edition of a similar magazine will furnish comparable examples.

Presentation: Rhetorical Devices

The visual devices used in advertisements range from the simple to the very complex, and fall into four main types. The most simple is:

1. *Product Presentation* where the article advertised is one of the central elements of the picture. The product is put forward, offered, presented, usually together with illustrations regarding its usefulness and value and the understood message 'Buy this'. Presentation in this simple form occurs in clothing advertisements in which the model *wears* the clothes which *are* the product, but not where the model wears the face she has created from the cosmetic product. This latter comes within the scope of what could be termed (1a) *Product Transformation*. These illustrations do not merely show a result of the product being used, for almost all advertisements show results in some form or other, for example the room with the carpet in it, the fat baby fed on certain baby foods or the attractive model enclosed within a particular girdle; but they show an end product in the form of the product itself transformed. For example, the tin of concentrate transformed into soup, the ball of wool into a knitted jumper, the lipstick into rosy red lips or the tin of paint into a bright new wall. This device is generally restricted to food, cosmetics, wool and decorating materials.

2. *Typification* is concerned with actors and refers to the intended identification of the reader with the actor in the illustration, or at least the recognition in the actor of characteristics common to a very widely defined type. The models pictured are typifications of very general types of—in the majority of cases—women: young woman, mother, housewife, which avoid any particular features. Where the illustration departs from general typification and pictures specific roles—nurse, bus conductress, vicar—the function is different: 'role-specific' in fact. The actor no longer asks for identification or a feeling of 'I am like you', but indicates that he or she is a particular person whose identity has specific connotations—for example, the policeman (in an advertisement for Pink Gin) is not a person with whom one identifies but a symbol for the law and the mobilizer of a particular set of assumptions and meanings, and as such belongs in the third category. In the same way celebrities and people taken from the world outside—'the public' (e.g. the 'Cookeen cook of the month', see plate 5a)—are too individual to be accepted under this heading straight. The device of typification works through its very generality and is in a way a form of metonymy—one 'young girl' is standing for all young girls, one 'housewife' for all housewives. There must be nothing special about the model or the reaction will be to say 'Ah, the girl with the turned-up nose' rather than 'Ah, a girl in her early twenties'. Typification works by balancing

between two extremes: between a portrayal so 'life-like' as to become
someone real rather than a type, and a person too idealized or too
specific to be regarded as a type: the debutant model or the celebrity.
Celebrities are a special case (see plate 5b–Belle Color), for although
they are ideal typification, they are not simply *types*–but something
more. It may be that there is another distinction to be made on the
basis of projection: identification. The majority of actors function by
identification, while celebrities function through projection. There are,
however, very few magazine advertisements which make use of celebrities. Further, it is difficult (especially in borderline cases) to know
whether a reader will experience identification ('I am like her') or projection ('want to be like her'). This clearly depends, more than other
distinctions, on the individual reader. The use of celebrities or wit-
nesses from the public forms a sub-category:

2b. *Testament.* If the celebrity is unknown to the reader then the
picture may retreat into simple typification, as may also happen if the
illustration does not indicate quite clearly that the portrayal is a documentary 'from life'.

Product presentation and product transformation are dependent on
the presence of the product in the illustration, and typification and testament on the presence of actor or actors. The following category is more
closely connected with objects and settings.

3. Beyond typification is the area of *Association* in which the techniques are derived from verbal rhetoric. These devices are figures of
speech as employed by writers but transferred into the visual medium.
They are used to clarify, to give added strength or impact to meanings
in the picture, to draw attention to certain aspects or to introduce completely new ones. The most important and common is, of course,
metaphor–the transference of ideas or meanings from one context to
another, but there are subsidiary types: synecdoche, metonymy, hyperbole, euphemism and pun, together with 'non-classical' devices involving the use of the incongruous or the puzzling. Bonsiepe (see above)
maintains that verbal mediation is always necessary for the metaphor or
similar device to work, but this does not seem to be a theory which is
upheld in practice as some examples may show. Verbal mediation may
be present or may help to make clear the full meaning of the metaphor
but is not a universal requirement. Some metaphors may be quite
specific–a match taken from its context of box/cigarettes, etc. and
placed in the context of a fire-insurance policy clearly means damage by
fire–whereas a rose taken from its context of other flowers, or vases,
gardens, etc. and placed in the hands of a blonde model is still acting
as a metaphor, but one which is not at all specific. Furthermore, items
may work metaphorically quite without intention on the part of the
advertisement's creator, an item included for its literal meaning may

have quite complex metaphorical meanings for some of the readers of the illustration.

4. The *Supervisual* depends solely on the visual nature of the illustration. The picture functions by virtue of the impression it makes as a picture, not through the arrangement of its contents. It may be the power of the lighting or the colour, the size of the close-up–but it is not just that these things in themselves are transmitting messages, though this may be a part, but that they are underlining and making inescapable the object (or objects) that is pictured. It is, in many cases, nothing to do with extraordinary visual techniques, but merely the power of the image itself with which we are concerned. Perhaps it is useful to adopt Barthes' voice as he interprets the photographic image in 'Rhetoric de L'Image'. 'The photo establishes in fact not a consciousness of the *being-there* of the thing (which any reproduction could provoke), but an awareness of the *having been there*. It is a matter then of a new category in space-time: spacial immediacy and temporal anteriority; in the photo there occurs an illogical conjunction between *here* and *then*. It is thus at the level of this denoted message or message-without-code that one can understand clearly the actual unreality of the photo; its unreality is that of the *here*, for the photo is never experienced as an illusion, it is never a *presence* . . . its reality is that of the having been there.' The mechanical means of reproduction and the space-time disjunction present the onlooker with the perceptual problem of the real which is not real–the photograph confronts us with the reality of something which is not present. Wollen uses both Barthes and Metz to explain this concept: 'He [Barthes] describes how the photographic icon presents "a kind of natural being-there of the object". There is no human intervention, no transformation, no code, between the object and the sign; hence the paradox that a photo is a message without a code.' And quoting Metz: 'A close up of a revolver does not signify "revolver" (a purely potential lexical unit) but signifies *as a minimum*, leaving aside its connotations, "Here is a revolver". It carries with it its own actualization, a kind of "here is (*voici*)". It is this self-actualization, this "*Voici!*", the presence without substance, the being-there or the having-been-there–or the having-been-here–which we are endeavouring to identify as one of the qualities of the photograph–which though part of every photographic image (like focus or light/shade) is in some instances revealed or stressed as the potent force that it is.' My use of the term being-there, for example, is not strictly the semiological usage which Barthes would make, and might be better replaced by a term which had served previously to refer to this phenomenon, namely 'isness'.

In practice these devices referred to overlap and cross-fertilize one another. Some examples may clarify the basic types of rhetorical device available. The Valspar advertisement (colour plate 1) is supervisual–it is the use of colour which enables this picture to function, and the actual items in the illustration are of secondary importance. Alongside the supervisual in this advertisement runs the device of product transformation–the paint transformed into brightly coloured furnishings and decor. The New Zealand Lamb advertisement (plate 3a) exemplifies the quality of 'isness' in its pictorial immediacy, its complete self-sufficient existence which is nevertheless ephemeral. In the category of association there are examples of hyperbole (the long-boat laden with flowers in the advertisement for Morny Soaps (see plate 6c)), euphemism Noble Lowndes (see plate 6b) and metaphor as in Scot Towels (17 February 1968) where a rose and the roll of paper towels are juxtaposed. The rose's softness and femininity and yet its toughness are qualities which are transferred to the paper towel. And in the Maxwell House illustration (plate 6a) the naturalness, the coffee-ness of the beans is transferred to the cup of coffee and thence to the product.

Typification is used in the Electricaire (plate 13b) illustration–which refers to the generic type: young mum. The device of testament can be seen in the advertisement for Cookeen (plate 5a) and the advertisement for Belle Color (plate 5b). The woman in the latter–to a person who was unaware of her identity as Linda Thorson, star of the 'Avengers'– would be merely typification (which the linguistic message is quick to guard against in its anchorage of the various messages of the illustration). Product presentation can be seen in the advertisement for Maxwell House referred to previously, and is a common feature of countless other advertisements.

CONTENT

The Four Elements of the Illustration

The first task is to note the presence or absence of these four main elements: the product, the props, the setting and actors. This is a fairly mechanical operation but needs some ordering in order to be manageable. There are fifteen possible combinations altogether, not all of which are equally likely to occur. Previous investigation had shown that illustrations with *only* props, *only* setting, or *only* props with setting, were very rare, and the following grid was developed to take this into account.

	Product (A)	Product + Actor(s) (E)	Actor(s) (I)
Props	+ props (B)	+ props (F)	+ props (J)
Setting	+ setting (C)	+ setting (G)	+ setting (K)
Props and setting	+ setting and props (D)	+ setting and props (H)	+ setting and props (L)

The grid provides the possibility of perceiving, not merely lists, but combinations and relationships. Beyond this simple level the nature of these elements must be specified in terms of denotation rather than connotation. However, as has already been mentioned, the line between the two is not easily drawn. To make classifications of any significance some interpretation is essential. At this stage I am, therefore, departing from the strictly denotive, so that both enumerative (sex and number of actors) and interpretive (expression of actors) are present in the system of classification.

No system is drawn up to deal with the larger connotive meanings to be handled subsequently as this is the stage at which the material is allowed to break out of the restrictions of classification. This does not mean a complete abandonment of efforts at objectivity and substantiation, for the interpretation of meanings is founded on the evidence provided by the preceding classificatory work. This exercise is of varying difficulty with regard to these four elements, and the experience of previous investigation and study was invaluable in determining the most useful modes of approach and organization.

Product

The breaking-down of the range of products advertised in women's magazines can be done in many more or less specified ways. The following breakdown was derived from experience as a feasible but not necessarily the only way of operating.

Cosmetics, hair preparations, slimming aids, sanitary towels and tampons.

Clothes (top-clothes), underclothes, tights and stockings, shoes and wool.

Food and drink.

Furniture, kitchen equipment, floor coverings, decorating materials, soft furnishings and household accessories.

Offers (and competitions), careers, medical preparations, business (banking and insurance), baby and children's products and children's clothes, cigarettes and miscellaneous.

Cosmetics is taken to include facial beauty aids—creams, lipsticks, eye shadow and so on—and also similar preparations not limited to application above the neckline, for example, perfumes and deodorants, bath lotions and talcum powder. Hair preparations are dealt with separately partly because of their large number and partly because previous investigation, together with the importance of hair itself as noted previously, indicates that hair preparations are treated rather differently from other beauty aids subsumed under the heading 'cosmetics'. Slimming aids were felt to be similar to cosmetics but with rather different associations and indeed some connexions with medicinal products. Sanitary towels and tampons are undeniably feminine, like cosmetics, but have even closer associations with the medicinal and are rather different items from lipstick and eye-shadow, and hence have been given a category of their own.

Clothes as a category includes all top-clothes, while underclothes includes also nightclothes. It may be that some distinction should be made between these, and in a survey attention should be paid to this possibility, but previous work has so far indicated that these products do hang together. Tights/stockings, shoes (including sandals, etc.) and knitting wool are straightforward categories.

Food and drink as a category includes all constituents for cooking or eating, whether needing preparation or not, and drinks both alcoholic and non-alcoholic.

Of the fourth list, furniture includes articles such as tables and chairs but excludes items covered by other categories, such as kitchen equipment, which is taken to mean large items of kitchen machinery such as cookers and washing machines. Such items as wall can-openers or carpet cleaners are taken to be general household accessories rather than items of equipment in the same class as washing machines. Floor coverings are simply rugs, mats, carpets, linoleum and so on, and decorating materials are such products as paint and wallpaper. Soft furnishings include towels, linen, curtains and similar products.

The remaining categories provide little difficulty. It would have been possible to extend the number of specific categories *ad infinitum* in order to decrease the number of products which fall into no other category than miscellaneous, but a line has to be drawn at some point and there seemed to be no other major types of product warranting individual attention. One difficulty which was presented and only half-solved was that of mail order advertisements. It would be possible to have a separate category for these, but the complicating factor is that a considerable number of them are centrally concerned with clothes, rather than a whole range of diffuse products. It was felt that the clothing factor was of greater importance than the mail order factor— although this, of course, is open to dispute—mainly in regard to the desire to get a full picture of clothes advertisements in such magazines as *Woman* and *Woman's Own* where a large number of the clothing advertisements are for mail order companies. Where the advertisement was specifically concerned with fashion or clothes it would be placed in the clothes category, and where concerned with general products or the running of a mail order 'club' it would be placed in the miscellaneous category.

In the case of overlap between product categories the advertisement should be closely scrutinized in order to ascertain the function of the product which is being stressed. In other words a shampoo which is presented as specially for children and with a picture of a woman washing her child's hair might be better placed in the category of products for children than in the one for hair preparations which are primarily 'feminine' in character.

Products do have connotations, although these are constant in a way the connotations of props are not. Some of the connotations of products like cosmetics and hair preparations have been considered above, in the earlier part of the preceding chapter. The significance of other areas – such as Food – has received scant attention, though one might guess that the world of Food/Nourishment/Communion is at least as complex as that of cosmetics. Perhaps it is because items like food appear to be so much more tangible than items like cosmetics that their deeper associations have been (comparatively speaking) neglected.

It is true, also, that the product stands apart from the other three elements in the illustration, and the props, settings, actors stand as modifiers to the product, drawing out any latent connotations which it might possess.

Props and Settings

Props occur widely and in a host of different forms: as specific articles of central importance, for example the barbed wire mask in the Sunsilk advertisement (plate 7a) or as part of a series of props comprising a background, for example the grandfather clock in the Valspar advertisement. They can be large, small, foreground, background, emphasized or vague. In the same way that poses, expressions and clothes carry meanings, so also do objects – especially the objects inserted into the advertisement illustration, for most if not all will have been selected and deliberately included as necessary or helpful to the overall advertisement message. In the above examples the mask might be said to mean 'keep off!', 'danger', or 'un-touchability', and the clock to mean something much less specific – sophistication and good taste. Props may be used to say something specific about the product, to add style or sophistication, to make-up a background, to draw attention and inspire curiosity, or as a functional necessity (e.g. the plate on which the bread and cheese toasted sandwich stands (plate 3b).

Similar things may be said of the setting. By no means all advertisements are set in some wider context: many, even those with actors, have a neutral, plain background, for example the advertisement for the WRAF (plate 7b) and most cosmetic advertisements. The absence of settings in many of the advertisements makes their inclusion in others the more interesting. Once again, these settings are not value-free neutral backgrounds, but carriers of meaning. 'To set the scene' is a telling expression and can be as relevant to the advertisement as to the theatre. The setting qualifies the items, actors and action of the foreground and puts everything into a context—like the backdrop on the stage. Actors shot against the background of meadowland and sunlight will clearly give a different impression from those same actors shot against the background of a living-room with armchairs and aspidistras.

Props

The props in an illustration cannot all be viewed in the same way. They are sharply divided into functional and non-functional. An example of the former would be the cup and saucer containing coffee in the Maxwell House advertisement (plate 6a) and of the latter, a pistol laid across a Mekay shirt. The pistol in the shirt advertisement is a metaphorical usage, while the coffee cup has almost no metaphorical meaning. In between these two polarities, however, there is an area which is less well defined. There are many items, which while being functional also have a metaphorical usage which puts them beyond the merely functional. In an advertisement for Sunhouse fires there are glasses containing an amber-coloured liquid which are functional as seen on one level, and yet—because they are cut-glass with a certain style and distinction marking them out as *not* mass-produced Woolworth's tumblers—they have a meaning beyond the functional which has to do with good taste, appreciation of the finer things in life and status. In the same way as the candelabra on the table in the New World advertisement (plate 8a) may be functional in the sense that it is there to light and decorate the table but it clearly has meanings and associations beyond the merely illuminating. It is interesting to compare this advertisement with the one for the Electricity Council cooker (plate 8b).

There seem, therefore, to be three categories in terms of which we can see the props in the illustrations. These are the functional/non-metaphorical, the functional/metaphorical, and the non-functional/metaphorical, or more simply functional (F), functional-metaphorical (F-M), and metaphorical (M). These categories are clearly sectors demarcated along a continuum and the line between two categories will at times be difficult to draw with certainty. It is at this point—along with many other similar points in this survey—that the analyst must fall back on his own knowledge of and feeling for the culture. These qualities will be in play always, but only at certain 'frontier' points will they be crucial.

Settings

The setting is the background or backdrop, the context in which the action takes place. In visual terms it is what appears behind the actors or product, but may in many cases surround or encircle them. The background qualifies the foreground, and the more obtrusive it is the more it affects and qualifies the main action.

In some cases–domestic interiors, for example–a large part of the setting may comprise individual items which will have been designated as props. In terms of the setting, however, these props are being viewed as a whole, as an integral part of the complete setting which includes the floor, the walls and the design of the room. Far more than individual items, settings communicate an overall atmosphere, a tone of voice which underlies the actual words.

One of the first levels on which to consider the setting of an illustration is that of style or presentation. We might pose this in two ways. First, does the setting appear to be documentary or staged? This must be a subjective judgement, but is by no means as difficult a question to answer as might seem. Many outdoor settings, as one would expect, appear to be documentary–'real', 'from life'–although this is not universally true. Interior settings provide more variation; the setting for Valspar (colour plate 1) is staged, the setting for Cookeen (plate 5a) is documentary. From a slightly different angle, one might ask–how familiar is the setting–or how strange? Regardless of its documentary nature or otherwise, is it part of our everyday lives, or does it take us to unusual, exotic places? At one end of the scale one can identify the quite familiar and well known, and the fantastic and utterly strange at the other. In between one might place another category; that which is a little distant from direct experience but which is not cut off from it nor entirely foreign to it–in some respects a wishful-thinking interpretation of reality.

The three categories would therefore be on the lines of the following:

The familiar, known, real, that which we know and can experience or have experienced for ourselves.

The wishful, slightly unusual, imaginative, at one remove from direct experience.

The fantastic, exotic, very strange, improbable, dreamlike, far from daily, conscious experience.

To look at them in a slightly different way: a fantastic setting is one which the reader would never rationally expect to inhabit, a familiar one he or she would expect to inhabit, and a wishful one he or she might hope to inhabit.

Obviously here the analyst must hold in his head an idea of what is familiar to the average person, and his idea of what is familiar and what constitutes the 'average person' may differ from another person's. Nevertheless one does have an idea of what is common in the culture and what is not, and though one person might well consider wishful what another thought familiar, it is unlikely that one person would consider familiar what someone else thought fantastic. The citing of examples is essential to any part of the analysis, but it is especially necessary in these areas of subjectivity, for the reader to assess the bias of the analyst.

The next area with which we are concerned is that of *Mood*. One's efforts here are directed towards discovering the mood evoked by the setting, which provides the atmosphere in which the product or action is experienced. The mood of the setting is an important element in the building up of an overall message. Any list of categories of mood or atmosphere must in its nature be arbitrary. The breakdown which immediately suggests itself is some sort of parallel to the familiar-fantastic classification, but when this was applied to a previous sample the result was not completely satisfactory. A homely everyday mood and a romantic-sentimental mood seemed to fit the demands of the material, but the fantastic-unusual mood seemed to be too general to describe the variations within it. That there appeared to be more variations within that category than in either of the others is interesting in itself.

The description of the sort of mood vaguely covered by the word fantastic or unusual thus divides into three separate–though connected–categories: the bizarre (dreamlike, surrealistic?); the extravagant (glamorous, luxurious?); and the exotic (exciting, to do with far away places with strange sounding names?).

Concentration has so far been centred on the abstract and atmospheric aspects of the setting, and attention should now be turned to the more accessible and concrete. Distinction has already been made between the indoor and the outdoor setting, but there are more detailed classifications that can be made, with regard to the type of outdoor setting, and the sorts of interiors depicted.

Outdoor settings. The first distinction to be made is between settings in this country and settings in (or purporting to be in) other countries, i.e. between home and abroad; (the opposition familiar/exotic seems to recur with great frequency). In terms of actual situation, settings can be divided into urban and rural, plus what might be termed greenbelt, to include parkland, gardens and countryside mixed with buildings. Combining the two categories provides six descriptions; for example, urban-exotic would cover settings such as Montmartre or the Kasbah, and rural-home would cover English fields and woods.

This classification takes care of the major distinctions, but room should be available for the insertion of important details like the presence of sea, rivers, mountains, etc. as seems appropriate.

Indoor settings. Interiors can be divided into domestic and non-domestic, the latter being any part of the inside of a building which is not the home–shops, public buildings, workplaces, theatres and so on. Domestic interiors, which from work carried out so far appear to comprise the majority, can be sub-classified on the basis of their style.

The following categories emerged from a survey of interiors in advertisements in *Woman* and *Ideal Home* (March–October 1968): traditional, ritzy, mod, camp, conventional.

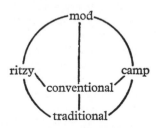

Traditional: styles and ornaments of long-standing, old-fashioned designs of continuing elegance, much bric-à-brac, heavier darker and more ornamented furniture than in other styles . . . perhaps floral wallpaper, leather-bound books and brass candlesticks, paintings in thick, gilt frames, sober colours.

Ritzy: connected with the traditional but blending modernity with old-fashioned sturdy quality. Furniture heavy and quite dark in colour, but less ornamented; plain, solid styles . . . often fairly luxurious.

Mod: streamlined furniture, sometimes painted instead of being 'natural' colour . . . bold primary colours, accentuation of simple geometrical shapes, use of synthetic materials and mod styled objects: clocks with giant numbers, psychedelic tea-trays, bright orange enamel mugs . . .

Conventional: a mail-order modernity, an everyday home in the suburbs, clean lines and bright but not too bold colours, natural wood colours prevalent, but lighter, fewer odds and end lying around than in other styles except possibly for the ritzy . . . comfortable but not luxurious.

Camp: use of old-fashioned furniture or other objects painted up/renewed/framed and sometimes imitated–or merely cleaned up *objets trouvés*; delight in ornamentation tending towards the baroque/art nouveau . . . any colour, brass bedsteads and wicker chairs.

The Actors

The three areas with which we are concerned are manner, appearance and relationships. The problem with each is not that there is little to say but the difficulty of finding the terms with which to say it. The following are suggestions which are not intended to be rigid or unalterable, nor are they expected to encompass every aspect or categorize every freckle.

RELATIONSHIPS. How is the actor related to the rest of the illustration, to other actors, or to him or herself? Where there are two or more actors in one picture there must be some sort of relationship between them unless they are separate shots, in which case it is usually apparent from the style of the photograph (see Tampax advertisement, plate 4b). These four categories deal with most of the relationships which occur, and although most easily applicable to two actors, can be adapted to apply to three, four or more. They are reciprocal, divergent, object and semi-reciprocal. The *reciprocal* is a simple two-way relationship in which each person is the centre of the other's attention (see the WRAF, plate 7b). The *divergent* relationship occurs where each person's attention is directed towards something different as in the G-Plan advertisement (colour plate 3). The *object* relationship applies where the attention of each person is directed towards the same object as the children in the advertisement for American Rice (plate 1a) (with allowance being made for the fact that this 'object' may be out of the picture). The *semi-reciprocal* is a relationship in which one person's attention is concentrated on the other, whose attention is elsewhere as in the WRAF (plate 7b foreground). In this and the following instances attention can only be deduced from the face and particularly the eyes of each actor; in those (rare) instances where an actor's face is not visible to the camera the position of the head may be the only indicator.

ATTENTION. The action in the illustration depends very largely on the attention of the actor(s)–to whom or to what it is being directed. It may be directed towards other *people* (see above), to an *object* (possibly the product), to *oneself*, to the *reader*, or into *middle distance*, as in a state of reverie. In some cases it may be that the nature of the actor's attention is *invisible* to the reader.

There is another dimension of attention beyond that signified by the eyes, and that is that of touch. The quality of *tactility* is applicable not only to hands, but to hair, face, shoulders and any other part of the body. The receivers of this attention may differ from the person or things being looked at and are limited to *self*, *objects* or *persons*.

APPEARANCE. Here we are referring back to the earlier discussion where appearance was separated from manner. Appearance is fairly constant over time and has to do with social status and racial and sexual characteristics. Here, then, we are trying to disregard the expression of the moment and concentrate on what underlies it. In a situation as artificial as the advertisement photograph the likelihood of the underlying 'type' being true of the actors real nature is small, but also irrelevant. The actor is being a *sort of person* for the advertisement as well as adopting a particular expression and pose. From previous investigations of the nature of actors–especially women–in advertisements, the

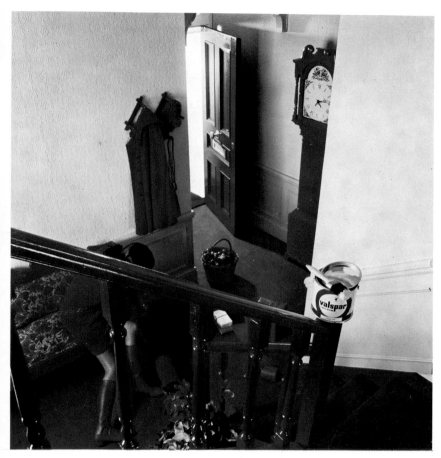

1. Advertisement for Valspar paints from *Woman*, illustrating the special effect of a predominant colour. Note the interior setting and the props.

important and defining axis in terms of appearance seemed to be that of sophistication. Hence one can develop a series of delineations from the very sophisticated to the naïve and the plain, thus: superior: sophisticated: plain: naïve. The 'plain' appearance should not be taken to apply to actors who are unattractive in appearance but to the sort of person who gives the impression of not being naïve, of understanding the possibility of sophistication, but rejecting it in favour of the simplicity of being a 'straight-forward guy'. At a tangent to this axis, however, there is the sort of appearance which is so unselfconscious, so unconcerned with sophistication or lack of it–one might almost say, so neutral–that the term 'plain' will not suffice, and one must substitute something of the order 'detached'.

MANNER, in contrast to appearance, is concerned with the indication of behaviour or emotion at any one time, and under this heading one must take into account the actor's expression, pose, hair and clothes. In these cases the same descriptions will not apply to both sexes: in some there will be equivalents, in others complete differences.

EXPRESSION. The types of expression suggested here derive from extensive studies of the material and experimentation with various sets of categories designed to reveal the relevant and the irrelevant. While no two expressions are identical the types explained here are designed to grasp in some measure the essence of a particular cluster of expressions which share certain basic similarities.

Female expressions:

(i) Soft/introverted: eyes often shut or half-closed, the mouth slightly open/pouting, rarely smiling; an inward-looking trance-like reverie, removed from earthly things.

(ii) Cool/level: indifferent, self-sufficient, arrogant, slightly insolent, haughty, aloof, confident, reserved; wide eyes, full lips straight or slightly parted, and obtrusive hair, often blonde. The eyes usually look the reader in the eye, as perhaps the woman regards herself in the mirror.

(iii) Seductive: similar to the cool/level look in many respects–the eyes are less wide, perhaps shaded, the expression is less reserved but still self-sufficient and confident; milder versions may include a slight smile.

(iv) Narcissistic: similarities to the cool/level and soft/introverted looks, rather closer to the latter: a satisfied smile, closed or half-closed eyes, self-enclosed, oblivious, content . . . 'activity directed inward'.

(v) Carefree: nymphlike, active, healthy, gay, vibrant, outdoor girl; long unrestrained outward-flowing hair, more outward-going than the above, often smiling or grinning.

(vi) Kittenlike: coy, naïve (perhaps in a deliberate, studied way), a friendlier and more girlish version of the cool/level look, sometimes almost twee.

(vii) Maternal: motherly, matronly, mature, wise, experienced and kind, carrying a sort of authority; shorter hair, slight smile and gentle eyes—mouth may sometimes be stern, but eyes twinkle.

(viii) Practical; concentrating, engaged on the business in hand, mouth closed, eyes object-directed, sometimes a slight frown; hair often short or tied back.

(ix) Comic: deliberately ridiculous, exaggerated, acting the fool, pulling faces for the benefit of a real or imaginary audience, sometimes close to a sort of archness.

(x) Catalogue: a neutral look as of a dummy, artificial, waxlike; features may be in any position, but most likely to be with eyes open wide and a smile, but the look remains vacant and empty; personality has been removed.

Male expressions:

There are fairly direct parallels with the above—the carefree, practical, paternal, seductive, comic and catalogue. The other two male expressions selected as types—the thoughtful and self-reliant—have similarities to the female 'introverted' and 'cool', though the thoughtful is far *less* introverted, and the self-reliant more smug than aloof or reserved, but there are no counterparts to the narcissistic or kittenlike. (For the latter a type 'boyish' might be postulated, but it remains potential.)

POSE. The same explanation regarding origin applies to this and the two subsequent areas of hair and clothes as was noted above with regard to expression. There is a certain correspondence between some expressions and some poses, but this is not universal, nor do corresponding poses and expressions always occur in conjunction.

(i) Composed/controlled: akin to the controlled 'relaxation' of a cat, an impression of balance and potential force; legs often slightly apart, hands together and head level or raised.

(ii) Carefree/active: engaged in some physical activity or movement, the arms and legs lead outwards and the head is often tipped back.

(iii) Narcissistic: self-caressing, limbs lead back to the body, often in a sitting or crouching position, head tilted downwards.

(iv) Dramatic/unusual: strange or exaggerated poses, unnatural, rarely encountered except in drama, poses intended to attract attention by virtue of their unusual nature.

(v) Relaxed/leisurely: an attitude of comfort, rest, recuperation, being 'at ease'; limbs drooping or supported; usually sitting, leaning or lying.

(vi) Functional: the body is object-directed, with limbs arranged to expedite the exercise in hand, to carry out a specific purpose.

(vii) Seductive: the come-hither pose, often sitting or lying, legs curled up or stretched out together; arms held back from the body, or one shoulder pushed forward, head erect.

(viii) Dummy: neutral, wax-like, stiff, lifeless–as a shop-window mannequin an inanimate object.

MALE POSES correspond to the above fairly closely although they tend to be a little more restrained. There is, however, no narcissistic pose nor any pose which is specifically seductive, as far as material studied so far has shown. These, together with similar omissions in expression, are interesting in themselves.

CLOTHES: WOMEN. It would be possible, perhaps, to classify clothing on the basis of the actual items worn, listing sweaters and skirts and comparing them with the number of shirts and jeans and so on. However, the method chosen and tried with some success is derived from a functional and stylistic base. Function and style are clearly related: we wear certain styles of dress for certain occasions. One can move from play/relaxation at one extreme to work/regimentation at the other, from styles less defined by conventions to styles almost completely defined by conventions, from the idiosyncratic and exotic to the uniform. The greatest concentration occurs near the middle of this spectrum, where the two areas of informal dress and dress for everyday in the office can be seen as parallel rather than to one side or another in the spectrum.

(i) Exotic: the unusual, idiosyncratic, very glamorous ... long evening dresses, extravagant party dresses, fancy dress, foreign costumes ...

(ii) Snazzy: the smart and very fashionable in a respectable and expensive way ... suits of impeccable cut, elegant dresses, hats and gloves ...

(iii) Office-wear: worn by the woman white-collar worker, neat, quite fashionable, not unusual, clothes to suit a multitude of informal social occasions ... dresses, skirt and blouse, a little jewellery? ...

(iv) Informal: worn about the house, in the garden, for walks in the country, comfortable and casual, maybe a little sloppy ... slacks/jeans, shirt/jumper ...

(v) Dirty-wear: clothes worn for cleaning, doing messy jobs of work, protective clothing ... overalls, aprons, jeans, old clothes ...

(vi) Uniform: defined vocational dress, the clothes of the girl in the WRAF when on duty.

(vii) In the case of the clothes being worn also being the product there seems little point in using this classification and the clothing in such cases can be described simply as product.

(viii) On investigation it became quite apparent that a further category on a different axis was necessary–to take account of the instances in which the actor was wearing no clothes or very few clothes: hence the simple classification: None.

CLOTHES: MEN. Men are both less common than women in the advertisements being studied and also exhibit less variation in their dress. A fairly simple breakdown on similar lines to the above would be the following:

Mod: clothes in bright colours, shirt and slacks/jeans, trendy styles, jackets not cut on conventional English lines, interesting ties . . .

Conventional: suit, or dark jacket and trousers, possibly neat pullover or cardigan, collar and tie, white or other sober coloured shirt . . .

Casual: pullover and slacks, check or coloured shirts, sports jacket perhaps, and cravat . . .

Working: clothes used to avoid spoiling better ones, for manual work, old clothes, overalls, etc. . . .

Uniform: defined vocational dress–that of the soldier or the waiter, for example.

HAIR: WOMEN. Enough has been said about hair to explain why a special note should be made about it, and the most important criterion to be applied is obviously that of length. This can be combined with a description of the naturalness or the artificiality of the style in the case of women: is the hair allowed to fall naturally or is it set or permed? The description does not relate to the way in which the style was obtained but the appearance it gives now. Thus a style described as freeflowing may have taken ten days and six coiffeurists to perfect, but the *appearance* is none the less free, natural and loose. The dichotomy between long/freeflowing/natural/loose and set/artificial/short is filled out by an intervening middle category which describes styles which contain elements of artificiality and setting but which retain some freedom and length. The artificial style, on the other hand, has no freedom, is completely controlled and firm: its pattern is manifestly a man-made construction. The three categories, then are freeflowing, shaped and moulded.

HAIR: MEN. Male hair styles can also be classified on the basis of length–although the range is much more restricted–but the question of artificiality does not commonly arise. A description involving tidiness as against untidiness can however be introduced: short/tidy, medium length/slightly unruly, long/untidy. The concept of untidiness never seems to occur in the sphere of women's hair–the nearest approach being freeflowing hair when it is windswept. This should not, of course, prevent one from noting untidiness should it occur. As in all the classifications one cannot make allowance for every possibility at the outset. Material which will not fit any of the categories in a given area has to be appreciated as the more interesting for that and given due weight in the examination of distribution and correlation.

The detailed inventory of the actors, props and setting completed, one returns to a consideration of the meanings expressed by each and by the image as a whole, involving as it does the meanings and connotations of all the actors, props, and the setting, and the relationships between them. At this point the analyst is–to a large extent–on his own. The meanings of an image, especially one containing all four of the elements, may be many and various, and a really deep and intense investigation might cover many pages with nuances, references and allusions. In the restricted time available, the analyst, using the evidence of the closed bone-by-bone investigation already completed together with his own sense of priority and significance, has to select those meanings which are not only apparent to him but which have some concrete point of reference in the material (e.g. to derive the meaning 'headmaster–hence authority' from a picture of a bowl of oranges because these happen to have some connexion in the analyst's mind is not justifiable, while to derive the same meaning from a picture of a large desk and a cane is justifiable and substantiable in general terms). It is impossible, though to substantiate unquestionably every decision about meaning that is made. Neither semiology nor iconography has provided a fool-proof 'scientific' procedure at this stage–although one control might be the reference of each picture to a panel of widely differing people for their interpretation of meanings. However, one should not imply that the interpretation of meanings from the illustrations is completely shrouded in mystery. The majority of pictures are not of overwhelming complexity, and the analyst with a mind tuned to the culture and with experience in dealing with this sort of problem should not encounter insuperable difficulties. In ambiguous and indistinct cases one should make note of *all* possible meanings, bearing in mind that one is not seeking merely the creator's *explicit* meanings (though these form part of the whole meaning-complex).

One could, if it were thought useful, go on from this point to isolate those meanings which are anchored by the linguistic message of the advertisement: those meanings which the advertisement intends to communicate directly, and to which it wishes to draw the attention. The intentionality of the advertisement does not necessarily end with these explicitly underlined meanings–other items in the picture may be intended to communicate although no reference is made to them. Indeed, in some cases, there will be little or no direct reference in the linguistic message to what is contained in the picture, though the picture is clearly not 'accidental'. The aim of a further study would be a combined linguistic-visual analysis. Beyond this there is an area of meaning which may have escaped intentionality, items the full meaning of which the creator(s) did not fully appreciate, but this difference is impossible to detect in practice.

MAGAZINES AND THE SAMPLE

Magazines, as entities distinct from newspapers on the one hand and books on the other, have been in existence since the late seventeenth century. Only during the present century, however, have they become items of mass circulation with national and international readership. Though they lack the immediacy of newspapers they have the advantages of topicality and continuity mixed with the opportunity to plan more carefully, to give lengthier treatment to items and to build up a cumulative impact. Magazines serve an immense number of special interests from *Hotel and Caterers Gazette* to *Angling Times* and *Parade*. The lack, it might be said, is not in magazines for specific interests or groups but in magazines for a general audience. This place was filled, prior to 1956/7 by magazines such as *Picture Post, Illustrated* and *John Bull*. The only contenders for this area now are the three newspaper colour supplements.

Only during this century also have magazines developed as a medium for intensive advertising worth many millions of pounds each year. Peterson, in his book *Magazines in the Twentieth Century*, establishes a clear link between the development of the mass circulation magazines and the growth of mass advertising. Each made the other possible. According to Peterson (speaking of the American situation) magazines of mammoth circulation became possible after World War I as a result of an expanding market both for the magazines and for the goods advertised in their pages, technical advances and improvements in the logistics of magazine publishing (plus, he suggests, an increase in leisure time, an increase in the general level of education and some redistribution of income).

From the point of view of advertisers, magazines offer less overall immediate impact than newspapers, but have advantages in the fact that they are less transient than papers, are read and referred to long after publication, have a high readership rate per copy and are read in a more leisurely and receptive fashion than newspapers. Certainly no other media have such large proportions of their space taken by advertisements, with the exception of pure advertising media such as advertising papers, boardings and direct mail. The percentage of advertising material to total space can rise to 60 per cent and over in many magazines, which is more than the 30–40 per cent of most newspapers, and substantially greater than the proportion of time allotted to commercials on television or in the cinema.

In terms of advertising expenditure magazines and periodicals account for a substantial but not major part of total advertising expenditure. They accounted for £50m in 1968, while trade and technical journals accounted for £44m in comparison with the £99m spent on national newspaper advertising and another £99m on regional newspaper advertising.[3] Television advertising accounted for £132m in 1968, poster and transport for £20m, outdoor signs £15m, cinema £6m and radio £1m.

Advertising expenditure in magazines as compared with the total advertising expenditure has decreased slightly in the years 1960 to 1968, from 12 per cent to 10 per cent. Thus:

	%
National newspapers	20
Regional newspapers	20
Magazines and periodicals	10
Trade and technical journals	9
Other publications	2
Press production costs	4
Total Press	65
Television	27
Poster and transport	4
Outdoor signs	3
Cinema	1
Radio	–
	100

The majority of press advertising is of the display type, i.e. 56 per cent. The remainder comprises financial advertising (3 per cent), classified (27 per cent) and trade and technical (14 per cent). Of this display advertising, magazines and periodicals accounted for £46m in 1968.

One substantial sector of the magazine market is that of the various women's magazines. These range from IPC's four major weeklies (*Woman, Woman's Own, Woman's Realm* and *Woman's Weekly*) through magazines for a specifically younger age range like *Petticoat, Honey* and *19*, to sophisticated glossies (*Vogue, Flair, Nova*) and home management magazines like *Woman's Home Journal*. Of the fifty-nine magazines listed by the Institute of Practitioners in Advertising Readership Survey, thirty-six are women's magazines, and the list of general periodicals includes *Ideal Home, Homes and Gardens* and *Homemaker*!

The magazine division of IPC had in 1967–68 a total sales revenue of £48m of which advertising sales comprised £20m and circulation sales £22m. In food and soft drinks the revenue of the women's magazine press totalled £5½m in 1968, half the total spent in the press as a whole, and in cosmetics and toiletries £6m, 70 per cent of the total spent in the press. Housewives (reputed to control or have influence over 70 per cent of the money spent by consumers) are an obvious target for the advertiser, and what more direct avenue to them than their favourite magazine?

Women's magazines have been criticized vehemently and consistently by all shades of opinion, notably by some of the authorities quoted above in the section on women—Myrdal and Klein, Deutsch and Horney for example—who see women's magazines as contributing to the church, kitchen and children view of woman's role. According to this view such magazines contain nothing but trivialities and inconsequential items on fashion and the home. The publishers on the other hand claim that the magazines serve a real need in terms of basic advice and help and in providing relaxation and leisure-time entertainment for the harassed housewife. The only indisputable deduction to be made at this stage is that the magazines are extremely popular both with women and with advertisers—a situation which gives satisfaction to one of the parties at least.

Six magazines were chosen from which the advertisements for the analysis would be taken. The magazines were *Woman, Woman's Own, Woman and Home, Petticoat, Honey* and *Nova. Woman* and *Woman's Own* were chosen because of their immense popularity and undisputed domination of the woman's magazine world, and *Woman and Home* as the most popular monthly woman's magazine. It is an unsophisticated non-glossy magazine with which *Nova* was chosen to contrast, representing the expensive, glossy up-the-market sort of magazine. *Nova* was chosen in preference to such magazines as *Vogue, Flair* and *Vanity Fair* whose preoccupations are almost solely restricted to the world of fashion and might be seen as fashion magazines rather than women's magazines. *Petticoat* and *Honey* are magazines directed at younger (but nevertheless adult) readership—*Petticoat* being the most popular weekly of this sort and *Honey* the most popular monthly.

In this sort of selection some areas are found to be unrepresented or under-represented. Other areas from which magazines might have been chosen are the adolescent/pop group (such as *Jackie, Valentine* and *Rave*), the *True Story/Romances/Magazine* group or the supermarket distributed *Living, Family Circle* type of magazine. It is the advertisements and not the magazines that are the specific area of study, however, and the magazines have been chosen in order to obtain a cross-section of the advertising being promoted throughout the woman's magazine sector at any given time.

The advertisements studied consisted of all those published in the six magazines during the two months March and September 1969. *Petticoat* was held up by an industrial dispute for the latter half of September and the two preceding issues of August were used instead. There were thus nine issues each of *Woman, Woman's Own* and *Petticoat,* and two of *Woman and Home, Nova* and *Honey,* furnishing over 830 advertisements (having excluded the many duplications) the smallest size of which was half a page. Advertisements smaller than half a page were excluded for the reason that the analysis was being developed to deal with large display advertisements, and to have included all the quarter, eighth and sixteenth advertisements would have weighted the sample in one particular direction with no apparent gain.

The readership figures for the six magazines are as follows.[4]

Percentage of total population (estimated at 40,200,000) over 16 reading:

	%	
Woman	26	10,569,000
Woman's Own	23	9,304,000
Woman and Home	7	2,901,000
Honey	3	1,046,000
Nova	2	773,000
Petticoat/Trend	2	639,000

(there may be substantial readership of *Petticoat* amongst under 16s)

Percentage of women (estimated total 21,016,000) reading:

	%	
Woman	41	8,561,000
Woman's Own	35	7,404,000
Woman and Home	12	2,493,000
Honey	5	957,000
Nova	3	553,000
Petticoat/Trend	3	572,000

Readership of these women by social grade (in thousands):

	A/B =2,508	C1 =3,729	C2 =7,321	D/E =7,458
Woman	36%= 914	45%=1,673	46%=3,333	35%=2,640
Woman's Own	31%= 775	36%=1,352	40%=2,893	32%=2,384
Woman and Home	19%= 485	15%= 545	12%= 868	8%= 594
Honey	7%= 185	6%= 216	5%= 352	3%= 203
Nova	9%= 224	4%= 141	2%= 129	1%= 59
Petticoat/Trend	3%= 77	3%= 126	3%= 212	2%= 158

Female readership by age group (in thousands):

	16–24=3,493	25–34=3,207	35–44=3,406
Woman	55%=1,920	43%=1,381	42%=1,416
Woman's Own	47%=1,657	39%=1,253	34%=1,153
Woman and Home	9%= 318	10%= 307	15%= 501
Honey	17%= 592	3%= 87	3%= 92
Nova	15%= 163	4%= 143	3%= 98
Petticoat/Trend	11%= 395	1%= 19	2%= 73

	45–54=3,483	55–64=3,377	65+ =4,050
Woman	42%=1,473	35%=1,181	29%=1,190
Woman's Own	35%=1,229	32%=1,069	26%=1,044
Woman and Home	14%= 496	16%= 552	8%= 318
Honey	4%= 131	1%= 42	— = 12
Nova	2%= 79	2%= 53	— = 16
Petticoat/Trend	2%= 54	1%= 22	— = 9

In terms of absolute numbers the bulge occurs in the C2 class, with the exception of the readers of *Nova*, the greatest number of whom are in the A/B category. *Woman* and *Woman's Own* are remarkable for their ability to cross age and class barriers with little variation in readership. The other magazines, with the exception of *Petticoat*, seem to have an A/B–C1 bias. *Woman and Home* is clearly a magazine for the more mature reader, though not to such a great extent as *Petticoat* and *Honey* are magazines for the younger reader. *Nova*, perhaps surprisingly, is also read more in the younger age groups.

Brief Description of the Magazines

This review considers the magazines as they were at the time of the survey. Subsequent changes are not therefore taken account of–but in general these publications seem largely unaltered now (1973).

Woman is published once a week and at the time of the survey cost 10*d*. (4p). It is a non-glossy production, $12\frac{1}{2}'' \times 10''$ and varying between 72 and 116 pages in length. It has a few pages in colour, but fewer than the number of colour advertisements. The 'World's greatest weekly for women' divides its contents thus: special features, beauty, cookery, fashion, fiction, home, knitting and sewing, and regular features. The regular features include letters, two problem pages, two medical columns and a column by Godfrey Winn.

Woman seeks to cater for a wide audience, from teenagers to grandmothers, and to provide them all with useful and wholesome advice on matters corporeal and spiritual. It is full of tips, hints, bargains, offers and do-it-yourself information. Its centre can be seen to lie firmly with the home and family: Edith Blair reviewing 'Plastics around the Home', 'The Quiet Hell-Raiser settles for Home–our tribute to Trevor Howard and his wife on their silver wedding anniversary', the Thorns babies modelling their sleeping-bags, wine-making at home, knitting patterns, cooking tips, recipes, special non-stick saucepan offers, stories ('The Marrying Kind') and anecdotal letters. Beauty and fashion articles stand somewhat awkwardly in this environment, seeming to represent a world of glamour and sophistication unfamiliar to the magazine as a whole and yet often managing to accommodate the two worlds by the humbleness of the approach–tips for double chins, clothes for outsize ladies, making the latest fashion styles at home. One is always making the best of things. There is a constant preoccupation with slimming, and beauty preparations often concentrate on running repairs rather than gilding the lily. The 'Special Feature' section is the only one which varies from week to week, but it rarely includes topics from the non-domestic world. The articles are most likely to be about celebrities, royalty and famous families, but many consist only of a special offer of rose bushes and bulbs. Occasionally there are articles on less humdrum subjects: girls who leave home, or unmarried mothers – but these are the exceptions.

Visually, the magazine varies in standard from page to page. Some pages are crowded and messy in lay-out with an unimaginative use of illustrations – this seems to apply regularly to certain columns, e.g. the Godfrey Winn and the entertainment columns – while other pages have arresting and well-composed photography (e.g. The Art of Cooking, 20 September 1969) and startling close-ups (Beauty, 20 September 1969). Because of the way the magazine is laid out – odd columns plus continuations of stories and articles from previous pages alongside advertisements – one of the overriding impressions is that of bittiness, and the visual colour, excitement and skill of some of the opening pages is only maintained in the latter two-thirds of the magazine by the advertisements.

Woman's Own is very similar to *Woman* in its format, and the price, size and length are the same. The contents are divided in much the same way – though, as in *Woman*, the division is much clearer in the list of contents than it is in the rest of the magazine – medical, fashion, beauty, home, cookery, offers, fiction and regular features (letters, problems, pets, astrology . . .). There are two other major sections 'This Week's Specials' and 'Articles', but it is impossible to discover the difference between them. It does mean, nevertheless, that there are substantially more articles in this magazine than in *Woman*, though the topics covered are similar, and the focal point – home and family – is the same. The scope does range from vivisection and sleep to the Battle of Britain and a reconstruction of the story of Ruth Ellis who was hanged for murder in 1955, but the most widely announced and advertised series of articles at the time of the survey was 'an important new series of 8-page pull-outs that build into a complete encyclopaedia all about you . . . The Mystery of Being a Woman.' Visually *Woman's Own* is much the same as *Woman*, perhaps even a little more adventurous.

In these two magazines there is a tension between the desire for marriage and motherhood and all the romantic accessories, and the actuality of chores, work, routine and the restrictions of sewing patterns and more new recipes. So much emotion is invested in the search for the right man, his capture and the taking of the final vows that there is the great danger of subsequent let-down. How can the romance be maintained after marriage while coping with the (so worthwhile) duties and chores? The contradictions which can arise from this provide very real problems for Marge Proops, Evelyn Home and Mary Grant to deal with and for the rest of the magazine contents to try to tackle in their own ways. The easy way out is to answer 'children'—which leads to the reinvestment of emotion in them, a postponement and possibly an accentuation of the problem. Of all the magazines *Woman* and *Woman's Own* show least concern for the woman who wants to be married and a mother but who wants an individual life of her own as well.

Woman and Home. This magazine is published once a month (also by IPC) and at the time of the survey cost 2s. 6d. (12½p). It is non-glossy (apart from the cover), 12½″ × 10″ and varies in length between 100 and 160 pages. Its contents are divided into the following headings: cordon bleu cookery, fiction, special features, knit and sew, the well-run home, fashion and beauty, our regulars, and why not let us help you? Regular features include astrology, children's columns and advice columns, the Golden Club for mature readers (concerned mainly with clothes) shopping advice and miscellanies of quotes and comments. There is a section on the arts, but no letters, medical columns or problem pages. Special features include articles on celebrities, royalty, travel ('I visit the great island of Crete, by Godfrey Winn') and social occasions ('Little Guide to Weddings, pull-out Booklet'). The world is very much that of the settled married woman who does useful things in her spare time, but whose first and overriding concern is for the home (the well-run home). Articles do perhaps range further than is common in *Woman* or *Woman's Own*—a career in the WRAF, or modern tapestries in ancient cathedrals—but further examples are not easy to find, and the section in which some of these occur is called 'Real Life', as if the rest of the magazine were not. The atmosphere of the magazine is traditional, calm, confident and very comfortable. *Woman and Home* is neat and tasteful—but not really fashionable. The world is well-off—but not glossy or trendy—desiring the best but not necessarily the showiest.

Colour is used at intervals throughout the magazine—perhaps to a greater extent than in the two magazines described already. In general, however, the layout and visual presentation is inferior to *Woman* and *Woman's Own*. Most photographs are straight shots at eye level with little variation of focus, angle, lighting or colour textures. There is the same bittiness and lack of apparent organization, although there are plenty of reasons to infer that the bittiness is deliberate: by linking the different parts of the magazine together like a jig-saw, there is a likelihood of more of it getting read. The fiction, as in all these six magazines, is never illustrated by photographs, but by drawings and paintings.

Honey is a glossy monthly costing 2s. 6d. (12½p), 11½″ × 8¾″ and between 100 and 164 pages long. Its content headings are fashion, beauty, features, regulars and fiction—beauty being the smallest section comprising usually only one article. Fashion concentrates on gear for girls, very fashionable, trendy and completely unlike the majority of clothes covered in the three magazines above. Regular features consist of personal columns, problem page, astrology, letters, film and music reviews and 'Honey Club'. The features have a constant theme in pop music and those connected with it, and to a certain extent, film stars. This, together with a concern for places and amusements/entertainments, is however only half of the features section. The other half ranges over a variety of subjects, all sharing a certain trendiness but not fitting into any consistent pattern: witchcraft, fortune-telling, acting in a repertory company, girls who leave home, young people on the dole, mixed marriages, the poetry of Brian Patten ... Overlaying these diverse topics is an impression of continuous excitability, as if the pressure towards everything being a rave or a drag were breaking the magazine up into a visualization of the electronic feedback from The Who's guitars. This impression highlights the fact that the visual is inseparable from the verbal in *Honey*. This is not to say that the layout is always successful and is due in large part anyway to the large number of highly colourful and arresting advertising insertions: following the editorial text from page to page through illustrations inserts and adverts brings to mind McLuhan's remarks about mosaic media. *Honey* is a pop-art page-by-page collage with the same incoherent coherence as a Radio One record show.

Honey is for the single girl who wants to be sure she's not only trendy and fashionable but also having a good time. Having a good time means entertainment, and it means men. *Honey* offers opinions and advice on both. Entertainment involves parties, films and pop (shows, clubs, dances and records). But men are the overriding preoccupation (the secondary and closely connected obsession being virginity: yes or no, how far to go). Though there is some serious discussion regarding, for example, contraception, there is a considerable amount of use made of sex in a rather more gratuitous way–in fashion ('See through fashion –how far can *you* bear to bare?'), cookery ('The food of love: setting sexy, sauce seductive') and personalities ('Oozing oomph. Sex-appeal secrets of the stars'). But how to *look* sexy is given far more attention than how to *be* sexy. One of the contradictions within the magazine is that girls are encouraged to use sexual attractions as much as possible, but to follow this policy through to its logical conclusion is still discouraged.

Petticoat. This is a weekly non-glossy magazine selling at 1s. (5p) for forty $9\frac{1}{4}'' \times 12\frac{3}{4}''$ pages. In some ways, although it is aimed at the same audience (in terms of age) as *Honey*, it is very different. It is in fact read widely by girls under sixteen. Part of its function is to give advice on money, clothes, etc. to schoolgirls who are dollies by night. It is a small magazine when compared with other weeklies like *Woman* and the contents are limited both in number and in length of treatment. The contents are not formally divided but can be listed as beauty, fashion, fiction, regular features and articles. Regular features are medical advice, problem page, astrology, film and record reviews, a personal column and a page of miscellaneous letters and items on accessories, fads and people. The articles have a solid theme of pop and film personalities with diversions into love and sex fairly frequently ('Petticoat report on Sexual Promiscuity'). At intervals, however, there are items on problems such as illegitimacy and 'The young divorcee'. The emphases fall on men (getting them, how to treat them/deal with them, keeping them), clothes and pop music, in that order. Advice on careers is very rare and the depictions of girls with jobs in the columns and the fiction are glamorous or vaguely to do with undefined office-work. Mention is not made of shops, factories or long-term careers.

Though there is a certain exuberance about some parts of the magazine, the sustained excitement of *Honey* is nowhere apparent–this being due in part to the fact that there are fewer pages, fewer articles, fewer advertisements and no glossy finish, and in part to the fact that *Petticoat* is simply a less sophisticated magazine. The use of colour is restricted in most editions to some of the fashion pages (plus, of course, the advertisements) and the visual side of the magazine is of uneven quality. The fashion photographs are rarely very original or striking and much of the rest of the illustration is in the form of a lot of small inset photographs which are messy and unattractive. In contrast to *Honey*, there are few pages which one would expect to see torn out and pinned on the wall.

Nova is a glossy magazine published once a month at 3*s.* 6*d.* (17½p). It is large (13″ × 10″) and in length varies from 90 to 140 pages and over. Its contents are divided into features, regulars and living. The living section includes items on fashion, beauty, cooking, travel and the home, with a concentration on the first two. The regular features exclude most of the regular features in the other magazines except astrology and a personal column (Kenneth Allsop). Apart from these there are sections on antiques and some rather irregular regulars–'profile', 'moneysworth', 'appraisal'.

The magazine deliberately avoids too great a concentration on the items which dominate other magazines of the *Woman–Woman's Own–Woman and Home* type or the *Petticoat–Honey* type. The *Nova* reader is above advice on make-up or knitting. Its sections on fashion, though important, are only a minor part and articles about the home are neither regular nor central. The articles concentrate quite heavily on personalities–whether in politics (Mme Ky and Mme Binh), the 'arts' (Mailer, Warhol) or show-biz (Vera Lynn, John Lennon and Yoko Ono).

The articles seem to reveal a desire to be a little unconventional, a little daring, but rather trendy; its non-personality items are on such issues as venereal disease, abortion and narcissism – although the treatment is often sensitive, lengthy and detailed. The fiction in *Nova* is different from the stories in all the other magazines in that it does not concentrate on romance and domesticity and is quite clearly meant to stand as serious literature. The difference between *Nova* and *Woman* is encapsulated in the titles of their respective fiction: 'Un Peu Comme Orson Welles' and 'Come Home, Darling'. Obviously the magazine does not see itself as just another woman's magazine but as a more sophisticated more modern, exciting and yet serious journal written primarily for women (both intelligent and affluent) but likely also to be read by men. Visually the magazine is interesting without being *avant-garde*: both photographs and drawings are used throughout to good effect, although colour is not as widespread as one might expect. The layout of the magazine and of the individual pages is clear, and very unlike the layout in a magazine such as *Woman*: advertisements intrude less into the features, which in themselves are more self-contained and do not have to be pursued through a labyrinth of tail-end pages. The adverts, in fact, fit neatly into the magazine because their colour and glossiness are similar to *Nova's* colour and glossiness. *Nova* has none of the excitement of *Honey* nor the crowded busyness of *Woman and Home*. It is measured, cool and self-aware, exciting when the need arises, serious when it seems applicable – and possibly a little too slick and clever. There is, none the less, an air of incipient nervous breakdown – as if the tension is about to snap, and the independent, clear-thinking career woman is about to come to blows with the competitive fashion-dominated society creature . . .

References

[1] References to previous investigations refer to pilot studies carried out prior to this particular survey by the writer. The purpose was to test methods and approaches, ways of classifying, and to obtain a general impression of the material and the practical problems involved.

[2] Literally, this means a group of letters cast in one piece, as for Belle Color (see plate 5b), Pretty Polly (see plate 11a).

[3] *I.P.A. Forum*, 28 October 1969.

[4] Figures from *I.P.A. Readership Survey* January–December 1967. It is to be borne in mind that the figures and percentages have been rounded up and down to the nearest whole figure. The social grade of the informant is normally based on the occupation of the head of the household, and in the event of the head's being retired it is either the previous or estimated occupation which is considered. The social grade of boarders, lodgers and resident domestic servants in private households and members of institutions is based on the informant's occupation.

grade A = Upper middle class; higher managerial, administrative, professional, £2,000 + p.a.

grade B = Middle class; intermediate managerial, administrative, professional, £1,000–£2,000 p.a.

grade C1 = Lower-middle class; supervisory, clerical, junior managerial, administrative and professional; £1,000 p.a.

grade C2 = skilled working class; skilled £14–£22 p.w.

grade D = working class semi-skilled and unskilled £6.10.0–£14.0.0 p.w.

grade E = lowest; old age pensioners, widows, casual low grade under £6.10.0 p.w.

2. Advertisement for Phensic from *Woman's Own*, the use of colour and expressions emphasizing the 'before and after' concept. (Detailed analysis in Appendix I.)

5

An Analysis of the Advertisements

The terms used in this chapter have all been defined fully in the preceding chapter, and if the meaning of words or the difference between terms is unclear, the reader should refer back. A résumé of the pattern of the classification and the terms used follows as a more concise guide to the chapter.

Products and Magazines

The products are classified into twenty-four categories and are subdivided into four clusters: the feminine, clothing, food/household, and 'others'. The advertisements are taken from six different magazines: *Woman*, *Woman's Own*, *Woman and Home*, *Petticoat*, *Honey* and *Nova*.

These two types of classification have a special relationship to the others. They are the ones which have the power to define the range of variation within the other classifications; they are *limiting factors*. For example, the product type 'hair preparations' will involve, in the great majority of cases, the use of a female head and of close-up. Clothing, in the same way, will necessitate the use of a model and a full-length shot. Some factors remain *independent* of the nature of the product–e.g. whether the model regards the reader or looks into middle distance, whether she smiles or scowls, and so on. Similarly, the type of magazine limits the range of variation–for example, advertising in a publication produced for readers under twenty-one will clearly tend to feature young actors rather than older ones. *It is in the areas where meanings cannot be said to be pre-defined by the product or the magazine that our interest lies, or in what sorts of meanings are made within given confines.* Given that clothes advertisements need actors to wear the garments, what sorts of actors are chosen, what sorts of settings do they appear in? This is the nature of question to be asked.

Presentation

(a) Style

Three categories: crowded, basic, streamlined; style refers to the layout and general appearance of the whole advertisement, the classification being based on a scale from a crowded, disordered look through to one which is streamlined and homogenous.

(b) Techniques

Focus, close-up, cropping, colour, lighting, angle, special effects, drawings and multiple pictures. These are photographic techniques, except–obviously–the use of drawings, and the splitting up of the illustration into separate pictures.

(c) Rhetorical Devices

Typification/testament, product presentation/transformation, super-visual devices and devices of association. Rhetorical devices make up the basic visual strategy of the illustration, typification and testament deriving from the actor(s), and product presentation/transformation from the product. Association derives mainly from props and setting– and is closely akin to metaphor in general terms. The supervisual derives entirely from the pictorial qualities without regard to the content of the illustration.

Content. I – The combinations of the elements

The elements comprising the picture are four in all: *product, actors, props* and *setting*, which can occur in fifteen different combinations. A 3×4 grid numbered A to L is the shorthand means of referring to these combinations. (see p. 88).

Content. II – The elements in themselves

(a) Props

A threefold classification is used: functional (naturally part of the scene being depicted), functional-metaphorical (part of the scene but with other, associative, meanings) and metaphorical (solely included for the purpose of association).

(b) Settings

PRESENTATION: staged/documentary (how true to life, how convincing, does the setting seem to be?).

Familiarity: familiar/wishful/fantasy–(how real or how strange is that depicted world?).

Mood: everyday, romantic, bizarre, exotic, extravagant (what is the evocative quality of the setting?).

PLACE: indoors or outdoors.

Indoor settings: domestic or non-domestic, domestic consisting of five sub-categories: traditional, ritzy, conventional, mod and camp.

Outdoor settings: exotic/familiar (or local), and rural/greenbelt/urban are the two sets of classifications.

(c) Actors

GENERAL: noting the number and sex of the actors featured and the presence or absence of children.

ACTIVITY: the *relationships* between actors, four categories: object/reciprocal/semi-reciprocal/divergent.

Attention: may be directed to the reader/camera, or be confined within the depicted scene. Attention within the scene can be given to any of the following–people, objects, self or middle-distance–or the direction of the actor's attention may not be discernible to the reader.

Tactility: where it occurs, may be directed towards three different items. The classifications are thus: self/people/objects/(nil).

APPEARANCE: the overall impression and style of the actors forms five categories: superior, sophisticated, naïve, plain and detached.

MANNER: *expression*–the ten female categories and eight male categories are enumerated and explained above (Chapter 4).

Pose: similarly, there are eight female and six male categories.

Clothes: there are seven female categories and five male ones.

Hair: female hair is classified by length/style and by colour, thus: freeflowing/shaped/moulded: blonde/non-blonde. Male hair is classified by length: short/medium/long.

Interpretation

The whole is interpreted as a complete piece of visual communication in terms of the meanings expressed.

The description of the survey is organized in the following way. The first step is a numerical breakdown of the material within each classification. This is given in Appendix II. The second step is a correlation of classifications, based on the selection of those correlations which seem fruitful, or on the elimination of those which are irrelevant or of no consequence. The remainder of this chapter comprises this analysis. Consideration of the meanings expressed, the interpretative stage, follows in the next chapter.

COMPARISONS AND CORRELATIONS

The difficulty when making comparisons and correlations–even on a relatively simple level–is that of order: it is the task of converting the mosaic into the linear. Something is inevitably lost in the process, but as the original is only held in the head of the investigator, it is a necessary process. However, it is also the job of the investigator to present those correlations which have some meaning and to leave aside those which have none–unless the actual lack of meaning is itself felt to be

significant. Although the format of the following pages may impart
a certain awkwardness to their reading and make the initial comprehension of their content overall a little difficult for those who are not
familiar with the material or its treatment, this form of presentation is
felt to be a *necessity*. In accordance with the method sketched out above
we are dealing here, not with the interpretative but with the descriptive level, in as far as we are able to maintain that distinction. Unless
the flow of the investigation is to be disrupted and the arguments diffused, deductions and interpretations for meaning must be held in
abeyance until this descriptive stage is completed. The intention is to
present–as 'straight' as possible–the ways in which the numerous
factors by which the material has been analysed relate together
and the patterns that thereby emerge. And the interpretations and
hypotheses can be expressed, drawn together and related to a wider
context.

Some sections of the following might at this stage be omitted by the
more impatient reader and referred to when subsequent discussion
makes it necessary or helpful. In terms of the development of the complete and coherent method, however, the best procedure is to follow the
descriptions sequentially and also to use them for reference at the interpretative stage. The intention is to take each group of products in turn
to establish some sort of character profile. A full account of these correlations will be found in the thesis from which this book has developed.
Any reader with a special interest in a particular area can refer to the
work in the University of Birmingham Library.

Correlations By Product

Cosmetics, Hair Preparations, Sanitary Towels, and Slimming Preparations

The first three of these four product categories seem to hang together,
while the last is opposed to them in many of the correlations. The first
group has an above average proportion of streamlined advertisements,
and makes use of many techniques–cosmetics and hair preparations
making especial use of close-up, see Cutex and Vaseline examples.
Slimming advertisements, on the other hand, tend towards a more
crowded style and a minimal exploitation of techniques. In terms of
rhetoric there is more variation: cosmetics are high on the supervisual
scale and use product transformation widely; hair preparations are also
above average on the supervisual scale while both sanitary and slimming
preparations make more use of associative devices. Typification is common in all four categories. In terms of elements, the actor alone and the
actor plus props occur most widely throughout, though there is more
emphasis on settings in slimming advertisements.

The props in cosmetic and hair illustrations tend to be functional-metaphorical or metaphorical, of all types in sanitary preparations and functional in slimming advertisements. Settings are few in the first two product categories, tend to be wishful or fantastic, outdoor, and romantic in mood. In advertisements for sanitary products the settings are even more likely to be outdoors but also familiar and either romantic or everyday in mood; settings in slimming product advertisements are similar but are situated indoors *and* outdoors.

The personnel in the vast majority of these illustrations consists of the woman alone. In an above average number she gives her attention to middle-distance or herself, except for slimming where a higher percentage direct their attention to the reader. Tactility is self-directed to an extent which is above average (see Bidex illustration, plate 9b.)

The sophisticated type predominates in both cosmetic and hair illustrations; in sanitary product illustrations the types are more widely differentiated, and in slimming ones the plain type is more common. The most youthful age distribution occurs in hair and sanitary preparation advertisements, a slightly older emphasis (though nearly all actors are under thirty) in cosmetic advertisements, and a very wide distribution through all ages in slimming advertisements. Cool, soft, kitten and narcissistic expressions have an above average incidence in cosmetic advertisements and there is a similar pattern in hair preparation advertisements (with fewer soft expressions). Practical and cool expressions in sanitary preparation advertisements, and catalogue expressions in slimming product advertisements show above average incidence. Seductive, dramatic and narcissistic poses occur to an above average extent in cosmetic and hair illustrations. In the former category one should add composed and relaxed poses, and in the latter, carefree ones. Carefree and functional poses are above average in incidence in sanitary product advertisements, and likewise narcissistic, dummy and functional poses in advertisements for slimming products.

A high proportion of exotic clothes is common to cosmetics, hair and sanitary products, and an absence of clothes to cosmetics, hair, and slimming product advertisements. Informal wear occurs widely in hair and slimming preparations. Cosmetics, hair and sanitary preparations exhibit a high incidence of free and blonde hair. Hair in slimming preparation advertisements tends to be free (though to a lesser degree) but less frequently blonde.

Clothes, Underclothes, Tights, Shoes, Wool

In style, the first three of these product categories tend to be streamline and the latter two, basic. Techniques are not widely exploited except in the illustrations for tights, and to a lesser extent, underclothes.

Actor plus product is the most common combination of elements in all these categories save shoes, where product plus props is the most prevalent. Product presentation/transformation is used very often, except in the case of tights, and typification is well used in wool, clothes, and underclothes illustrations. Supervisual devices are made most use of in the advertisements for tights, and association in tights and underclothes advertisements.

Props are most likely to be functional-metaphorical in clothes and underclothing advertisements, and more various in the other three categories. There are few settings in tights and shoe illustrations, and those tend to be outdoor, wishful and everyday or romantic in mood. Wool settings are very different with mainly interiors (often conventional) familiar, and everyday in mood. Clothes settings are mostly outdoor, (and tend to be urban) or non-domestic interiors; a high proportion are wishful and romantic. Many settings in underclothing advertisements are also wishful, but there is a high incidence of the fantastic as well. The mood is more exotic than in the other categories, with a high incidence of country locations.

The basic personnel of the illustrations is the woman alone, but women together (e.g. Berlei, plate 10a), are more common in clothes and underclothes illustrations, and man and woman together, in wool illustrations (e.g. Laird Portch, plate 10b). Relationships with men tend to be semi-reciprocal, and between women, divergent. Attention is mainly directed towards the reader or middle distance, with noticeable attention to the self in shoe and underclothes advertisements. There is a high incidence of self-directed tactility in the first three categories, which is less marked in wool, and not at all the case in shoe illustrations, where object-directed tactility is more common.

The detached type is much in evidence in all categories except tights. There is a high incidence of the superior type in clothes advertisements, the naïve in shoe advertisements and the plain in wool advertisements. The catalogue expression and dummy pose predominate in clothes and wool illustrations. In underclothes the soft and cool expressions are above average in distribution, in tights advertisements the cool, carefree and kitten expressions, and in shoe advertisements the soft and carefree expressions. Relaxed, carefree and seductive poses show a high incidence in tights and shoe advertisements; and the dramatic and narcissistic in tights and underclothes advertisements. The composed pose occurs to an above average extent in shoe and underclothing illustrations.

Clothes constitute the product in most of the clothes, underclothes and wool advertisements. In the case of tights, clothes tend to be exotic, informal or absent, and for shoes it is informal or office-wear. In underclothing and shoe illustrations there is a high proportion of free hair-styles, but in the other three categories, while the free style is predominant, there is an above average incidence of the moulded style. Ages are mostly below thirty, but with greater concentration in the older part of the age range in wool advertisements than in the other categories.

Food

There is a high percentage of streamlined advertisements, but apart from a great use of colour and close-up, other techniques are under-employed. The product alone and the product plus props account for nearly 60 per cent of the illustrations; only 36 per cent include actors, and only 17 per cent include settings. Product presentation and transformation are common, testament is relatively common, and supervisual devices are used to an extent much above average.

Props are mainly functional, and settings tend to be documentary, familiar, and everyday in mood. Of the indoor ones, most are domestic, and conventional or mod in style. Outdoor settings tend to be local but non-urban.

There are quite a number of children in the illustrations (see American Rice and New Zealand Cheese), and some men alone. There are very few instances of man and woman alone but quite a high percentage of family groups. Relationships tend to be reciprocal. Attention tends to be directed towards people or objects, and tactility to objects.

The plain type is predominant, and in expressions the practical and carefree are most common. Poses tend to be functional, clothes of the office-wear type and there is a high percentage of moulded hairstyles. The majority of actors is over twenty-five and three-quarters seem to be over thirty.

Household

Style tends toward the basic pattern; decorating materials and kitchen equipment being more streamlined than the other categories. Techniques are used much less widely than in most of the product categories so far considered, but there are wide variations between the types of household product. Most household illustrations include the product, while only a third feature a setting. Nearly half do *not* include actors. There is a high percentage of product presentation, and of product transformation in the case of decorating materials. In the use of associative devices all save household accessories and kitchen equipment are above average, and the supervisual devices are much exploited by the advertisements for decorating materials and floor coverings.

Props are mainly functional and functional-metaphorical, but floor coverings include quite a number of metaphorical ones. Overall, settings tend to be staged, wishful, everyday, and indoors. Variations within that picture include a stress on the familiar in kitchen equipment and household accessories settings, and on the bizarre, exotic or extravagant in furniture settings. The style of indoor settings is predominantly mod, save for kitchen equipment and household accessories.

The personnel in the household illustrations is similar to that in the food illustrations. Floor coverings and decorating materials tend to be more 'female' (see Valspar, colour plate 1) (i.e. a high proportion feature women alone), and furniture illustrations provide more instances of man and woman alone than any other single category (see for example, G-Plan, frontispiece). There is a very small number of instances of attention directed towards the self and a high incidence of attention directed to objects (except in the case of floor coverings and household accessories) and of attention directed towards people (save in illustrations for decorating materials). Tactility is mainly object-directed, most emphatically in furniture, kitchen equipment and household accessory advertisements.

There is a high incidence of the sophisticated type, with a bias in the case of kitchen equipment and household accessories towards the plain. Practical expressions are above average in extent, as are carefree and soft expressions. Catalogue expressions are numerous, but the remaining types are almost completely absent. Catalogue expressions are concentrated in the kitchen equipment and household accessory advertisements, and the soft and carefree expressions in the furniture illustrations. The predominant poses are functional and relaxed, the former most common in kitchen equipment, household accessory and decorating material categories, the latter in furniture and soft furnishings.

Exotic clothes show a fairly high level of occurrence (save in kitchen equipment and household accessories). Informal wear is common, as also in office-wear. Free and shaped hairstyles are about equal in occurrence, while moulded styles (mainly in kitchen equipment and household accessories) make up only 14 per cent. Kitchen equipment and household accessory illustrations show a low incidence of blondeness, while decorating materials and furniture show a high incidence. Most of the actors fall into the middle of the age range (twenty-five to thirty-five) except for those in kitchen equipment illustrations who tend to be older.

Offers and Careers

Style tends to be crowded in both, and techniques are not widely used. In career advertisements the commonest arrangement of elements is actor plus props, and in offers, product alone or product plus actor. Supervisual and associative devices are underexploited, rhetoric concentrating on product presentation in offers, and typification in career advertisements.

Props tend to be functional in both categories. Settings are rare in offers illustrations, mainly familiar, everyday and outdoor; in career illustrations they tend to be familiar, everyday or romantic, and indoor, though non-domestic. The personnel in illustrations for offers tends to be women alone, while in career advertisements they are more likely to be mixed, and often occur in threes. Attention in the former is mainly given to the reader or middle-distance and in the latter the distribution of attention is about average. Object directed tactility is the norm in both categories.

There is a high incidence of the plain type in offers and career advertisements with a high proportion of the naïve type in the latter also. In both categories there is a high percentage of the catalogue and practical expressions and of the dummy pose. In career advertisements carefree and functional poses are also above average in occurrence. In the same advertisements clothes consist of uniforms or office-wear in the majority of cases, and of office-wear in those for offers. In the career advertisements there is a high incidence of the moulded hair-style but in offer advertisements there is a preponderance of the shaped style. In age most of the actors in the former are under thirty, and in the latter there is an average distribution throughout the ages.

Baby and Children's Products, Medical and Business

There is a tendency to the basic style in all these categories, though medical advertisements also tend to be crowded. Techniques are not much used for baby and children's products, but are widely used in business advertisements, and to a lesser extent in medical ones.

Actor plus props is a common arrangement of elements in all three product categories, though the actor alone is more frequent in medical, and actor plus product in children's clothing advertisements. All make use of typification and all save baby and children's products use associative devices to quite a high degree. The majority of props in children's and baby products illustrations are functional, in business advertisments they are functional-metaphorical, and in medical advertisements a mixture of both. Settings are rare, but where they do occur tend to be familiar and everyday.

Children occur in all categories and the personnel tends to be mixed –except in baby product illustrations where there are no instances of a man and a woman together. Attention is directed to people (and to the self in medical illustrations) and tactility to objects (also to people as in baby advertisements, and to people and the self, as in medical advertisements).

All types are to be found in the baby and children's product advertisements while the plain type predominates in medical advertisements illustrations, and the sophisticated in business ones. Expressions also differ widely. Only the carefree expression has a slightly greater than average incidence in business advertisements, while in baby product advertisements the soft, maternal and comic are all high in incidence. The carefree, practical, narcissistic, maternal and 'pained' (a literal description of a type only found in medical advertisements, e.g. Phensic) expressions all occur to an above average extent in medical advertisement illustrations.

The functional pose is the most common in all three categories, but the composed pose too is common in baby advertisements and the relaxed pose in business advertisements. Clothes tend to be of the office-wear or informal type. There is a high proportion of moulded hairstyles in business and medical illustrations, and of free hair-styles in baby product illustrations.

Almost all the women in baby advertisements are in the twenty-five to thirty age group, below thirty in the business advertisements and distributed through the age groups in an average pattern in the medical advertisements.

Cigarettes

The advertisements are mostly streamlined, but make little use of techniques, save for close-up and special effects. Most of them have a product alone or product plus props arrangement of elements, and make extensive use of product presentation, association and supervisuality. The majority of props are metaphorical and the few settings tend to be rural. Actors occur only rarely and there is an insufficient number to make a description worth while.

The table opposite resumes the relationship between products and elements in schematic form. As there were no instances of illustrations in the Product+ Setting group (C) it has been omitted. The figures show the incidence per element as a percentage of every product (to the nearest whole figure.) Most of the correlations have been noted under style, technique and rhetoric. Other connexions which can be traced are due mainly to the particular products which comprise each category—rather than to a direct relationship between, for example, the incidence of the bizarre and a Props + Actor combination.

	A Product	B Product+Props	D Product+Props+Setting	E Product+Actors	F Product+Actors+Props	G Product+Actors+Setting	H Product+Actors+Props+Setting	I Actors	J Actors+Props	K Actors+Setting	L Actors+Setting+Props	M Props
Cosmetics	5	8	—	5	8	—	4	32	22	8	5	4
Hair preparations	3	6	—	6	3	—	—	45	21	8	6	2
Sanitary products	9	—	—	—	—	—	—	27	18	27	18	—
Slimming aids	—	16	—	13	—	—	13	16	15	13	13	—
Clothes	1	—	—	38	10	28	22	1	—	—	—	—
Underwear	—	—	—	28	13	18	39	—	3	—	—	—
Tights	—	33	—	22	22	7	17	—	—	—	—	—
Shoes	9	55	9	3	6	—	15	—	—	—	—	3
Wool	—	—	—	57	17	6	20	—	—	—	—	—
Food	15	44	1	5	11	—	13	2	2	—	3	4
Kitchen equipment	31	28	—	10	7	—	10	—	—	4	10	—
Floor coverings	18	29	—	—	18	—	23	6	6	—	—	—
Decorating materials	—	11	16	11	11	—	47	—	—	—	—	5
Furniture	—	20	7	—	—	7	67	—	—	—	—	—
Household accessories	33	44	—	3	7	—	3	7	3	—	—	—
Soft furnishings	—	20	15	15	15	—	30	—	5	—	—	—
Offers	40	11	3	20	3	6	6	3	3	—	6	—
Cigarettes	21	64	—	—	—	—	—	—	—	7	7	—
Baby products	4	7	—	15	30	—	4	15	26	—	—	—
Careers	—	—	—	—	—	—	—	15	45	15	25	—
Business	7	7	—	7	—	—	—	7	53	7	13	—
Medical	8	—	—	12	—	—	4	27	35	4	8	4
Miscellaneous	12	12	2	22	6	8	—	12	10	6	8	4

Correlations by Style and Techniques
One would expect there to be a connexion between the overall style of an advertisement and the techniques employed in the illustration, though there is no direct mechanical connexion which is imperative.

It has been noted in passing, but should be stressed here, that techniques seem to be of two types: those which tend to increase impact, excitement and unusualness in the illustration (colour, focus, angle, close-up and special effects) and those which detract from the impact, excitement and indeed general appeal of the picture, namely multiple illustrations and drawings. Cropping appears to occupy a neutral position in this distinction. The correlation with style substantiates the dichotomy.

In fact most techniques are used decreasingly as the style becomes more crowded and vice versa. Only the use of multiple pictures and drawings increases as the style becomes more crowded. The use of cropping is a constant (cf. Phensic, Pretty Polly, and Sunsilk illustrations).

One would also suspect a connexion between style and rhetorical devices of the supervisual type. This is certainly so: Supervisual devices are directly connected to the style of the advertisement. The incidence of 'Supervisuality' is directly proportional to the degree of streamlinedness and inversely proportional to crowdedness. There is, further, a direct connexion between the supervisual and the use of close-up, colour and lighting techniques.

There is some connexion between style and the use of associative devices although this is less outstanding. The use of association is more common in streamlined and basic advertisements than in crowded ones.

Some advertisements definitely seem more *sophisticated* than others. It is not merely a consideration of form, for it affects content at least on the level of association.

Surprisingly, those illustrations most basic or simple in constituents (A, E and I categories) (see tables on pages 88 and 123) tend to a higher incidence of crowdedness. Correspondingly, the incidence of the streamlined style in categories G and H (the fullest in terms of constituent elements) is quite high. This lends some substantiation to the previous statement that sophisticated advertisements, which are highly developed in terms of form, are often also more complex in terms of content. Although the illustration may contain a lot, and be quite complicated in content, the overall style of the advertisement may well be uncluttered and streamlined. This is not to say that all simple (A, E, I, etc.) illustrations occur in crowded or unsophisticated advertisements. Indeed, many make great use of a variety of techniques, especially close-up.

Close-up is most frequent in categories A, B and I, least frequent in G and H, and angle occurs to a greater extent in the E–H sections than elsewhere – but these are examples of somewhat direct mechanical connexions. The former is due to the fact that close-ups are bound to be less frequent when settings are included and most frequent when just the product or the product with props is featured. The latter is due to the preponderance of clothing advertisements in the actor plus product column, which feature the whole (full-length) actor or actors and lend themselves to the use of techniques involving angle. It is of some significance perhaps that the actor alone category coincides with close-up treatment to such an extent (i.e. the actor alone equals the face in close-up).

Props

Style and props are directly related in that the incidence of functional props is inversely proportional to the degree of streamlinedness, and the incidence of functional-metaphorical and metaphorical props is *directly* proportional to the degree of streamlinedness.

In other words, simplicity in content does *not* parallel simplicity in form, and frequently the opposite is true. A sophisticated advertisement may be simple in form but complex not only in content but in intention and meaning. A sophisticated advertisement may be streamlined, use many techniques, associative or supervisual devices, and be complex in terms of constituent elements and type of props.

Settings

In mood and familiarity crowdedness is coincident with the everyday and familiar, and the restricted use of techniques likewise coincides with the everyday (see Cookeen and Vymura illustrations). In other moods colour, lighting, focus, angle, close-up and special effects occur in 90 per cent or more of the illustrations, but in illustrations with an everyday mood the figure is 50 per cent.

There is *no correlation* between style or techniques and the type of setting.

Actors

There are some interesting correlations between style/techniques and the type of actor featured in the illustration, further substantiated by expression. Plain types and practical, carefree and to some extent catalogue expressions are more likely to be found in crowded advertisements, and sophisticated types and cool and soft expressions are more likely to be found in streamlined or basic advertisements. This is not a definite one-to-one relationship, for the streamlined 'modern' style often does not accompany sophisticated fashionable women. Further, there is a strong correlation between younger actors and streamlined advertisements, and between older actors and crowded ones (cf. Cookeen (5a) and Electricaire (13b) advertisements).

There is a stronger relationship between techniques and actors. Colour, focus, angle, lighting and special effects show a 35 per cent incidence in illustrations featuring plain types, and a 58 per cent incidence in those featuring sophisticated types. There is a similar correlation in terms of practical-carefree-catalogue and soft-cool expressions. This adds yet another dimension to the profile of the sophisticated advertisement.

Correlations by Rhetorical Devices

There is an important difference to be noted between, on the one hand, typification/testament and product presentation/transformation, and on the other, association and the supervisual. The former occur in the great majority of cases where there is an actor or the product in the picture, and the occasions when they do not occur fail to show any significant correlation with any other factor, except that they are less likely to occur in illustrations with a greater number of constituent elements (e.g. less likely in G or H than A or E). Product transformation is merely the form which product presentation takes in many of the illustrations for food, cosmetics, wool and decorating materials. Testament is not very common. It occurs mainly in food and slimming illustrations, and accompanies less streamlined advertisements. Supervisual and associative devices are, however, far more variable in occurrence, and it is with these that we are primarily concerned.

Something has already been said about the use of the supervisual and of association in connexion with style and techniques, and in connexion with specific products: that there are, for example, more supervisual devices used in illustrations for decorating materials and food than clothes and careers. One might pause here to consider whether there is any pattern to be distinguished from the relationship of product to rhetoric.

One pattern can quickly be seen by correlating the list of products on the supervisual scale with elements (see also below); Supervisual devices are used mainly where actors are absent and attention is focused on the product. Most of the products low on the supervisual scale make a lot of use of actors. The exceptions to this scheme would seem to be cosmetics and tights. The latter are often in fact illustrated without the whole person (see above), but the former product almost invariably uses faces. The explanation behind this may lie in that (i) there is an *over*-emphasis on the face, which involves a large number of very close-up shots; and (ii) that the face is being presented much as food is presented: the completed article, artistic creation. The face is reified, made object in the way that food on a plate is–both are photographed in delicious close-up (cf. Bread with Cutex). It is also true that product transformation is common to three of the 'top four' products on the supervisual scale: cosmetics, food and decorating materials (an analogy with decorating materials might also be drawn, perhaps).

The use or non-use of supervisual devices is not wholly a factor explicable in connexion with the presence or absence of actors. It does also indicate a certain exuberance in presentation, or the lack of it. Many of the products at the lower end of the scale, are, it seems, presented in a rather more drab fashion than others higher up. This is substantiated by the tendency of these same products to crowdedness and the limited use of techniques. Careers, medical and baby products, offers, furniture and soft furnishings come to mind in this connexion. The exception would seem to be clothes–but on examination (see above) clothes can be seen to be less excitingly portrayed than many other items. Their presentation is very calm and restrained.

Supervisual Scale:

decorating materials
food
floor coverings
30 %
cosmetics
tights
household accessories
cigarettes
kitchen equipment
20 %
hair
shoes
slimming
business
miscellaneous
wool, underclothes, children's clothes
10 %
sanitary preparations
offers
furniture
medical
baby
soft furnishings
clothes
careers

Using the degree to which products employ devices of association as the basis for a comparative scale, it is clear that they are not arranged in anything like the same order that they take up on the supervisual scale. It is possible that products towards the lower end of the scale tend to be those either with simple things to say, or complex messages which are not always best conveyed by association, but by atmosphere or nuances of pose and expression. This would leave those 'In between' cases with messages that can be conveyed by association at the top of the scale.

'In-between' – messages that can be conveyed by association	cigarettes[1] furniture[2] tights floor coverings[2] business slimming[3] sanitary preparations[3] decorating materials[2] medical[3]
Complex	underclothes shoes clothes cosmetics hair
Simple	soft furnishings household accessories miscellaneous children's clothes careers food kitchen equipment
Very Simple	wool offers baby

[1] Part of the pressure towards the use of association would be the legislative pressure against showing people smoking.

[2] Messages connected with these three products may be most easily conveyed by association because they are not explicit and difficult to state overtly (because they are connected with taste and status?).

[3] Similarly messages connected with these products may be best conveyed by association rather than more directly because each has a slightly delicate or potentially discomforting quality.

The main burden of association is carried by props (q.v.), though it may also be articulated through settings or people–for example, a desert, or a policeman. Associative devices are most common where props are present and least common in the categories A, E and I. The correlation of props with associative devices tells us little, however, other than that there is a *slightly* greater tendency for functional-metaphorical and metaphorical props than functional props to be present in illustrations using associative devices. In many cases where functional-metaphorical props are present, so also are functional ones.

There are not many correlations between rhetoric and settings or actors which are very meaningful. In terms of familiarity, association is common to all categories, the supervisual occurs mainly in the wishful and familiar categories and product presentation and/or typification *alone* occur mainly in the familiar category. Regarding actors, only in the case of testament are any differences distinguishable: there tend to be more plain types than average in this category, with expressions of the naïve or catalogue type.

Correlations by Props

To resume what has been said already – types of props vary widely with the sort of product they accompany. Functional props and streamlinedness do not go together, while functional-metaphorical/metaphorical props and streamlinedness do. There is a strong link between props and the use of association, and those props have a slight tendency not to be functional.

In addition to the foregoing, props considered in conjunction with settings and actors reveal the following patterns.

(i) The main comparisons to be made are between functional and functional-metaphorical props, as the number of illustrations with both metaphorical props and settings is small (only 13 per cent of illustrations with metaphorical props contain settings). Functional props occur in settings which are familiar, everyday in mood, mainly indoors (conventional in style), and where outdoors, familiar rather than exotic. 46 per cent of illustrations with functional-metaphorical props also include settings (against 32 per cent for functional props), and 57 per cent are staged. The distribution between familiar, wishful and fantasy is roughly average, but the incidence of bizarre and extravagant moods is notably above average. A large proportion are indoor and mod or traditional in style. The number of conventional style interiors is well below average.

Metaphorical props, in brief, inhabit settings which are not familiar, which are romantic or exotic, and outdoor.

The contrast between the everydayness and familiarity accompanying functional props, and the bizarre and extravagant moods accompanying functional-metaphorical props is clear and marked. It is also clear that the majority of functional–metaphorical props are part of domestic room settings. Functional-metaphorical props take on a crucial significance. At the same time it is interesting that there should be so close a tie between functional props and the general familiarity and 'ordinariness' of settings. It leads one to hypothesize the existence of two major types of settings: (a) the familiar, everyday setting–reality, or a one-stage-up reality; and (b) the unfamiliar, unusual setting–unreality, or reality several stages up.

(ii) Comparing types of props with female appearance, expression and hair-style reveals some definite and consistent patterns. Functional props are accompanied by plain appearance rather than sophisticated, a tendency to practical expression (and away from soft and cool expressions), a higher incidence of older than younger actors, more moulded hair-styles and fewer free ones than average. Functional-metaphorical and metaphorical props present, in general, the opposite of this pattern, metaphorical props going furthest in the other direction. One representative table will serve as an indication:

	Functional	Functional-Metaphorical	Metaphorical	Average
superior	0	5	6	3
sophisticated	21	50	44	44
naïve	7·5	10·2	21	11·5
plain	64	26·6	16·5	32
detached	7·5	8·2	12·5	9·5

It appears that sophistication in actors is accompanied by a complexity and sophistication in the communication of meanings. A hypothetical model offers itself, taking as its basis the opposition between the familiar/ordinary/simple and the unfamiliar/sophisticated/complex:

'sophisticated woman' *
+
functional-metaphorical or   (=complex and often subtle mean-
metaphorical props   ings, though some are explicit)
+
settings with non-everyday moods
+
streamlined style
use of techniques
greater number of constituent elements

is opposed to
   'ordinary woman' *
     +
   functional props   (=simple and explicit meanings)
     +
   familiar settings with everyday moods
     +
   crowded style
   lack of techniques
   smaller number of constituent elements
  * A concept to be examined below.

What seems to be indicated is that sophistication in actors accompanies sophistication/complexity in the communication of meanings.

Correlations by Settings

Detailed descriptions of the setting typical for each sort of product have been given above. To recap and generalize a little, 'feminine' product settings tend to be outside, while food and household ones tend to be inside and domestic, clothing being in between–often indoors but non-domestic. The remaining products vary widely, many having few settings anyway. Cosmetic and hair preparation settings tend to be romantic while food and household ones are everyday. Clothing settings vary from the romantic and everyday to the exotic. Most of the remaining products have everyday, and to a lesser extent, romantic settings. They are generally familiar, but elsewhere the familiar-wishful-fantastic distinction breaks up these clusters of products–food settings are familiar but most household ones are wishful, for example. Fantastic settings occur here and there, notably in cosmetics and underclothes illustrations.

There is also some correlation with style and techniques (the familiar and the everyday tend to be found where advertisements are more crowded and use fewer techniques) but no correlations of great significance with the use of rhetoric. The connexion between functional props and everyday/familiar settings, and the contrasting connexion between other sorts of props and non-everyday settings has been discussed above (under props).

It remains to examine how the various factors comprising the settings interrelate, and to relate the settings to the actor.

How far is the staged/documentary distinction based on the difference between outdoor and indoor settings? Certainly most staged settings are indoors and 88 per cent of outdoor settings are documentary as one would expect, but 15 per cent of staged settings *are* outdoors and further, a third of documentary settings are *indoors*. What sort of interiors constitute these documentary settings? Many of them are non-domestic (44·5 per cent) and of the domestic ones, 40 per cent are *conventional*. The remaining styles are all correspondingly a little under-represented.

The staged/documentary distinction has no significant correlations with the familiarity/unfamiliarity distinction. However, there is an interesting correlation with mood – but as this is closely paralleled by a comparison of mood with indoor/outdoor it is probably more meaningful to look at it under that heading. Romantic and exotic settings tend to be outdoors while bizarre and extravagant ones tend to be indoors. Everyday settings lean towards the indoor as well. The following schema suggests itself:

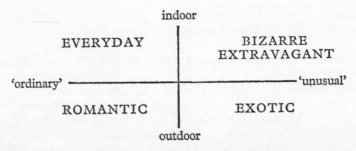

The correlation of indoor/outdoor with familiarity reveals that the familiar settings have a greater tendency to be indoors than outdoors, and the wishful vice versa, while the fantastic settings may be either indoors or out of doors.

The relationship between familiarity and mood can best be illustrated by means of a diagram. It shows that although there is a considerable tie up between the familiar settings and the everyday mood, the coincidence of mood and familiarity is elsewhere much less marked. The wishful category is the most wide-ranging in mood, embracing the everyday, exotic, extravagant and bizarre in roughly equal parts, while giving the major emphasis to the romantic mood. Although it emphasizes the romantic, this accounts for under half of the whole. Fantastic settings are fewer in number and they are mainly exotic or bizarre in mood.

Indoor settings

Most indoor fantasy settings are non-domestic (75 per cent), and in the same way most romantic and bizarre settings are also non-domestic. Conventional interiors are familiar and everyday without exception, and

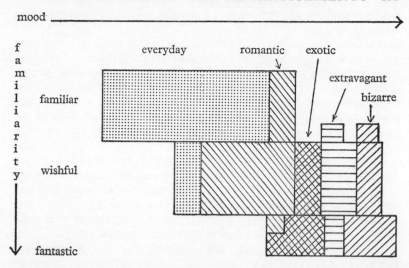

mod interiors also tend to be everyday in mood but are more wishful than familiar. Ritzy settings vary between the everyday/familiar and the extravagant/wishful, while trad interiors are wishful and extravagant. Camp settings are not sufficient in number to reveal any overall pattern.

Outdoor settings

The bizarre and extravagant moods are rare in outdoor settings (and the exotic mood is uncommon in indoor settings). Local settings tend not to be fantastic, or exotic in mood–and exotic settings tend not to be familiar or everyday in mood. Local urban settings are familiar and everyday, while local greenbelt settings are familiar-wishful and every-day-romantic. Local country settings tend to be wishful and romantic.

Exotic urban settings tend to be wishful and romantic-exotic in mood, exotic greenbelt settings similar, and exotic urban settings to be wishful or fantastic, and exotic in mood.

The correlation of exotic settings with exotic and romantic moods rather than everyday mood is hardly surprising, nor is that of local settings and everyday or romantic moods. The tendency for country settings to be towards the wishful-fantastic end of the scale, and urban settings towards the familiar end is of slightly greater interest, for there is no ostensible reason why exotic urban settings should be any more familiar than exotic country settings.

Correlations of Settings with Actors

In indoor settings attention and tactility directed towards objects, and attention directed towards people is most predominant, while in outdoor settings attention directed towards middle distance is most common.

Attention and tactility directed towards people tends to accompany the familiar and the everyday mood, and the same is true of attention and tactility directed towards objects. Attention directed to middle distance is accompanied by a romantic or exotic mood and is wishful or fantastic. Self-directed tactility is mainly wishful, and is accompanied by a romantic or exotic mood. Attention directed towards the reader, however, tends to be familiar and attended by the everyday mood.

Children occur in conventional interiors and local exteriors, and are familiar and everyday. There are no children in the fantastic category.

Where the illustration features women together the mood tends to be romantic or exotic (the settings are often fantastic), the interiors non-domestic and the exteriors exotic. In contrast the woman alone tends to occur in domestic interiors and local country exteriors.

In the man plus woman situation, a greater than average proportion is wishful, and set in local non-urban (mainly greenbelt) settings or interiors which are not conventional. Groups of men and women are accompanied by a higher percentage of all moods except the everyday and are often in non-domestic settings.

Relationships do not exhibit a lot of variation in connexion with setting. In terms of familiarity, however, divergency increases towards the fantastic end of the scale and decreases towards the familiar. Reciprocity exhibits the opposite pattern. There is, further, something everyday about the reciprocal and romantic/exotic about the divergent.

There is a strong correlation between the appearance of the actor and the type of interior. The sophisticated type is found in non-domestic and mod interiors (and to a lesser extent traditional ones), while the plain type is found in conventional interiors. There is, however, no corresponding correlation with exterior settings. In terms of mood there is a high degree of correspondence between the plain actor and the everyday, and between the sophisticated actor and the other moods. In the same way there is a correlation between sophistication and wishful/ fantasy, and plainness and familiar settings.

Expression, Pose, Clothes and Hair

Maternal and practical expressions tend to occur in familiar settings and soft expressions in wishful ones. Fantasy settings mainly comprise cool, soft and catalogue expressions. Similarly functional poses tend to be in the familiar settings, while relaxed ones are accompanied by wishful and dramatic ones by fantastic settings. The other poses occur in approximately equal proportions.

Office-wear and informal clothes occur mainly in familiar settings, while exotic clothes occur mainly in fantastic settings. Hair is more likely to be free and long in fantastic settings and more likely to be moulded in familiar ones.

Mood is in this instance closely parallel to familiarity. Maternal and practical expressions tend to be everyday in mood, and cool ones to be bizarre, exotic or extravagant. Incidence of the soft expression increases as one moves from everyday through to the extravagant. Functional poses are mostly accompanied by the everyday mood, while dramatic and composed poses tend to come from the bizarre-exotic-extravagant area.

Office-wear and informal clothes occur mainly with everyday moods, and exotic clothes with bizarre-exotic-extravagant ones. The incidence of no-clothes or nearly no-clothes is lowest at the everyday end of the scale. Moulded hair is most prevalent in the everyday category and least in the bizarre and exotic. Approximately the opposite applies to free hair.

No significant patterns emerge from a correlation of types of interior and exterior with relationships, attention or tactility, except for a slight tendency for attention to be directed more toward middle distance or the self in country than in urban settings. Generally, however, these are factors unaffected by the nature of the setting.

In terms of expression and pose, there is a connexion between both the practical/functional and the catalogue/dummy and urban settings; while carefree, soft and cool expressions, and carefree, relaxed and composed poses tend to be found in non-urban settings. Indoors the soft expression and relaxed pose occur in ritzy settings to an extent which is above average, and the same applies to friendly and maternal expressions and functional poses in conventional settings. There is a high proportion of functional poses in mod settings also.

Exotic clothes tend to occur in non-local and non-urban settings, while office-wear and informal clothes occur in local exteriors. Inside, exotic clothes occur mostly in non-domestic and mod settings, while office-wear and informal clothes occur more in conventional settings.

There is a strong correlation between the free hair-style and non-urban settings. In interiors the proportion of shaped hair-styles increases to equal that of the free style, but with the moulded style still only half as common—except in traditional and conventional settings, where it predominates.

Age

The ages of the female actors reveal interesting patterns—they tend to be older in indoor domestic settings than in non-domestic or outdoor settings, and women in country settings are most likely of all to be under twenty-five. Conventional interiors reveal the most mature age structure, and camp ones the youngest.

There is a greater proportion of younger women in fantastic settings than in wishful ones, and more in wishful than in familiar. In the case of mood the pattern is less simple. Women in everyday settings tend to be older and women in romantic and exotic ones to be younger. However, bizarre settings are less inclined to youth and extravagant ones exhibit a definite bias towards the late twenties and early thirties.

What is remarkable is the coherence of these patterns – the close relationship between settings and actors – and more than that, between kinds of expression, pose, relationships, attention, etc. and types of domestic interior, exterior, moods and so on. The existence of two distinct poles, two major clusters of meaning, stance and perspective becomes quite clear. They can be expressed as two opposed paradigms.

urban	country
indoor	outdoor
familiar	wishful (+ fantasy)
everyday	non-everyday
conventional interiors	non-domestic/traditional interiors
local exteriors	exotic exteriors
reciprocal relationships	divergent relationships
children	non-children
attention to objects/people/reader	attention to middle-distance/self
plain	sophisticated
maternal/practical expressions	soft/cool expressions
functional poses	relaxed/dramatic poses
office and informal wear	clothes tending more to the exotic
moulded hair-styles, non-blondeness	free hair-styles, blondness
older	younger
plain, ordinary, simple	sophisticated, unusual, complex
The normal, daily, family inter-acting with the world of things and people, concrete, functional, housewifely.	The wishful, dreamy, internal, isolated, self-involved, exotic, abstract, dissociated from things or people.

Taking into account the opposition expressed above (p. 131), one could add:

functional props	functional-metaphorical and meta-phorical props
crowded style	streamlined style
lack of techniques	full use of techniques
small number of constituent elements	greater number of constituent elements

Correlations by Actors

Comments on the tables (see Appendix II)

The predominance of female actors has already been noted, and is in accordance with expectations. It should be remembered, therefore, that in the case of comparisons between the sexes the male sample comprises a far smaller total than the female.

Men are more likely to direct their attention to people than are women, whereas women are far more likely to direct their attention to middle-distance or themselves. A similar pattern emerges in the case of tactility. Male tactility is more likely to be directed towards people and less likely to be directed towards the self, while the opposite holds for female tactility.

Men have a slightly greater tendency than women to be plain, and are less likely to be sophisticated or detached. In general, they fall more easily into a plain/sophisticated dichotomy.

Male actors exhibit an above average number of carefree, comic and practical expressions, while of the directly comparable expressions, female actors show a larger proportion of the catalogue type. Only a small percentage of female actors exhibit overtly the narcissistic or seductive expressions while large numbers have the cool or soft expressions.

There is a large proportion of functional and dummy poses in both male and female categories, there being less dummy and more functional in the former, vice versa in the latter. The relaxed pose provides a contrast in that it occurs to a wide extent amongst males and only to a small extent (8 per cent) amongst females.

An interesting factor concerning both male and female actors is the very low incidence of real working clothes, suitable for dirty or manual work. Male costume is largely conventional or casual, in contrast to the exotic nature of most of the female actors' wear.

Male hair is rigorously controlled – there are no instances of its being long or untidy, and in the vast majority of cases it is short and neat. With women, freeflowing hair is the most common, and there are slightly more instances of the shaped style than the moulded.

Men are consistently about the same age or older than women, where they occur together, and indeed, overall men tend to be older than women.

Further Correlations

The relationship of the number and sex of actors can best be demonstrated by means of a block graph; which indicates amongst other things the predominance of the woman alone:

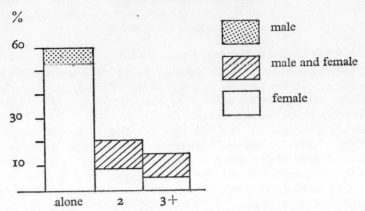

Actors by themselves are likely to look at the reader. Women accompanied by women tend to look into middle distance, while women in mixed groups are more likely to look at people (though *less* so than men are). Women alone tend to regard themselves or to look into middle-distance, and the tendency to self-tactility in women is pronounced—regardless of whether they are alone or accompanied.

Semi-reciprocal relationships are especially common in the situation of man and woman alone. In most cases it is the man who regards the woman and she who looks away. Reciprocal relationships are also mainly composed of male + female but with slightly less tendency to be alone (there may be other people or children present). Divergent relationships occur mostly in situations where there are two or more women together.

Narcissistic and seductive poses and expressions and cool expressions are more likely to accompany the (female) actor alone, while accompanied actors are more likely to exhibit the carefree, practical and maternal expressions and the carefree and functional poses.

Attention in reciprocal relationships is directed to people but tactility is as likely to be directed towards objects as persons, or indeed to be non-existent. Tactility is not likely to be self-directed.

In semi-reciprocal relationships the attention of the person being regarded is equally likely to rest on objects, middle-distance, the self or the reader, and tactility is equally diverse. In divergent relationships the attention tends to be turned towards middle-distance, and tactility, though varied in direction, tends to turn to the self or to nothing. In relationships where the participants look out at the reader, tactility tends not to be directed towards people; and in most object relationships tactility as well as attention tends to be directed towards the object(s).

In terms of manner and appearance, relationships correlate most clearly with expressions and least with clothes, though in all cases the connexions are only tentative. Carefree and friendly expressions and functional and relaxed poses are most common in reciprocal relationships, while soft, cool and catalogue expressions are rare. Carefree and soft expressions, freeflowing hair and exotic clothes are common in semi-reciprocal relationships, while catalogue and cool relationships are common in object/camera relationships. Soft, catalogue and cool expressions, dummy and composed poses and sophisticated appearance typifies women in the divergent relationship.

Attention and tactility are clearly closely connected. Object-directed tactility and object-directed attention tend to occur together, and similarly with people and the self. Self-tactility and no tactility often accompanies attention directed towards middle distance and attention directed towards people often occurs alongside tactility directed towards objects. Where attention is directed to the reader, tactility is either non-existent or directed towards objects or the self, and the same is true of those cases where the direction of attention is undiscernible or the object of it hidden. This last, being a 'don't know' category, is excluded from most comparisons. The relationships can be seen as falling into two parts – one inward and self-involved, the other outward and concrete – thus:

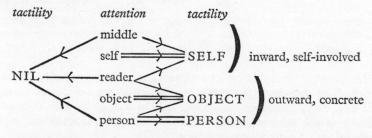

The correlation of expression and pose with attention emphasizes the pattern indicated above. *Self*-directed attention tends to be accompanied by soft or narcissistic expressions and poses of the narcissistic, composed or relaxed type. Attention directed towards *middle-distance* tends also to be accompanied by soft expressions and similar poses as well as by some catalogue and carefree expressions. *Object*-directed attention is most often attended by practical as well as some catalogue and carefree expressions. Poses tend to be dummy or functional. Attention directed towards *people* correlates with maternal and carefree, and to a slightly lesser extent, practical and catalogue expressions. Poses, again, tend to be dummy or functional, with the addition of some of the carefree type. Attention directed towards the *reader* is similar to these last two in one way: the high proportion of the catalogue expression and dummy pose, but different to *all* the above in the predominance of the cool expression, accompanied by composed and dramatic poses. The relationships between pose and expression, touched upon here, will be dealt with in more detail subsequently.

To correlate clothes and hair-styles with attention adds further depth to our picture. Taking the type of clothing occurring most frequently in each of the five categories we get the following:

self – none
middle-distance – exotic
reader – office/informal/exotic
object – office/informal
people – informal/office

Thus there is a definite progression through from the absence of clothes at the inward end of the spectrum to the predominance of informal wear at the outward end.

Hair-styles offer a similar progression with freeflowing styles most common (and moulded styles least common) at the self end of the scale and the opposite at the object and people end.

%	Self	Middle-distance	Reader	Object	People
free	66	53	45	43·5	41
shaped	24	32	30	30·5	29
moulded	10	15	25	26	30

In the case of attention and appearance the relationship is less direct. The detached type occurs to an above average extent in the self and middle-distance categories, and to a degree which is below average in the other categories, and plain types are more common in cases of attention to objects and people.

Most of the expressions and poses pair off together, as indicated in the section on the system of classification: cool with composed, soft with relaxed, carefree with carefree, practical with functional, catalogue with dummy, narcissistic with narcissistic and seductive with seductive. There are some connexions beyond these one to one relationships. Narcissistic poses are quite likely to accompany cool and soft expressions, and functional poses occur with the catalogue, carefree and maternal, as well as with practical expressions. Further, the composed pose is quite common with the soft expression, as is the dramatic pose with the cool expression.

Expression, clothes and hair are related in ways which might by now be expected. Office-wear tends to be accompanied by the practical, maternal or catalogue expression and informal wear by the catalogue or carefree expression. Uniforms are accompanied by practical and catalogue expressions also. Soft, cool, and to a lesser extent, carefree expressions occur alongside exotic clothes, and cool, soft and narcissistic expressions where clothes are absent.

A high incidence of moulded and shaped hair-styles accompany the catalogue, maternal and practical expressions, while carefree and cool expressions are characterized by a low incidence of moulded and high incidence of freeflowing hair-styles. Soft, seductive and narcissistic expressions all show a very high incidence of the free style and very few examples of the moulded type.

Rounding off, this leads us to a brief consideration of the connexions between hair and clothes, the outlines of which should already be clear. The three hair-styles occur to an extent which is about average in the case of informal wear. With office-wear there are fewer free styles and more moulded, while all uniforms are accompanied by the moulded hair-style. The proportion of moulded styles is low in the exotic clothes category but the shaped style is represented to an extent which is almost equal to the freeflowing. The absence of clothes tends to be accompanied by the freeflowing style.

Almost all superior types, of which there are few, exhibit cool expressions, while almost all the detached types have the catalogue expression. The sophisticated type is characterized by cool, soft or catalogue expressions, the plain type by catalogue, maternal, practical or carefree expressions, and the naïve type mainly by soft expressions, but also to some extent by carefree and kitten expressions. Most seductive expressions occur in conjunction with the sophisticated type, and most comic ones with the plain.

The denseness of the cross-permutations should make it necessary only to outline the remaining correlations. *What is surprising is the consistency of the patterns exhibited by the material.* Presumably, using each investigation as a pilot for a further one, categories and areas of classification could be so sharpened as to make some of the emergent patterns even clearer.

The functional pose correlates with office-wear and uniforms, while at the other extreme the narcissistic pose correlates with the absence of clothes. Between these, dummy and carefree poses tend to be accompanied by informal wear, and composed, dramatic, relaxed and seductive poses by informal or exotic clothes. At the functional end of the scale hair-styles show a greater tendency to be moulded, while at the narcissistic end they tend very much to be freeflowing.

The superior type is characterized by exotic clothes, composed pose and a tendency to shaped hair-styles. The detached type is characterized by the dummy pose, office-wear or the absence of clothes and, again, a tendency to shaped hair-styles. With the plain type functional, dummy and carefree poses are the most common, as is the moulded style of hair and informal or office-wear (uniforms also fall within this category). In the case of the naïve type, clothes tend to be informal or exotic, pose to be relaxed or carefree and hair to be free. Free hair-styles and exotic, informal or lack of clothes are common in accompaniment to the sophisticated type, together with a variety of poses: composed, relaxed, dramatic, narcissistic and dummy.

Some explanation should be made here regarding hair colour, about which little has been said so far. The pilot study revealed fair or blonde hair to be an important factor in women's magazine advertising, especially with the 'feminine' products (see above). Correlations of blondeness with other factors does not reveal much of significance—except in the sphere of appearance and manner, with which we will now deal. With regard to the style of hair itself, blonde hair is far more likely to be freeflowing than brunette hair (70 per cent of blonde hair is freeflowing in styles), and only 6 per cent is moulded). There are two departures from the average in terms of clothes: office-wear being below and the absence of clothes being above average in correlation with blonde hair. With blonde hair there is an above average incidence of cool, soft, carefree and narcissistic expressions, and of composed, relaxed (and to a lesser extent) carefree and narcissistic poses. As far as appearance is concerned, over 60 per cent of blondes are of the sophisticated type, and only 16 per cent of the plain type. Nearly 16 per cent are of the naïve type, however, which is an above average proportion.

Age

Female actors whose attention is directed towards themselves or middle-distance tend to be younger than those whose attention is directed towards objects or people. Similarly, tactility directed towards the self is a feature of younger female actors, while tactility directed towards objects or people is a feature of older ones.

In the case of appearance, the plain type tend to be older, and the sophisticated type younger—i.e. below thirty. The naïve type also tends to be younger: generally under twenty-five. Expressions and pose also correlate fairly definitely with age. Soft, kitten, narcissistic and seductive expressions are more common with younger actors and maternal and comic ones with older actors. The practical expression is also a little more common at the older end of the age scale, while the cool expression is rarely found in the over thirty-five sector. Composed, narcissistic, seductive, dramatic and carefree poses are more common with younger actors, and functional poses with older ones. The relaxed pose has its highest incidence in the twenty-five to thirty-five age group.

Exotic clothes and the lack of clothes are common at the lower end of the age scale, while office-wear is clearly found at the other end of the scale. Snazzy clothes are likely to be worn by those over thirty, and informal wear is found throughout the age range. In the case of hair-styles, the freeflowing clearly accompanies the younger actors, and the moulded style the older.

Men

So far it has been established that male actors tend to be older than women, to be plain more than sophisticated, and to direct their attention to people rather than to themselves or middle-distance. The most common male expressions are the comic, thoughtful and carefree–and of poses, the relaxed and functional. They tend to have short neat hair and conventional or casual clothes.

Correlations are more difficult to establish because of the far smaller number of male actors in the sample, but there are some connexions of interest. Uniforms tend to accompany the plain type, while formal, mod and exotic wear accompanies the sophisticated type. Hair-styles do not show much variation in conjunction with other factors, but medium-length hair does seem to accompany casual and mod wear more than other types of apparel. Further, the sophisticated type shows a high incidence of glad-eye and self-reliant expressions, and relaxed and dramatic poses. Plain types show a high incidence of comic, catalogue, carefree and paternal expressions, and functional and dummy poses. Similarities to the pattern exhibited by female actors will be apparent:

sophisticated/formal, mod, exotic/glad eye, self-reliant/
relaxed, dramatic

as opposed to

plain/uniform/comic, catalogue, carefree, paternal/
functional, dummy

In the case of male actors, however, there is a far greater middle area: a model which includes elements from both of the above, but which is centrally as follows:

sophisticated or plain/conventional, casual/thoughtful,
practical/composed . . .

Correlations by Magazine

As the six magazines used in the analysis have some important differences (see section in preceding chapter) some idea of the relationship of the more basic variables which we have been considering to these publications might be useful. First, some basic facts: the total number of magazine pages in the March/September sample was 2,692 and advertisements of half page size or over took up 42 per cent of these. Each magazine contributed a different amount of advertisements to the sample, of course, there being differences in size, and number of issues per month. The proportion contributed by each was as follows:

	%
Woman	28·4
Woman's Own	34·8
Woman and Home	7·2
Petticoat	8·5
Honey	12·2
Nova	8·9

While the variations in proportion mean that some magazines have a greater 'representation' than others, the samples do represent a block of reading matter available in these two months in newsagents and bookstands. This, as far as we can be representative, is the world offered by women's magazines in these months.

The percentage of advertising (half page and over) to total magazine space was as follows in each of the magazines:

		%
Woman	March	39·0
	September	45·5
	all	41·7
Woman's Own	March	44·5
	September	46·5
	all	45·5
Woman and Home	March	40·0
	September	33·1
	all	36·8
Petticoat	March	26·5
	August/Sep- temper	26·6
	all	26·5
Honey	March	52·0
	September	52·3
	all	52·2
Nova	March	46·0
	September	43·5
	all	44·6

Noticeable are the high figures for *Honey* and the very low ones for *Petticoat*. The breakdown by product is, however, the most useful and illuminating.

	Woman	Woman's Own	Woman and Home	Nova	Honey	Petticoat
cosmetics	7·5	8·4	6·8	29·5	27·5	25·6
hair preparations	7·7	7·4	7·4	4·0	22·2	22·5
sanitary towels and tampons	1·2	0·7	—	1·0	2·2	5·3
slimming preparations	3·0	2·5	4·3	2·0	0·7	—
all 'feminine'	19·5	19·0	18·6	36·5	52·5	53·4
clothes	1·9	3·8	3·7	25·0	13·0	7·8
underclothes	5·2	5·2	3·1	8·0	5·1	2·1
tights	2·3	3·6	2·5	2·0	4·4	2·6
shoes	7·7	3·6	5·0	—	4·4	2·1
wool	4·5	2·9	3·1	—	1·5	—
all clothing	21·6	19·0	17·4	35·0	28·2	14·6
food	23·4	17·0	15·5	8·0	0·7	1·0
kitchen equipment	1·6	6·0	6·8	3·5	1·8	8·5
floor coverings	2·2	4·2	2·5	1·0	—	1·0
decorating materials	2·5	3·1	1·2	1·0	—	—
furniture	3·1	2·2	1·2	1·0	—	—
soft furnishings	3·1	1·8	1·8	2·0	—	—
household accessories	3·1	5·7	8·7	1·0	—	0·5
all household	15·6	23·0	22·2	9·5	1·8	10·0
offers	4·7	6·1	4·3	1·0	2·5	1·6
business	0·9	1·5	1·8	—	1·5	2·1
career	0·8	1·4	0·6	—	7·2	9·5
medical	2·0	4·0	4·3	—	1·5	3·6
baby/children's clothes	2·8	2·6	5·6	—	—	—
cigarettes	2·8	2·0	—	5·0	—	—
miscellaneous	6·0	5·4	9·7	5·0	4·1	4·2

Notes

In general terms *Woman, Woman's Own* and *Woman and Home* concentrate on the food and household sector while *Honey* and *Nova* concentrate on clothing and feminine products and *Petticoat* gives greatest emphasis to feminine products. *Nova, Honey* and *Petticoat* are far more restricted in their product range than are *Woman, Woman's Own* and *Woman and Home*. The distinctions between the magazines are far less clear than these outlines suggest, and the extent of the variations can be seen from a closer perusal of the above table.

Petticoat has no slimming advertisements but an above average number of sanitary towel/tampon advertisements. There are a lot of cosmetic and hair preparation advertisements, but a below average number of clothes and other sorts of clothing advertisements. The incidence of advertisements for food and all household goods except kitchen equipment is low, while the incidence of career advertisements is very high.

Honey has a high incidence of feminine and clothing advertisements, except for slimming preparations and wool. It has a low percentage of advertisements for all other products save for careers.

Nova has a lot of feminine and clothing advertisements (especially clothes) but this includes a less than average number of advertisements for hair preparations, wool and shoes. The incidence of advertising for the remaining types of products is low, with the exception of cigarettes, kitchen equipment and soft furnishings.

Woman and Home has a slightly below average number of advertisements for feminine products, though the proportion of ones for slimming preparations is high. Clothes and underclothes advertisements are rarer than average while household goods, especially kitchen equipment and household accessories, occur to an above average extent. The magazine is noticeably low on advertisements for careers and high on those for children's clothes.

Woman's Own has a below average number of cosmetic and a slightly above average number of slimming advertisements. Advertisements for clothing are average or below in incidence while those for food and household products are above average.

Woman is similar to *Woman's Own* on feminine products, shows a very low incidence of advertisements for clothes but an above average proportion of ones for underclothes, shoes and wool. There is a high incidence of advertisements for food, and the remainder are about average, except for careers and business which are below.

Some products occur to a degree which is roughly equal over the six magazines – underclothes, and tights for example, while others vary a great deal, e.g. the large number of sanitary products in *Petticoat*, the large number of clothes in *Nova*, the small amount of food in *Honey* and *Petticoat* and so on. There are some very limited seasonal variations: more shoe advertisements in *Woman* and *Woman's Own* in March, and more floor covering, decorating and soft furnishing advertisements in the same magazines in March. Otherwise the two months do not exhibit any marked differences.

Elements

There are few correlations of significance. The *Woman* and the

Woman's Own distribution is average, and the *Woman and Home* distribution is similar, with perhaps a greater emphasis on category A (product alone). *Nova* shows an emphasis on illustrations with actors/ actors with product *with* settings but without props (i.e. G and K), probably because of the large number of clothes advertisements in that magazine. *Honey* has a greater number of illustrations in the K and L categories than average, connected probably with the number of careers and cosmetics advertisements. *Petticoat* shows an emphasis on the actor alone column (again to do with careers and cosmetics) and a low incidence of illustrations in the actor plus product column (see p. 123).

Rhetorical Devices

Testament occurs mainly in *Woman, Woman's Own* and *Woman and Home* while typification is especially accentuated in *Petticoat* and *Honey*. This latter probably derives from the preponderance of feminine and clothing advertisements, which need actors, in those magazines. The use of association is greatest in *Nova* and least in *Woman*, but they only differ by 9 per cent. Supervisual devices are also fairly evenly distributed, lowest again in *Woman* and equally high in *Woman's Own* and *Nova*–but again the difference between them is small–only 3½ per cent.

Style and Techniques

The correlation of both style and techniques with magazines reveals the same basic pattern. Taking those magazines with the highest proportion of streamlined and least of crowded advertisements, we have, in order, *Nova, Honey, Woman's Own, Woman, Petticoat* and *Woman and Home*. In terms of the degree of use of focus, colour, lighting, angle and special effects, a similar list emerges, with *Petticoat, Woman* and *Woman's Own* bunched together:

Nova/Honey/Woman's Own–Petticoat–Woman/Woman and Home

There is, then, a definite correlation between the magazine and the style of the advertisements, and the techniques used in the illustrations. *Nova* and *Honey* are the most streamlined and make most use of techniques, *Woman and Home* is the most crowded and makes least use of techniques. In between are *Woman's Own, Petticoat* and *Woman*.

Props and settings show no correlations with magazines that do not derive from the products typical to the publication. Similarly, comparisons of actors through different magazines reveal patterns which are traceable back to the product types. Nevertheless, there is a larger proportion of 'sophisticated' types (with all that goes with that umbrella description) in *Nova* and *Honey* (and to a lesser extent, *Petticoat*) while plain types occur more often in *Woman, Woman's Own* and *Woman and Home*.

6

The World of Woman

The task now is to reconstitute the message with the emphasis on meaning. However, 'a consideration of the meanings expressed' (above p. 115) is by no means the simple exercise this brief phrase suggests. On this level we are concerned solely with *connoted meanings*. These have to be interpreted by the analyst, who can give no proof of the accuracy of his interpretations. The most that can be done is to produce examples which support the reading offered, but which also allow the reader to make his own judgement. The meanings will be expressed by *all* the elements analysed above, working individually and in combination. A single object, a tortoise for example, may connote longevity and slowness. In conjunction with another element, a carpet, the meaning 'longevity' stands out. Alternatively, an expression, a pose, and a setting may together signify a meaning–say, carefreeness.

Here the analyst is using his own sensitivity–to the nature of visual communications, to the material, and to the whole world-of-meanings– in order to pick out global meanings, and to name them.

It is necessary to put names, which may range quite widely in their nuances, to these meanings. The difficulty is that the reader may interpret different, idiosyncratic meanings from these names–the sheer number of which makes it impossible to undertake definitions for each of them. One relies, then, on a fairly general level of agreement as to the nature of such descriptions as 'elegance', 'serenity', or 'happiness' and should not be unduly dismayed if differences between two closely connected meanings are not clinically precise. Distinctions between some meanings cannot by their nature be crisply drawn.

We will begin by looking at the connotations of the props used, subsequently broadening our frame to take in the connotations of settings and the actors. The connotations of the props fall, broadly, into six categories, or clusters, if we disregard those meanings functionally specific to a product (e.g. plates in food advertisements, or knitting needles in wool advertisements).

(i) Meanings connected with femininity: flowers, furs, ear-rings, ribbon and so on. For example, flowers in Atkinson perfumes (plate 12a), jewellery in Noble Lowndes (plate 6b), or fur in Enkasheer (plate 11b).

3. Part of an advertisement for G-Plan furniture from *Woman's Own*, the woman beautifully merging into the surroundings with the props of good taste and luxury conspicuous. (Detailed analysis in Appendix I.)

(ii) Meanings connected with good taste, culture and discrimination: original paintings, coffee-table books, wine, candlesticks, etc. For example: the decanter in the New World advertisement (plate 8a) or the candelabra in G-Plan furniture (colour plate 3). Or meanings connected with status or luxury, signified for example, by the sculpture in the Belle Color illustration (plate 5b) or the items (purse, miniature, etc.) accompanying the Kleenex tissues (plate 13a).

(iii) Meanings connected with naturalness or closeness-to-nature, signified by things like flowers, plants, birds, sun. For example, the grass and blossoms in Polyherb shampoo (plate 14), a rose in Wella hair spray (*Nova*, March) or birds, bees, flowers and butterflies in Robertson's Honey advertisements (*Woman and Home*, March).

(iv) Meanings connected with childhood and babyhood, signified by items like satchels, toys, rattles and nappies: the feeding bottle in the Electricaire advertisement (plate 13b), the satchel in the Vymura illustration (plate 12b) or toys and rattles.

(v) Meanings connected with fun, recreation, excitement are signified by props such as go-karts, balloons, and footballs. Some examples are a snow sled for Peter Stuyvesant, the 'champion' car and crash helmet for Laird-Portch (plate 10b) or the bow and arrow in the Tampax picture (plate 4b).

(vi) Meanings connected with domestic ritual, like the paraphernalia of washing up in Oxo 'tea-towel offer' illustrations or the iron and completed stack of ironing in the Phensic illustration (colour plate 2).

It should be noted that meanings will overlap. For example, the ironing in the Phensic illustration also signifies, specifically, the completion of a hard job of work, recovery and success. There are, further, other meanings which are particular to a specific advertisement, conveying a specific–often unique–message; e.g. universality signified by a globe: mystery and the exotic signified by a 'yashmak' or the barbed wire which signifies untouchability (plate 7a).

The connoted meanings of the *setting* can also be seen in terms of these six groupings. This should not be taken to suggest the existence of six rigid and self-enclosed categories, however. We are dealing with areas and directions of meaning, not with precisely defined units.

(i) Settings have to do with femininity and romance. For example, Morny (plate 6c) and Atkinson's Félice (plate 12a).

(ii) Those settings connoting good taste, elegeance, luxury, tradition and so on. Two examples are G-Plan (colour plate 3) and Belle Color (plate 5b), where a wide, richly carpeted staircase leading up to an arch and a bust on a pedestal can be clearly discerned behind the actor.

(iii) Settings have connotations of wholesomeness, freshness or naturalness; for example, Polyherb (plate 14) and Maxwell House (plate 6a).

(iv) Settings having connotations of childhood, of softness and brightness. For example, the playroom in the advertisement for Vymura and the swing in the advertisement for New Zealand cheese (plate 2b).

(v) Settings having to do with excitement, fun, colourfulness or the exotic; two examples being Silhouette: the sun-scorched Mediterranean coastline, and Laird-Portch (plate 10b).

(vi) Those settings connoting domesticity, functionality, and to a lesser extent, modernity and simplicity. For example, Horlicks, Vymura (plate 12b) and Cookeen (see above).

As in the case of props, there are a number of meanings, many of them idiosyncratic, which fall into none of these groups, and further, there are many which cross the boundaries between two or more of the groupings. As far as relative frequency of occurrence is concerned, it should be noted that in contrast to the meanings connected with props, feminine meanings are much rarer and natural ones more frequent. Femininity tends to be connoted not by location, but by props or actors. The other groups are roughly similar in incidence, with perhaps a greater proportion of (ii) than is the case with props.

When we turn to the actors we can distinguish both roles, and attributes of those roles, a double set of meanings. The male and female roles presented in the illustrations are as follows:

Female		*Male*	
i	mannequin	i	husband and father
ii	self-involved woman	ii	friend/boyfriend
iii	wife and mother	iii	mannikin
iv	hostess	iv	specific work roles
v	carefree girl	v	buffoon
vi	career/independent woman	vi	he-man/hero

The roles are arranged in order of frequency of occurrence, but the total number on the male side make the distinction between most and least common less extreme than is the case with female roles, where (i) occurs about six times as frequently as (vi). The attributes, or connected meanings of these actors can be subdivided into six groups on the lines of those described above in the discussion of props and settings. Examples of these will be given below.

(a) Sensual, narcissistic, seductive, introverted, beautiful.
(b) Elegant, sophisticated, discriminating, trendy.
(c) Natural, healthy, delicate, flawless.
(d) Gentle, loving, serene, innocent, concerned.
(e) Active, carefree, exuberant, youthful.
(f) Competent, capable, homely, cheerful.

Although the connexion between these groups and particular roles is often well defined the correspondence is nowhere absolute. Hence the sections (a) to (f) above should *not* be taken as having a direct relationship with the female roles i–vi.

These meanings are the distilled meanings, the recurrent meanings, the reinforced meanings. Though their significance can only be properly understood when we view them in terms of their relationships, nevertheless the simple fact of their emphasized status in the advertising gives them a significance in themselves. In some ways the values implicit in the advertising can be seen here at their most transparent and unadorned. The meanings point to the importance of certain areas of life, of certain styles or interpretations of life, as presented by the medium of advertisements in women's magazines. In this connexion it is vital that we realize that these meanings are implicitly awarded a positive status, they are *approved values*.

Approved activities are housework, child-rearing and having a good time while one is young; while the approved stances towards life are those of the discriminating connoisseur, the clean and wholesome outdoor girl, and the soft and sentimental self-involved woman. These will all receive further attention in the subsequent sections.

As has been explained before, the advertisement communication is not merely a selling message, it is a complex collection of meanings both directly and indirectly connected with the specific sales persuasion. These meanings may be deliberate, partly realized or wholly unconscious on the part of the advertisement's creators. The meanings are not just taken from a limited range, to do with the qualities of specific products, but draw upon the whole cultural world available to the creators. Given that the meanings are manifested, objectivated, in the visual material, they are amenable to study and analysis. Taking the findings of the analysis up to this point, the purpose is to set into context, to interpret in the light of the wider culture, and to reveal the nature of the underlying patterns and the values contained in them.

It is not useful to retain all the divisions and categories used previously, for the purpose is now one of reuniting, of perceiving interrelationships, seeing the world which is being presented, as a whole. To do this we will regard our interpretations from three viewpoints: the actors, their location, and the products for which they have been created.

We begin with the actors and their worlds as this follows most immediately from the preceding chapter, but the order is otherwise not of crucial importance. Interpretations from the advertising are made on the basis of the findings described in the previous chapter. Where possible and convenient, reference is made to the particular points from the survey which are relevant to the comments being made, and at other times the reader is free to refer to the survey material as necessary. Examples are available as further assistance to the reader (see plates), and detailed notes on a cross-section of them are provided, by way of general elucidation, in Appendix I.

ACTORS AND THEIR WORLDS

We have two opposed sets of characteristics which arise from consideration of the detailed analysis of female actors. The general nature of each will be apparent, but the detailed picture can now be completed. It should be emphasized again that these sets of characteristics are not the result of *one* group of correlations, but the outcome of a whole series of interdependent and mutually validating correlations.

There does exist, between the two opposed types, a middle ground which provides the skeleton of a 'neutral' type. However, with these illustrations and the women portrayed in them, the tendency in the majority of cases is towards one of the two extremes, not towards the middle area.

Inward/self-involved:	*Outward/concrete:*
attention to self, middle-distance	attention to objects, people
tactility to self	tactility to objects, people
narcissistic, soft expressions	practical, maternal expressions
dramatic, relaxed, narcissistic poses	functional poses
freeflowing, blonde hair	moulded, non-blonde hair
exotic clothes and lack of clothes	informal or office-wear, uniforms
younger	older
sophisticated	plain

Neutral:
attention to reader
no tactility
catalogue, carefree (and cool?) expressions
dummy, carefree (perhaps composed) poses
shaped hair
exotic, informal, office-wear

The two main sets can be seen from differing perspectives, and we here choose to take two oppositions which seem crucial to them, namely (i) the distinction between inward-looking-ness and outward-looking-ness (which contains something of the unreal/real and ethereal/concrete oppositions) and (ii) the distinction between the public and the private, the social and the personal. The qualities can then be grouped on the two axes in order to generate four types, an arrangement which seems to summarize the relationship to each other of the most recurrent roles or ways of life which are presented in the illustrations:

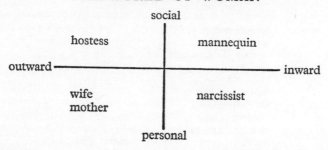

Sophistication, or lack of sophistication, is another of our major perspectives. This can also be shown on the schematic arrangement we have just made. The sophisticated/non-sophisticated (or most sophisticated/least sophisticated) axis would run diagonally and the division between more and less sophisticated would run through the middle of the hostess and the narcissist roles as shown below. The manniquin remains the most sophisticated and the mother and wife the least so. Expressed in detail the arrangement would look like the chart on p. 154, though the terms obviously remain general.

The *mannequin* is the least lifelike of the roles. She is in an artificial world, often obviously so in the way she stands and looks (dummy poses and catalogue expressions). She is on show, on exhibition–but, crucially, on exhibition in a competition with others. Backgrounds, props, expressions even–seek to add to her sophistication, fashionableness, or uniqueness. Although in a social/competitive situation, sometimes with men present, but more often with women, the mannequin is essentially interested only in herself and the impression she is making. She does not condescend to notice her associates and thereby admit her ordinary stature. She is aloof, haughty, and ostensibly sufficient unto herself, while relying on others to reinforce her self-image. Her outdoor surroundings tend to be exotic, and her indoor ones, non-domestic. The relationships which involve her are divergent, and her attention is rarely directed towards things or people. The props accompanying her are not functional, and the presentation is streamlined, complex, and fully exploits visual techniques. The evidence supports the view expressed by Murray Wax (above, Chapter 3) that clothes are essentially social, and explains his inability to account in the same way for the use of make-up, which he also thought to be socially oriented, but which he knew was widely used by women spending the whole day on their own. The evidence of the preceding chapter suggests that clothes are predominantly social in nature, while cosmetics are primarily private and personal. This does not mean that a substantial number of cosmetic and hair preparation illustrations, for example, do not portray the woman as mannequin, but it does point to a significant distinction

1

Society hostess
lady of leisure,
aware of fashion and
good taste.
Cool, composed,
clothes tending to
the exotic;
children rarer,
surroundings more
wishful.

2

The mannequin, assured,
competitive, beauty on display,
cool, composed, dramatic.
In exotic, wishful/fantasy
surroundings

Surroundings
familiar
Practical, and
more carefree.
The little home-
maker, wanting to
be 'modern'.
Hard-working, with
children; clothes:
informal, office-wear.

3

Mother and wife
housebound, dutiful
plain, practical.
Older
in conventional
interiors, everyday,
familiar.

4

Narcissistic woman,
completely self-
involved, sensual.
Soft expression,
narcissistic poses.
Lack of clothes,
free blonde hair.
in exotic, some-
times fantastic
surroundings.

Romantic,
idyllic;
sometimes with
men. Self-
involved, less
sensual, more
youthful and naïve.
Soft/kittenlike free
blonde hair. Surround-
ings romantic.

between the crucial functions of cosmetics and clothes. Examples are common–but see the advertisements for Berlei and Sunsilk (plates 10a and 7a) for two typical variations.

There is perhaps a greater variety of products represented in the *narcissistic* sector. The most central, nevertheless, are cosmetics and hair preparations, though underclothes form a substantial part. The narcissist–'self-involved female' is perhaps a better, less exclusive term– varies from the woman who is literally and metaphorically wrapped up in herself, to the girl deep in a reverie. Even when being seductive, she is (perhaps more than ever) aware of her own femininity and sensuality rather than of the presence of any potential lover. At the periphery of this type is the girl in a haze of romance–perhaps with a man–but who is in the last resort more bound up with aspirations and dreams of her own than with the actuality of the man. The ubiquitous diamond engagement ring advertisements are almost all perfect examples. This is odd, because engagements *are* relationships with men. Yet more attention is paid to the girl's feelings about herself in this aspired-to situation than to the bond itself. The self-involved female has, typically, a soft expression and directs her attention and tactility towards herself. She is sophisticated or naïve–her hair is frequently long and blonde and she often wears very few clothes or none at all that the reader can make out. She is alone with herself, involved in her body and her own beauty.

Mention has been made of the proliferation of nakedness in the media. In this respect the advertisements are obviously in line with a general change in standards of 'acceptability' or 'decency', or at least with a change in the media. The numerous nudes are not merely a feature of an allegedly permissive society, however. In the first place, nudity, even if not as blatant as currently portayed, has been common in women's magazine advertisements for some years. Second, its occurrence is restricted to certain fairly well-defined areas and is by no means used to sell everything and anything from careers to cornplasters. Nakedness is a feature of advertisements for products of the 'feminine' sort and to a lesser extent of tights and underclothes. It coincides with features outlined above–long blonde hair, for example; but also, and equally crucially, with such factors as self-directed tactility and self- and middle-distance-directed attention, and most especially with intro-version and the narcissistic role. It is not the same sort of nudity as that which graces the pages of magazines for male readers such as *Playboy*, which is brazen, directly suggestive in a rather arch way, and has far more in common with the inaccessibility of the mannequin type. This type of nudity is private, isolated, and the source of wonder, pleasure and satisfaction to the subject. It does not differ, however, from the *Playboy*/stripper variety in its experience of the body as alienated/object rather than integrated/subject. The body is reified, something seen as an object to admire or even revere in a quasi-religious way. The use of dramatic, isolating shadow, mysterious darkness, the ethereal mistiness of focus are common techniques of transporting the female to a personal world of reverie and self-contemplation. The Enkasheer illustration is a good example as are also the illustrations for Cutex and Bidex (see above) and the Félice advertisement shows the introspection of the girl even when accompanied by a man (in a typical semi-reciprocal relationship).

The *hostess* has much in common with the mannequin. Like the mannequin she sees action on the social front: her peers may in fact be her competitors. She moves in a domestic world, however; the house is her realm and her *raison d'être* is to exhibit, not herself, but herself externalized in the form of food and decor. The house, its furnishings, its decoration, and the food served in it, are marks of her sophistication, fashion awareness, sense of good taste and status. Sometimes she may veer to the extravagant (with luxurious furnishings and exotic cuisine); at other times she moves more securely in a modern, tidy, neatly decorated house. She is aware that her surroundings are speaking for her and must therefore be on her guard lest they open their mouth in the wrong place or say the wrong thing. Because what they say is very much altered by the passing of time, she must be constantly alive to changes in styles and fashions. She is proud of this world, which is her creation. Nevertheless, although she has produced this world, she cannot possibly escape *from* it. The alterations she can make to it are marginal and not structural, its basic nature remains firmly intact, restraining and resisting every effort at reconstituting its function. She is more object oriented than the narcissistic or mannequin, more often sophisticated than not–frequently exotically dressed but older–just a little more staid–than the two roles already considered. The example, New World (see plate 8a) is extreme but not uncommon or untypical.

A similar situation surrounds the *wife and mother*, but the actual concrete environment is of much less importance. The home is important, crucially important, but it is not the decor nor the fashionableness of it that is important so much as the duties that are carried out in it: those of being a housewife and a mother. Interiors tend to be far more conventional, everyday and familiar than those accompanying the hostess–and exteriors, where they occur, are local witness Dr Whites 'everyday is much the same'. The wife and mother is older and plainer than the women portrayed in the other main roles, unsophisticated, and practical in outlook. She dresses more functionally, though rarely in really workmanlike clothes. Her relationships are more often reciprocal than in the case with other women and she gives her attention to objects or people–often children. The props that accompany her are functional in the main, and moreover, the style of the advertisements in which she appears tends to be crowded, with fewer techniques and a smaller number of constitutent elements. It is a busy, plain and simple, honest world. Her task is a private, non-competitive one. The home may be beautiful, but only as a backcloth to the role being played by the woman. Her creative drives are not to be wasted on fashionableness or status-seeking, but to be channelled into the loving and cherishing of husband and children, and the running of the complex mechanism called the household. It is a demanding job and a challenging one, it requires effort, skill, endurance and knowledge to be executed successfully. The reward, the satisfaction, is personal and private. There is a contradiction, nevertheless, between the presentation of woman as a real hardworker and the idea of a calm, satisfied, attractive woman. In fact, the work is never too gruelling. It is skilful, creative and needs a great deal of love and care–but it need not make you ugly–just more mature and fulfilled. See advertisements (plates 5a and 13b) for Cookeen (kitchen-mum), Electricaire (baby-centred-mum) and there are the fun-mums and grans for different aspects.

Of the roles enumerated at the beginning of this chapter, those un-accounted for in the scheme so far are the *friendly/carefree girl* and the *independent or career woman.* The former is balanced between sophistication and unsophistication–for the girls are often fashionable, but perhaps rather naïve–not dowdy, but not chic; between the social and the personal, and the inward and outward. The carefreeness or friendliness is social by its nature to some extent, and outgoing as well, and yet the exuberance and the cheeriness is rarely directed to anyone or anything in particular, rather to an image held only in the actor's mind (see Tampax). The role takes up, therefore, a central position in the schema.

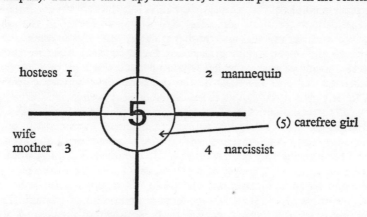

In a way it is a mock carefreeness, for the freedom is not the freedom to *do* anything specifically. Further, the carefree female is always a *girl,* which gives one a sense of a short spell of deceptive freedom before the inevitable decline into one or other of the roles on either side. It is, by its nature, a transitional role. She is the fluttering butterfly which has not yet decided where to settle. She is 'having fun while she's young', but she too will (and she knows) settle down quite soon, and in fact looks forward to it.

At no point does the schema allow for the social woman to be doing anything that is more constructive or indicative of an independent personality than hostessing or being beautiful (showing off, in either case), or for the private woman similarly to be doing anything more than admiring herself or carrying out household duties. The *independent woman*, or the *career woman*, is the remaining role presented in the illustrations. She is the only woman to be involved in something not to do with social success, home and family, or her own femininity, who has any stability or substantial nature. First, it must be realized that she is infrequently portrayed. The schema cannot accommodate her without considerable disruption.

A major part of this role stems from illustrations for career advertisements and it is clear that, outside of (dull) career advertisements, females in jobs – whether unmarried girls or working wives – are hardly ever represented. The impression gained from the roles offered is that women are of sufficiently noble birth to have means of their own, or that they are provided for by men, be they boyfriends or husbands.

Who is the independent/career woman? What is her portrayal like? Her very scarceness makes any overall portrait very difficult to draw. As has been mentioned before, a fair proportion, if not most, of these women are members of the armed services or (less frequently) the nursing profession. These are careers, certainly, but they allow very limited independence. They are complete, self-contained worlds in the way that the world of the wife and mother is. They offer the extreme alternative to any of the feminine roles previously discussed and preclude any composite alternative which would take account both of a job *and* a normal social life. They can be the complete opportunity for opting out for anyone who cannot meet the demands of the other roles, because they offer a total identity, a world which is completely self-validating. It is significant that in this way the career becomes irreconcilable with other roles – with being married, with having a good time or good taste, etc. What remains? An office-worker or two, women as comics, women setting off to travel, a couple of more mature ladies. From the picture presented by these illustrations one could not begin to grasp the fact that one-third of the total labour force is composed of women. The 'working woman' is simply omitted from the world of meaning of the illustrations. No one would think that women ever participated in any pastimes, hobbies, sports or any non-domestic interests. The girl in the Tampax illustration (plate 4b) is one of the few instances of the exception. (The advertiser might ask why the advertisement should refer to such things. The Tampax advertisement replies: why not?) The WRAF illustration (plate 7b) is representative of the picture presented by career advertisements. The impression given is that of a life which is dull, unfashionable and regimented.

How far is the type of role portrayed a result of the type of product advertised? Product type and role are connected, and closely connected, but there are sufficient variations to make a one-to-one correspondence impossible. Clothes might have been presumed to correspond fairly completely with the mannequin role but the correspondence is in fact not at all complete, and products such as tights and underclothes, cosmetics and hair preparations, are to be found in several differing sectors. The nature of these links will become clearer when we turn to consider the products.

A further mechanical/economic connexion needs to be examined. Is it perhaps that the limitations of role options available is due to the need to sell those products which those sorts of women on whom the roles are based are most likely to buy? Is the selling of femininity or housewifeliness a necessary corollary of selling 'feminine' or household goods? A proper response to this theory is that there is no reason why frying pans and shampoos could not be sold with an emphasis on the time-saving, efficient qualities which would leave one free for other things (Brillo took this approach a year or so ago). Nor is there any reason why illustrations for products which make people look nice are obliged to concentrate on elements of introversion and passive femininity. (However, would such products sell as well to an audience tuned to a world of equality, wage-earning and extra-domestic interests? How would expensive 'special' cosmetics body lotions, and false eyelashes sell in such a world?)

The clusters of meanings derived from the props when examined more closely, fit into the well-defined world of woman as so far described. The largest grouping is that of good taste, status, discrimination, etc. and following that, naturalness and femininity. The other three areas are childhood/babyhood, domestic ritual, and fun/excitement. One can see how these correspond to the explanatory scheme that has been derived, and it becomes apparent that these meanings relate to each other in broad but important ways. The meanings may or may not correlate fully with illustrations portraying the corresponding roles. Where they do, there is extra reinforcement, but it is with the overall pattern, the underlying structure, that we are concerned. Recreation connects with the concern for nature and the outdoors, which itself links up with the naturalness of femininity. Femininity leads on to maternity (babyhood) and hence to the domestic ritual of wife and mother. On the other hand excitement, and the enjoyment of the good life connects with sophistication and fashionableness, with fashion and style in the home, concern with the domestic, and back again to the domestic ritual.

If we take into account, not female roles, but female life patterns, moving from carefree youth through to the responsibilities of home and family, and superimpose these dynamic relationships, two paths emerge.

A Guide to the World-of-Meaning of Advertisement Illustrations included in this survey

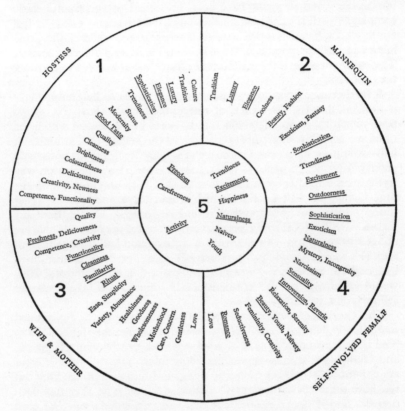

Underlinings indicate greatest frequency of occurrence.

Meanings are not restricted in occurrence to the zones in which they appear of course. Happiness, for example, occurs throughout, wherever women are pleased and satisfied with their present roles—but it occurs most of all in the area indicated.

All the meanings noted have positive values in the advertisements.

This is the world-of-meaning of the advertisement illustrations.

One path lies through sophistication, social competition and concern with fashion and style, into the home. The other moves through naturalness and femininity through to maternity and the establishment of the household. One is more assertive (competitive and public) and the other inward, 'sensitive' and private. These, one suggests, are the two paths offered to women as patterns for their lives. They move inevitably towards the same goal.

The absence of a link between sophistication and naturalness is interesting and may prove significant. There *is* a connexion of sorts in that many of the mannequin settings are outdoors and rural. Is this countryside-as-backdrop the same as or similar to the 'naturalness' of the more self-involved female, or are there important differences? In the case of the mannequin, the countryside *is* a backdrop, it is not integral—its purpose is to be exotic, exciting, fashionable—or merely to provide an interesting, colourful background. Second, in the more narcissistic cases the natural elements are more closely associated with the actor, the relationship is far more tactile.

MEN, if anything, are more stereotyped than women. They exhibit a far more restricted range of appearance and manner: their dress is conventional and their hair short and neat. The plain ones tend to be workers or husbands, and the sophisticated ones to be heroes or mannequins. There is a sameness about them, however, which gives an overall impression of characterlessness. The sophisticated type merely has more style to his characterlessness than the plain type.

Men, of course, are the opposite of self-involved. Their attention and tactility is most often directed towards people or things and their general manner is frequently practical/functional and outward going. It is in this respect that the men in advertising differ most radically from the women. Man is as noticeable by his absence as by his presence and it is the *aloneness of the woman* which is important in so many cases, as has been noted above. In contrast, the man is only rarely seen on his own. Most of the time he serves as an accompaniment to the female. Man either works or is concerned with the world of the woman in a supporting role. Most men alone are those with specific work roles; those with women are husbands, boyfriends, heroes . . . The worker is separate, in another world, unconnected to the woman by bonds of romance or family.

The male mannequin is more common than might have been anticipated in women's magazines. In many cases he is wearing and exhibiting clothes knitted by the woman, or clothes presumably bought by the woman. He is, in a sense, a projection of herself in a way similar to that in which the he-man/hero is a manifestation of her dreams. The husband and the boyfriend are real, while the mannequin and the hero are unreal, ideal, flawless, even if they *are* cut-out dummies. Their relationship to the woman is insubstantial and ephemeral. The ordinary often plain and simple, boyfriend or husband is more lifelike and more attainable. He is closer, concrete, fallible. The ideal is, perhaps fortunately, unreal–and the real is easily dealt with, for the men are but simple beings.

Frequently, as we have seen, the relationship between male and female is one-sided: it is a relationship in which the man is giving his attention to the woman while she is interested elsewhere, and that elsewhere is often herself. This occurs in all roles, but noticeably with the boyfriend. Nowhere is the female self-sufficiency and quiet contempt for the outside world more clearly stated (Félice, plate 12a). There are some occasions where the boyfriend is treated rather more romantically. The boy and girl (rarely persons of great maturity) signify this by looking dreamily into each other's eyes. The content of their communication is mysterious, full of what we assume to be the unspoken language of people in love.

As father, with the happy family, the man is more like a child himself, moving closer to the buffoon role. The father is one more responsibility for the woman to look after. As husband, he is served, waited on, and ministered to–the guest in the wife's house. He is the man whose main business and concern is elsewhere; his job–somewhere 'out there' where he becomes one of those workers pictured in other places, is removed from intimacy into the unconnected and unknown world of his work.

To the husband who cannot cope by himself, the father who is really just a kid himself, the buffoon who spills things and acts the fool, the boyfriend who is a slave and suitor–to all these the woman is superior, she is in control of the situation. On the other hand the man as mannequin, hero, or sometimes as boyfriend, is often but a cipher, a thing of no substance, something standing for 'a man' and little more.

Outside of these examples that we have considered at length, what other roles, stereotypes, caricatures even, are left? There are not many. Only a handful of the actors do not fit the roles already described. The occurrence of other roles is usually deliberate and purposeful–for example, a butler is used in order to add class and prestige, or a Chinese man to make a point about washing or the exotic East. Most work-roles have already been considered, but there are those which transcend just being a job, and seem to be a way of life–like the butler, and the vicar.

Of the men, the following can be distinguished. *Racial types*: Chinese (indicated by facial characteristics, exotic tunics, high collars: there is one old gentleman with a round Chinese cap, a long wispy beard and an inscrutable expression) and Arab (mounted on camels, dark and sullen, dressed in flowing white robes). *Elderly gentleman*: the refined gent (with neat moustache and three-piece suit), dashing gent (balding, with large moustache and glint in the eye), grandfather (surrounded by kids, white-haired, genial, serene, with newspaper, pipe and glasses) and the old man (with beard and glasses and a tweedy suit). *Special vocations*: butler (respectable, efficient, white-haired and fatherly), policeman (genial, stout, the honest Mr Plod) and vicar (grey-haired, black clothes and dog-collar, plus an ingratiating smile; or younger, comic, with a foolish awkward smile). The only other portrayal is that of a melodrama villain–with evil eyes, sleek black hair and a thin moustache.

All the women so far unaccounted for are middle-aged or older, apart from one portrayal of an innocent heroine from melodrama. The rest are, broadly, either 'grannies' or 'old wives'. The *grannies* have grey/white hair, short, often in bun or hairnet, sometimes wearing traditional black clothes, surrounded by children, plump and serenely smiling. There are various *old wives*: the shocked (maternal, respectable, prim, mouths open and hands flung in the air); the bumbly, fussy and nosy–usually thinner–and in one case accompanied by net curtains and aspidistra (well-known stereotypes are used to communicate messages clearly and quickly: the peering nosy woman is easier to identify as such if she has net curtains and an aspidistra as props); and the advice giver (comic, often a bit tatty, old-fashioned, sure and set in purpose). Apart from grannies and old wives there is only (a) the elegant woman–with dyed hair, neat but stylish clothes, heavy jewellery and rather neutral–and (b) the office woman–neat, efficient, strict, and rather formidable–and these are few and far between.

Location

A few pages will now be taken in considering the part played by the location–the background and props–against which the actors are seen, and which to varying degrees qualify their impact and impression. We can see what sorts of worlds are constructed and how they affect the picture that has already been described.

Interiors: Domestic

Generally, attention is more likely to be given to objects and people (and tactility to objects) than in exteriors. Interiors are more familiar and everyday, and have a greater tendency to feature reciprocal relationships and older, and if not always less sophisticated, rather more mature actors.

The majority are not settings one would expect to encounter in most of the homes one might visit. There are some, mainly of the deliberately documentary sort (which turn out to be 'conventional' in style) which do impress one with the realness of the background. Of the rest, they are reality one-stage-up as the agencies would say; or in many cases, two-stages-up. The more extravagant the interiors become, the less likely is anyone even to aspire to them. Conventional interiors are familiar and everyday, mod interiors are everyday but more wishful than familiar, ritzy interiors vary between everyday/familiar and extravagant/ wishful and traditional interiors are wishful and extravagant. We can see these factors correlated in the following way:

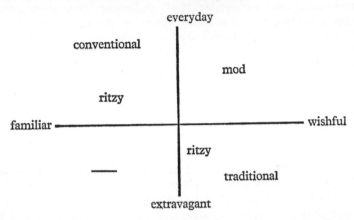

Where the ritzy takes the form of being one stage up from the conventional, it remains everyday and familiar, but when it is more expensive, more luxurious, it becomes extravagant, and leaves the realm of the familiar for the wishful. In the extravagant/wishful sector one does not even envisage oneself in such settings, except in moments of fantasy–though this may be a no less potent appeal.

Certain absences can be interesting if they are consistent. Wallpaper and heating devices, for instance, are rarely seen except where being advertised, windows and doors are not common, neither are televisions, newspapers, ash-trays or cigarettes. On the other hand, there are a vast number of tasteful objects–elegantly framed pictures, large and luxuriant plants, coffee-table books, vases and busts which look priceless– mainly in rooms which appear larger than those of an ordinary suburban house. The absence of doors and windows effectively cuts the room off from the outside world, and also often served to give the reader the impression that he is entering the room. Televisions, papers, cigarette ash: these are part of the daily bric-à-brac of life and their absence (as the absence of untidy day-to-day paraphernalia altogether) makes the scenes less life-like and promotes the idea that houses are ideally always tastefully spick-and-span. Neatness, tidiness, cleanness, order, taste– whether *avant-garde* or restrained–these are the messages expressed. Some of the absences will be due no doubt to the mechanics of the photographer's studio–large items, be they doors, windows, fires or televisions, are more trouble to set up, and there is no incentive to include them. Nevertheless, the fact that some factors are due to the mechanics of the business does not diminish their importance in terms of meaning: the result concretized in the picture, is the same.

Men are conspicuous by their absence–they are peripheral to the world of the home, and where present are passive, receptive, waited on. Their world is elsewhere. Even in situations involving house-decorating, for example, men are not common. Children occur quite frequently, though they are not as dominant as one might expect (they occur in about 25 per cent of the domestic interiors). They appear in ones and twos, rarely in great numbers. Where present they are clean, tidy, calm, sweet and under control. Children are less common in the more sophisticated settings, and those settings with three or more children are all of the more 'conventional' type.

Inside the home the woman has no one for company but herself or her children–the highest incidence of woman alone is in domestic interiors. Social gatherings large or small stand out because of their rarity. The woman is queen of all she surveys, but she only rarely shares it all with anyone outside the family. Her dominion over the home means her incarceration within it. There are no friends or companions, there are no indications of her individuality, or of *her* at all, rather than *her home*. In a lot of ways, in fact, the women match the home. They harmonize with the setting in texture and colour and attitude. In a functional kitchen or bathroom she is practical and efficient (Cookeen, plate 5a), in a soft and comfortable room, she is soft and relaxed (Electricaire, plate 13b), in a mod room she is mod (Schreiber, *Woman*), in a sophisticated elegant one she is sophisticated and elegant (G-Plan, colour plate 3), in a dark and mysterious room she is dark and mysterious (Silhouette, *Woman*), in a homely room, homely (Horlicks, *Woman*). In many interiors she matches the colour scheme so closely she is almost camouflaged (G-Plan, colour plate 3, Valspar, colour plate 1). She is an organic part of the home, and the cliché reproach 'I'm just part of the furniture' might be taken at face value. It is difficult to know whether to view the rooms she inhabits as extensions of her personality, or to see *her* as an extension of *their* personality.

Interiors: non-domestic

The non-domestic interior is a limbo area, a half-way house between indoors and outdoors. The settings are often not well known or recognizable places–they are strange, unusual: a mansion hall, a Victorian restaurant, an enormous greenhouse. The more recognizable tend to be places of entertainment (e.g. theatre or café) or travel (e.g. air terminals). The exclusions are as noticeable as the inclusions: shops, and places of work, for instance. Does the representation of the place of purchase destroy the atmosphere by rendering it too commercial, too overtly persuasive? And once the time for fun and freedom has passed (theatre-going and travelling), the home, the domestic interior, takes its place, not the wage-earning workplace.

It seems that in many cases the places chosen for settings are arbitrarily selected for the sake of nothing except a nice picture. In the same way the accompanying actor is artificial, pleasant but empty. This vague disconnected world has most in common with exotic exteriors, which frequently have no more connexion with the actors than the provision of a picturesque backdrop. These are places where people meet but do not communicate, exhibit themselves without giving anything of themselves.

Exteriors

In contrast to interiors, attention outdoors is more frequently given to middle distance, things are less familiar and the mood tends to be romantic or exotic. Relationships are more often divergent, and the actors younger. These tendencies are most emphasized in country settings.

As mentioned above, exotic exteriors are often only picturesque backdrops used to add excitement and sophistication to an illustration. The actor's interaction with the setting is minimal and she remains out of place, artificial, unrelated. The presence of men is more likely in the greenbelt and urban locations – and this also applies to local settings. Women in urban settings are frequently accompanied by rather shadowy males in the background.

Women look more out of place in urban settings than men. Men, whose attention and tactility is most often directed towards objects and people fit more easily into the town where people and things are more in evidence. In local country settings, however, women are frequently alone, and are a part of the scene rather than being set apart *from* it. They are integrated into the setting and more often than not have a tactile connexion with it. There is an almost mystical element of communion with nature which men do not share. Man, in fact, by fitting in more with town life, by being object-oriented, concerned with the concrete and practical is typically urban, out of touch with the older, natural world. It is the woman who maintains this connexion, who is in touch with the pastoral past, who guards the health of the community by her adherence to the old stable values, by her functions of childbearing, nursing and rearing, and of cooking and ministering, and the assertion of common sense drawn from the wisdom of the earth: age-old tasks which never change . . .

PRODUCT IMAGES

We come back now to the pivot of the whole process, the product. Here we are concerned with the meanings associated by the advertising with specific types of product. While often absent from or playing a small part in the illustration, the product is the *raison d'être* of the advertisement. The illustrations—in style, content and meaning—do exhibit strong correlations in terms of product type, so that one can say definitely that each product has a series of meanings associated with it— *which are by no means always directly derived from the function of the product.* The clusters of meanings and associations connected with the larger groups of products—'feminine', clothing, etc.—are more general and less homogenous, which is to be expected. Part of the homogeneity of the advertising for similar products from different agencies is due to the intense inwardness of the advertising/media world, and part to the existence of established ways of seeing a product, its particular function, and therefore the ways in which it should be sold—which boil down to established sets of meanings or world-views possessed collectively by the advertising business and its satellites.

Cosmetics

Cosmetics are bright, modern, streamlined and visually appealing in terms of style techniques and rhetoric. They emphasize and depend on the visual, possibly because the product's effect itself depends so much on the look it can create. The advertisement at this level is saying that the make-up can create a work of art, is startling, exciting, attention-getting. There is a tension in the presentation however, between the narcissistic and the exhibitionistic. One strand of the advertising emphasizes the intense femininity and narcissism (in pose, expression, lack of clothes, hair-styles and some of the props). It stresses privacy, aloneness, inwardness. There are few settings, woman is alone and her attention and tactility are directed towards herself. She is the subject of her own satisfactions, and even when with others the relationships tend to be of the semi-reciprocal type. She is immersed in her own sensuality. On the other hand there is the woman presented as a beautiful and glamorous object, worthy of adulation and emulation. Her clothes, her appearance and expressions indicate a sophistication and elegance which demands an audience as well as personal appreciation. Her poise is perfect, her face is perfect, the whole effect is perfection; but she can *do* nothing but stand and be wondered at. She has taken on the status of a work of art. (In some ways it seems that the woman—and her face especially—is presented much as food is presented: the completed dish—an artistic creation. The face is reified, made an object like food on a plate: all in delicious close-up which is almost real.) There is, also, a concern for the natural (seen in props and settings) and a denial of the world of the practical and everyday. The world of make-up, perfumes, body lotions, is one completely removed from familiar surroundings, removed from a definite slot in time and place. This is most clear in cases of explicit fantasy but extends far beyond overt fantasy into perhaps an even more unreal world because not obviously fantastic. It is not here and now, it is not in dreams, it is nowhere except inside the mind and the body of the woman.

Hair Preparations

The exhibitionist/narcissist opposition is present in the illustrations for hair preparations, but in a less marked way. There is a concern with sophistication and elegance, manifested in clothes and appearance and also an inwardness and aloneness similar to that described above (few settings, women tend to be alone, to lack clothes, and appear introverted in pose and expression). Overall perhaps, there is a tendency towards a middle ground, a more carefree, younger, less introspective emphasis. The element of carefreeness is given greater weight by the attention to naturalness in props and settings and the hair itself appears as a parallel to nature–its abundant healthy growth, its colour and texture. The hair-styles themselves tend to polarize: the exhibitionistic is characterized by the more elaborate styles and the latter by long and luxuriant hair which provides the pleasure of both tactile sensation and the sensation of personal beauty. Again, the world of hair and its care is a non-practical one however much the copy stresses real advantages and scientific differences. The world is partly pastoral, verdant, serene and blossoming, partly that half-known mystic realm beyond reality and fantasy. The importance of hair preparations is–generally–that they should be effective but unseen. Their purpose is to render to the hair the natural beauty and sensual texture which is its original birthright but which for vaguely understood and hinted at reasons has somehow been lost in the process of urbanization and artificial living.

Sanitary Towels and Tampons

Dealing with menstruation is no longer a topic wrapped around with euphemism and secrecy. With the commercial discovery of vaginal odour the taboos have receded even further (Bidex, 9b). The advertisements for sanitary towels and tampons do have a slightly different character from those for cosmetics and hair preparations, however. They are quite streamlined and visually attractive, without being extrovertly supervisual; they are if anything *modern* in style and stress. They are concerned with activity (especially manifested in props and pose) and with freshness and naturalness. It is a fact that there is a notably high incidence of blonde hair and of white clothes (Tampax, plate 4b), speaking of freshness, cleanliness, purity. While sharing the characteristics of introversion with the other 'feminine' products, the woman is not so much alone as private, independent–very self-sufficient. Furthermore, there is a certain amount of attention to the practical in evidence—in pose, expressions, and in settings, indicating that this is an area in which women need to have a smattering of the practical and efficient—that this is where the artificial is even more necessary to the maintenance of the natural in appearance and activity.

Slimming Preparations

The illustrations for slimming preparations exhibit something of the conflict between the private and the public worlds discussed above. One strand concentrates on the social and comparative aspect and the other on the personal, self-involved aspect. The former is characterized by the abundance of settings, type of dress, pose and expression and the attention given to people and the reader. It is competitive and concerned not so much with one's own feelings as with what other people will think. The latter is characterized by narcissistic expressions and pose, self-directed attention and tactility and the incidence of nakedness. It is less real—closer to the world of make believe where all women can be naked nymphs. There is, however, a strong element of the ordinary and everyday in the slimming advertisements—mainly found in conjunction with the social/competitive type. It is an ordinariness of style and techniques, of familiar settings, plain appearance and functional props, through which the woman is thrust swiftly back into a more concrete world. It brings home the daily chore of slimming—whether this is deliberate or not is unclear. Although the subject is the body, the social/competitive type of approach does not wish to be specific about it.

Clothes

On the whole the presentation of clothes is very calm and respectable. Visually the illustrations are modern and sophisticated, but not exciting. There is a deliberateness (often amounting to artificiality), almost a staidness, about the atmosphere: the static poses, the catalogue expressions, the moulded hair-styles, the neutral but elegant backgrounds and so on.

If cosmetic illustrations concentrate on the personal and give rather less attention to the social, the opposite is true of clothes. Women are often in groups although their relationships are hardly close (i.e. they tend to be divergent). There is little of the introspective woman about these illustrations (in spite of the self-directed tactility) although there is an element of romance and reverie—and sometimes mystery, manifested mainly in props and settings. The overriding impression is one of luxury and elegance in settings, and sophistication and elegance in women. This elegance is accompanied by a superior detachment, a cool aloofness, made obvious by appearance, expression and pose. This aloofness does not alleviate the underlying feeling of maturity and respectability. Some illustrations counter this aspect by emphasizing a more active and youthful approach, but these remain a minority, even in the magazines for a younger audience. Settings vary between the sophisticated traditional and the exotic outdoors. Even here, though, the countryside or the foreign streets are but a backdrop to the central actor or actors–used to add something extra to their personalities. The artificiality of the situation is rarely resolved–the whole enterprise is an exercise in showing off, competing in sophistication with other women. Yet the mechanical deliberateness of the illustrations seem to reveal the sterility and lack of real excitement or involvement in the endless competitiveness. One feels that the illustrations are trying desperately to maintain the spirit of high fashion in a context of widely available and mass-produced clothes.

Underclothes

The illustrations for underclothes are streamlined in style and visually inventive. There is a concern with the outdoor, with naturalness (revealed in setting and props) a sort of mysterious freedom (Berlei, plate 10a), the nature of which escapes analysis. The settings are far less natural and separate than in the case of clothes. They are full of atmosphere, sensitive of the woman's mood, sensuous, close. The division between private and public, narcissistic and exhibitionistic is present again in this product type, and is, if anything, more accentuated. The social role is characterized by the use of props to do with status and taste, the presence of others, and expressions and poses which are aware of onlookers. Even in the presence of others, however, the woman is withdrawn. With men her relationship is semi-reciprocal and with women, divergent. For the woman on show the underclothes are moulding her, presenting her, making the best of her. For the woman for whom pose, expression, hair, props, tactility and attention all come together to convey a narcissistic experience the clothes are close, intimate, tactile things, caressing her, holding her, softly and sensually. The atmosphere is moody and intimate, a creation of often bizarre or exotic settings and careful techniques of lighting and colour. It encloses the woman with her mystery and leaves her to herself.

Tights

In the illustrations for tights there is again a conflict or opposition present, though in a different form. It involves activity and sensuality. The latter is concerned with softness, tactility, isolation, the sensual qualities of the garment as experienced by the wearer. The frequently naked or semi-naked models, their pose and expression, their attention to middle-distance and self-directed tactility, and their aloneness, all contribute to these qualities. The tights (Enkasheer, plate 11b), more than underclothes, are closely fitting, snug, tactile in themselves and add to the tactile qualities of the body like a permanent and continuous smooth caress. The tights are an extension of the woman's body, but so intimate an extension as to be *part of* the body. On the other hand, tights are concerned with activity, vitality, freedom and the outdoors, as can be seen in the country settings, the carefree poses, and to a lesser extent in expression and clothes. The actors are more outward-going, youthful, energetic. The product is not strictly functional—more a conferrer of freedom, something which allows the female to find full expression in movement without artificial restrictions.

Shoes

The presentation of footwear is, in contrast, rather ordinary. The illustrations have, overall, none of the sophistication and pace of the ones for tights. There is, in fact, an everyday quality about the product, revealed further in settings and in clothes. Together with this, the women themselves, while not plain and ordinary, are certainly less sophisticated than in the other clothing sectors considered so far. If there can be said to be a tension in these illustrations it is between the person-oriented and the object-oriented. The former is concerned with looks, elegance, beauty and fashionableness (reflected in props, attention, pose and expression) while the latter has to do with the world of things, with newness, variety and with particular qualities like toughness and resistance to urban strain. This can be seen in the scarcity of actors, the object-directed tactility, the concentration on the product as object rather than as a part of the personality. This split is a version of the well-established *function* versus *fashion* argument in the world of personal adornment (Norvic, plate 16). This is one of the few places where it is manifested in the advertising, however.

Wool

The presentation of wool as a product is visually very ordinary in terms of style, techniques and rhetoric, and in atmosphere the illustrations are familiar and everyday. There is a strong feeling of the homely and conventional—in settings, appearance, pose, expression and hair-style. The world of wool is family-centred—with men and children joining women in substantial numbers, the woman presumably having created the garments worn by all members of the family. There is also something of the 'nice romance'—the safe and secure male–female relationship of the sort which culminates in a knitted pullover for him and for her. Nevertheless, the elements of deliberateness, artificiality of pose (similar to clothes) and of appearance and manner, permeates this pleasant world. The wives and husbands, mothers and children, are so clearly modelling dummies with catalogue expressions that their world of love and sweet affection is rendered unreal and the attempts to appear motherly, full of love, creative, seem somehow desperate and false.

Food

One knows that the way a meal or dish looks affects both the cook and the consumer. The illustrations emphasize this with their techniques (especially the use of close-up and colour) and the supervisual. The images of food in question are larger than life, present in as palpable a form as any representation can be (Bread, plate 3b); it is also characteristically associated with a simplicity and wholesomeness, naturalness, freshness, health, energy and growth reflected both in settings and in props (New Zealand Cheese, plate 2b). Accompanying this there is a homeliness, a feeling of the family, a reciprocity of relationships often rare elsewhere. The mother is the centre of this, of course, and children are much in evidence–personally, and through props (American Rice, plate 1a). As important as the appearance and the goodness of the food, seems to be the variety available, and the amount. Sheer abundance and multiplicity are constant features. It is not enough that the food be good and well-prepared–there must be more than enough of it, and if possible, a choice from many dishes. All this the good mother or hostess brings about through her skill and creativity.

In the rhetoric of advertising the world of food and cookery is a practical one, very much object-oriented, as props, attention, pose and expression indicate. This practicality goes hand in hand with an everyday familiarity which is common to settings, manner (especially clothes) and appearance, and a maturity in the actors–most of whom are over twenty-five. The preparation and the serving/eating of food and the occasions at which it is eaten are all enmeshed in a good deal of ritual, even in a familiar domestic context. In contrast to most of the product types already discussed, the world of food is an object–and people–dominated, rather than an abstract or self-dominated, one. It is concerned with practical and everyday things and with everyday people (the family) rather than with social occasions and special people (though this aspect too is present). More than anything it is concerned with variety, abundance and appearance. This last is a factor which connects it with the products so far covered. Clothing and 'feminine' products (even sanitary preparations) are concerned with appearances, cosmetics and hair preparations most of all. To achieve a certain (felt to be acceptable and desirable) appearance is an end in itself, for which the exercise of much skill and creativity is felt to be necessary. The face or the body must look like a well-prepared dish, elegantly served and adequately concealing its secret constituents and recipes. The connexions with naturalness are another link with preceding products, though the end result of cooking, as much as making-up or dressing, is often far removed from anything which could be called natural.

Household Goods

Kitchen equipment and household accessories are similar to food in their association with practicality and the familiar, but differ in that there is no delightful appearance, naturalness or abundance to compensate. The overriding impression is of plainness and ordinariness, which is manifested in every aspect of manner and appearance, in techniques and rhetoric, setting and props. Attention and tactility are object or person oriented and the values of functionality and efficiency are repeatedly stressed. The world is familiar, indoor, domestic, and decidedly mature.

The world of floor coverings and decorating materials contains strong elements of the practical (Vymura, plate 12b) and the concern for objects–but concentrates also on appearances: elegance, sophistication and good taste. Elegance and good looks are emphasized by the wide use of techniques and of supervisual rhetoric, and by the presence of more sophisticated actors. Pose and expression still stress the practical, as do attention and tactility, while clothes, hair and appearance stress sophistication and the importance of looks.

The illustrations for furniture are still object-oriented, but there is an even stronger element of sophistication and taste. This is not so much emphasized in the presentation as in the settings and the appearance and manner of the actors used. There is a strand of warmth and cosiness, even of romance, also present, and many of the settings are bizarre, exotic or extravagant: a strong contrast to the settings of other household goods.

Soft furnishings inhabit the area between floor coverings/decorating materials and kitchen equipment/household accessories, being almost equally concerned with practicality and modishness. The use of the actors' hair as an indicator is interesting here: in the former (floor coverings and decorating materials) hair-styles tend to be free, and in the latter (kitchen equipment and household accessories) moulded. In the case of soft furnishings the dominant style is shaped.

There is then, a tension between the practical and the modish, between function and fashion (as there is in the case of footwear). The products can be arranged into a continuum from kitchen equipment and household accessories, through soft furnishings, to floor coverings and decorating materials and to furniture. This progression is closely tied to appearances–in that kitchen equipment and household accessories have least to do with, and floor coverings, decorating materials and furniture have most to do with creating an appearance in the way that clothes and cosmetics do. The degree of appearance-consciousness exhibited by the inanimate decor is paralleled by that of the accompanying actors. One of the interesting things about these products is that furniture and kitchen equipment, which might both be considered large pieces of household furniture and thus very similar, are in fact poles apart.

Offers

Offers and competitions, no matter of what sort—whether for a dream house or a free plastic spatula—exhibit very similar characteristics. Visually they are crowded and unattractive, use few techniques and are almost never supervisual. This ordinariness is reflected in settings and the appearance and manner of the actors. Accompanying this is a stress on the functional (especially in props, attention and expression). The illustrations have something of the air of the market place: a lot of verbal persuasion, rather unsophisticated techniques, crowdedness, and a concern for the concrete rather than the abstract. There is, however, little of the gay and gaudy appeal of the market. The fact that this approach should be reserved for this area reinforces the impression one has of cheap offers, contests and competitions as rather unsubtle and old-fashioned (and possibly suspect) ways of selling. The illustrations and advertisements are working within an established tradition from which few of them seem able to free themselves.

Cigarettes

There is only a small amount of evidence regarding cigarettes—the props suggest quality, tradition, the discrimination of the connoisseur, while the visual aspect draws attention to size, making the product life-like or larger than life. The style of presentation is decidedly modern and streamlined. There is a slight conflict here between the stress on the modern and fashionable cigarette and the element of tradition and quality which so many are deemed to possess.

Baby and Children's Products

Illustrations for these products are, as one might expect, full of portrayals of motherhood in terms of looking after and caring for a baby, and are people oriented (as exemplified in attention and tactility). There are men, but never accompanying woman: children are –overall–a female preserve, and not a joint concern. Together with a homeliness and practicality (seen in props and manner) is the impression of ritual, of specific things to be done in certain, largely unalterable ways. The illustrations are not exciting or streamlined–they are restrained and generally middle-of-the-road. This restraint accompanies a certain serenity (manifested mainly in expression and pose) experienced by the mother.

Motherhood is satisfying, natural, a normal thing for a woman, something dealt with efficiently but carefully, and in no way an exceptional strain or harassment.

Medical

Illustrations in this category are also person-oriented (as can be seen, again, in attention and tactility). The world of cures and preventatives is one of ministration, concern, care. The mother takes on the nurse role, exhibiting competence and skill in the necessary practicalities (as shown in expression, pose and clothes). The practical exigencies are accompanied, as in so many cases, by an ordinariness–an everydayness, which is manifested in visual terms (style, techniques and rhetoric), in props and settings, and in the actors' appearance and manner. It is a domestic world, and a familiar one: illnesses are passing difficulties, cuts and bruises minor. Headaches appear to be the most upsetting and disabling sickness ... perhaps the only occasions in the advertisement illustrations when the woman is shown to be under considerable strain, unhappy, unable to cope. Cuts and bruises, measles and chills happen to men and children–headaches and period pains happen to women, and the latter are dealt with before they occur. Headaches prevent, amongst other things, the woman attending to visiting parents, dealing with children and doing the ironing. They are the deadliest enemy of the wife and mother in the carrying out of her duty. The illustrations suggest, however, that cures are speedy and simple and need not threaten the wife's role if the correct measures are taken. Illness is seen on the one hand as something which necessitates the care and attention of others and which therefore reinforces the wife and mother role and is not a real threat (serious illness is not considered), and on the other hand something which prevents the wife and mother from carrying out her role and which *is* a serious threat.

Careers

Career advertisements occupy a somewhat anomalous role amongst the rest of the advertisements as we have already remarked, in that they do not correspond with the major role categories derived from the advertisements as a whole. There is a strand of youth and innocence in the illustrations (to be seen in appearance and expression) which seems to express a naïve questing after new and worthwhile experiences. Something of the new, unusual, non-everyday is offered (as seen in settings and props) but hardly in overwhelming proportions. Generally the illustrations are people and object oriented, with a concern for efficiency and order. This can be seen in the props, settings, appearance, attention and manner–especially clothes and hair. The world is not a swinging one, but a staid and organized one. The presentation is mediocre in the extreme, being second only to offers in crowdedness, restricted use of techniques and low incidence of the supervisual. Careers are not exciting, but rather ordinary; not full of freedom but of restriction. As an alternative to the other feminine roles a 'career' does not stand out as the most attractive prospect.

Business

The businesses advertised consist mainly of building societies, insurances and banks. Their presentation is a little more visually oriented than that of careers advertisements, and on the whole the business world is slightly more sophisticated than that of careers or medicine (as can be seen in appearance), but is by no means swinging. It is familiar, functional and ordinary (this is reflected in settings and in manner especially hair and clothes). It is concerned with people and things and not with abstractions (as indicated by relationships, attention and tactility) and the high incidence of children may be due to their mediating role in that they can make concrete the abstract consideration of, and concern for the future. The ordinariness of the illustrations is a way of making the product accessible to everyone: taking away the exotic and emphasizing the everyday; it is also a reminder that the business in question is stable and reliable. There may also be elements of reticence; being unable to speak frankly about future eventualities, accidents, deaths – or even about money.

There is no point in repeating conclusions already stated regarding each product, but some general remarks are in order. (When talking about the products being this or having elements of that we are, of course, referring to the illustrations advertising the product.)

As mentioned above, there is in many of the products in this group a feeling for, and a stress on, the natural, against the artificial urban world of things, which is also the world of men. In the natural, biological world of women, a world of vital emotions and duties, she is the guardian of the real values of life. This world is set against and superior to the constructed, material, sordid, hard, lifeless world of men. Paradoxically, however, the rejection of this man-made world is accompanied by the reification by the woman *of herself*, which, furthermore, is achieved by *artificial* means. In the case of underclothes, tights, cosmetics, hair, sanitary and slimming preparations, something artificial/man-made is used in order to attain an appearance of naturalness.

The world is one in which a person has to be concerned about how things look, about what impressions one is giving. It is in this way a false and artificial world, evolved not from personal needs and desires but from received ideas of what is good and tasteful, of what is socially acceptable and what is not.

THE MAGAZINES

It can also be seen that the magazines themselves fit into the role-patterns derived from the advertising, though there are some interesting but fairly simple differences between them. *Honey* and *Petticoat* concentrate on the carefree, the mannequin and the self-involved woman, with *Petticoat* giving more emphasis to the last than *Honey*. *Nova*, on the other hand, pays rather less attention to the narcissist and more to the hostess, the mannequin–and uniquely–the independent woman. This magazine is the only one to offer an alternative view of woman's role outside the five main ones of the schema. *Woman and Home* concentrates on the hostess and the mother and wife, while *Woman* and *Woman's Own* include all five roles in their all-embracing pages, but give special emphasis to the mother and wife and (to a slightly lesser extent) the hostess. The range in these two magazines is the widest, and it is the widest also on the advertising side. The advertising (seen in terms of types of products advertised) broadly supports these patterns. There is a preponderance of food and household goods in *Woman*, *Woman's Own* and *Woman and Home*, of 'feminine' products and clothing in *Honey*, and of 'feminine' products in *Petticoat*. The advertising in *Nova*, however, puts it firmly back in the same area as the other magazines. Its concentration on clothes makes the mannequin role almost inevitably the most common. The incidence of the independent women in the advertisements from *Nova* is, it should be noted, no higher than in the other magazines. In this instance the advertising is acting clearly to bring into line an unusual attitude (self-consciously 'liberated') which the magazine's editorial content–in part–attempts to offer. This adds another conflict to the one already noted in *Nova* and makes its world even more precarious. In general, however, the magazine content and the advertising support each other. Sometimes the editorial content will even assist the advertising in other ways than the reinforcement of certain images of woman by stressing complementary values such as acquisition, novelty and fashionableness.

Finally, one comes back to the most broad question of all. What is the nature of the link between the world presented by the advertising and the 'real world'? To what extent are the meanings expressed by the advertisements a reflection, a distortion or a reinforcement of the real world? The first is certainly not the case; there is no one-to-one relationship of 'real facts' to 'advertising facts', as has been stressed already (Chapter 2). Distortion and reinforcement are terms which more accurately describe the relationship, though the best analogy might be that of refraction. The advertisements provide an interpretation of reality which reinforces certain aspects of it–but because certain aspects are singled out and others are not, and those that are selected can be presented in a variety of ways, there must be some distortion occurring as well. The transmission of cultural meanings by the advertising is both conscious and unconscious and is executed both by commission and omission. The process of selling a product, preparing a campaign, selecting a shot and so on—the mechanics of the business—also affect the content of the communication whether it be on the level of the need to find something 'new' to say or to stress, or on the level of the photographer's particular liking for pretty pictures. The use of a large sample should have helped to iron out idiosyncrasies, and those *consistent* factors deriving from the nature of the business should also be taken into account. It is only where recommendations or blame are being apportioned that it becomes imperative to understand what is due to the mechanics of the business, what is due to the guile of agencies and what is due to the nature of the media or the culture as a whole.

This sort of discourse must, by its nature, work with social types, but given this necessity there is as much room for variation between illustrations as there are different advertisements. There is a startling lack of this variation. The advertising *does* therefore confirm conventions of ideal types/stereotypes, as Goffman has suggested. It confirms that grannies are like this, that policemen are like that, that women are either like this or like that . . . and so on. It confirms the convention, incidentally, that England is a totally white country. It confirms—or even establishes, perhaps, along with other media—not only conventions regarding people but also regarding interiors, accessories and indeed anything which comes within the illustrations' sphere.

The suggestion made earlier that the reinforcement of certain styles and tastes meant in effect the reinforcement of the styles and tastes of a particular sector of the middle class of the Home Counties, seems to be amply borne out by the material. Certain fashions in decoration, types of interior and so on, recur in the illustrations to such an extent that one idea of what is acceptable and tasteful is broadcast as if it were the universal taste, or at least the *best*. Whether these tastes are those of the creators, or merely what the creators feel is the fashionable thing for the moment, is of no consequence. In the same way that these ideas of style and taste are broadcast and reinforced, values pertaining not to things but to people are also broadcast and reinforced, so that the worldview of the middle-class media men or the world-view they wittingly or unwittingly adopt gradually permeates the rest of the culture and attains the status of universality, acceptability and normality. And those things which are felt to be universal, acceptable and normal are things which are emulated, to which people aspire.

The advertising does *not* promote, however, a world of fantasy—at least in the usual sense of the term. It is a world more actual than that, yet in a crucial way distorted—like a slightly bent mirror, and thus not real at all. The part of advertising which is complete fantasy is small and immediately recognizable as such. The rest of the advertising is unreal in a far more subtle way.

The advertising in women's magazines (as elsewhere) acts as a moulder of female outlook and does serve as a legitimation of those roles in which so many women find themselves. The roles offered, the life-patterns indicated, the stances adopted, are all consistent in their occurrence and their form, and it must be remembered, cumulative. Not only this, but the magazines themselves in most cases support the advertising in the maintenance of these roles. Even when ostensibly turning over a new leaf, the magazines can be moving in the same old grooves. A pull-out section on careers in *Woman* seemed all one could wish for – but what were the four headings under which the jobs (twenty-six in all) were arranged – beauty, home, fashion and cookery! The reification of the female, loss of individual independence, introversion, the retreat into the womb of the home, woman as the natural half of humanity, guardian of the past and the future, the emphasis on sexual attraction, competitiveness . . . all these occur again and again, the same roles are proffered again and again, consistently and cumulatively. Although the woman as man's foil, his servant and subordinate, seems to be the opposite of the woman as a self-sufficient inward-looking being, these are but two sides of the same coin. The alternative coin would show woman as man's equal and woman as an independent spirit, and this is the missing image.

The advertising thus acts as a social regulator, to preserve the *status quo*. It is a part of the socialization of women, educating them to their roles. Stated as its most extreme, this process does serve a political purpose in maintaining the male domination of all the major sectors of society and an economic one in maintaining a corps of reliable con-sumers and an unpaid work force in the home (as well as a low paid one elsewhere). It need *not* be a conscious conspiracy to be powerful and effective. The level of consciousness of the exploitation of women should nevertheless not be underestimated. Consider this quotation from *Advertisers Weekly*; in the special supplement on 'The Women's Market' a two-page advertisement was placed by I P C women's weeklies, the first half of which went as follows:

'Taking the woman's point of view is always our business . . . that's why we could do so much for your business.

Yes, taking the women's point of view is just one of the special factors that make the big four – *Woman*, *Woman's Own*, *Woman's Realm* and *Woman's Weekly* – such a unique mass market medium, aimed exclusively at women. We get right close to them; sit down with them; talk to them intimately . . . about everything that goes to make them women.

So naturally, we get them involved. They spend time browsing over our magazines and take it all in. Nearly 12 million of them, every week of the year . . . and they're big spenders, too. What better atmosphere could you create for selling to women?'

Nor is this to suggest that men emerge unscathed from the impressions advertising gives of them and their roles. Although they are rarely the central subjects of these advertisements (unlike beer or tobacco advertisements, for example) their role is also defined in a limiting and often stereotypical way. If the man of the beer-drinking advertisements is tough, shrewd but silent, at home he is an extra, a subsidiary. Although acknowledged to be the boss, and served as a master, he is somehow out of his element, and has to be content to leave the real mastery of home affairs to the woman.

Clearly no one can say how far our estimates of ourselves and others and of what we think of as normal and acceptable is affected directly and indirectly by such external influences as the mass media. But unless the media are completely divorced from life, in which case it is difficult to see how they could function, values and assumptions and standards (often vaguely held and ill-defined) *must* be affected to some degree. It is therefore important to ascertain *in what direction* these pressures operate.

Anne Oakley, in her article 'Occupation Housewife', in *New Society*, wrote: 'A majority of women who are housewives apparently fail to realise this [that housework is unproductive, arduous, petty and excludes anything that would promote the development of the woman] or to suffer from it in any direct way. The solution to the paradox lies in the socialisation of women into the equation of femininity with domesticity. Through this socialisation, which various forms of social control serve to maintain, housework becomes a part of themselves: not only of their lives but of their identities.' Advertising is one of the forms of social control and one which stands to gain from the maintenance of this sort of socialization.

Is it the case, however, that the mass media or advertising in particular, must necessarily be opposed to all aspects of women's liberation? In the short term the answer might be no, for advertising is essentially adaptable and parasitic. However, if liberation for women from the situations, status and stereotypes of society means real changes in consciousness and real changes in economic and social relationships, then advertising must remain in opposition . . . their ideologies stand in too fundamental a disagreement. Moreover, advertising in any case remains the implement of those forces which seek to maintain the *status quo* and resist radical social and economic changes. Any acceptance of a more liberating posture towards women by advertising is likely to be of the most superficial, and ultimately damaging, kind. (Though one must bear in mind that in specific instances advertising can be the most contradictory of all the media.)

In the last few years one way in which advertising has reacted to changes in attitudes to women and of women has been the development of a sort of mediating or compromise model: a more sensual, overtly sexual woman–described at length in some of the sections above. Advertising can accept the development of a more 'permissive' society and indeed capitalize upon it, and while appearing *avant-garde* in this respect can maintain all the old social roles for women in slightly updated guises. Advertisements can change completely in outward style and in manifest content while retaining the same values absolutely. 'Permissiveness' is a godsend to the media in that it enables them to give the impression of daring without actually challenging established power in any important way.

It is still an open question whether advertising is more powerful or forceful when the society seems uncertain. In the period leading up to and covered by the survey recorded in Chapter 5 advertising did provide a façade of satisfaction and certainty. The widespread development in Britain of the movement for women's liberation has occurred since the completion of the major part of this work, and it remains to be seen whether advertising *will* attempt to turn it to its own ends in any way.

In general the idea–commonly encountered–of advertising being in the forefront of change and development is misconceived. It embraces change in the technological sense alone–not as a step towards human betterment or social justice but as an increase in efficiency or productivity. Advertising presents not an outward-going but an inward-looking world, not a wide vista but a view which is narrow and constrained. It does not open up more possibilities but restricts the perception of those which already exist.

In criticizing the medium, however, we are only commenting on the outward manifestations of a whole system of economic and social relationships. We have taken a close look at advertising as one way of penetrating to some of the values held by that system. Further research would show us how far other media purvey similar values and would enable us to see more clearly those which are the more powerful and recurrent. That done, we could indeed put the question–are these values *our* values? If they are not we might ask why they are so widely broadcast, and what sort of dissemination other values are allowed.

From the point of view of method, there are other things which have emerged from this study. The communication of meanings, even when the means of communication is visual, can be studied and can be studied in a way which is not merely selective and intuitive. The methods involved in such a study can be improved and sharpened, and there is room for much more work to be done in this and related areas. In this area particularly it would be useful to study the text *plus* the visual communication, to study advertisements from other magazines (the colour supplements for example) and from television, and to carry out an analysis over time. Within the confines of this particular study there are modifications one would wish to make, including perhaps, a different classification of appearance, another look at rhetoric, a refined classification of products, and a classification for children; but at this stage one has to be satisfied with having made a beginning, with having suggested paths that it may be profitable to explore further.

It has become clear that the analysis of the visual communication can yield a great deal—by no means all of which can be properly handled at present—and that to continue to ignore this aspect of communication is both illogical and unnecessary. We have become aware that factors such as appearance, dress, hair-style, and so on, can convey a lot of information—and not only that, but clothes, expression, the style of the advertisement, settings, etc. *all* together convey a large amount of mutually consistent information, much more than we have been able to pin down. It is the consistency of the evidence, the denseness of the correlations in the knitting together of the wide range of aspects of the illustrations which is impressive and important. It is important that patterns *do* exist—they may be hazy at the edges in some parts, some aspects may be obvious in some ways—but the patterns are coherent and extremely significant. There are patterns of meanings, patterns relating to types of products, patterns of types of advertisements (e.g. that complex content tends to go with simple presentation, that sophistication in actors is accompanied by sophistication/complexity in the communication of meanings) and so on. These patterns mean that the vocabulary of the advertising is restricted—by the mechanics of the business, by the ethos of the business, by the existence of traditions and stereotypes and received modes of behaviour which have been accepted unquestioningly. There *is* a great deal of variation—but, while we have not been able to capture *all* the differences and nuances, it is clear that the range of the visual vocabulary *is* restricted. It is the essential nature of this restricted vocabulary which we have tried to establish.

APPENDIX I. Notes on some examples

There follows a simplified and individual analysis of some pictures in order to give an idea of the complexity of the material, to indicate some of the main points that have been made above, and to draw attention to important and typical features. These examples are selected for this brief analysis for the reason that they illustrate well, certain factors with which we have been centrally concerned and for the reader may serve to add depth and insight to the picture he has managed to build.

1. G-Plan (colour plate 3)

The style is streamlined–there is a large picture bled to the edges, and a neat text arrangement which does not distract from the picture, and colour, focus and lighting are all used carefully and subtly.

Description. The scene is the ground floor of a house and the personnel is a man and a woman. Furnishings in the two rooms visible include a dining table and chairs, sideboard, settee and armchair and another smaller table. There is a spiral staircase, and a large window (an unusual occurrence) in the farther room. The man, bending over the table in the far room, wears a suit, but is otherwise indistinct. The woman sits at the dining table peeling an apple. She wears an ankle length green dress and her hair is shaped but not rigidly set. Though her attention is on the peeling of the apple her expression is soft and her pose relaxed and functional. There is a large vase of chrysanthemums, a wine decanter, a nearly empty wine glass, a condiment set, serviettes and two candlesticks with lighted candles on the table. On the sideboard is a vase and a pot-plant. The wall dividing the rooms contains a pattern of square holes; the floor in the near room is of bare glazed brick.

Interpretation. This is a domestic scene with man and wife having completed a meal of some sort together. He is a background figure at this point and she is the centre of attention. She is well–almost exotically– dressed, calm, serene, relaxed. The atmosphere is bright and lightly romantic. The furniture is the product. The flowers are luxuriant and extravagant, the dishes, decanter and candlesticks are elegant and expensive looking. Most of the props are luxury items, from the vase to the condiment set. Wine with a meal (and from a decanter, not a bottle), fresh fruit to finish, lighted candles, and the use of serviettes mark this couple out as well-off and well-bred. The house and the furnishings speak of money, but the accessories–the vase on the sideboard for example– speak of a refined and descriminating taste, and the design of the house–its spartan floors, unusual wall and spiral staircase–speaks of the *avant-garde* with a dash of daring–more fashionable than the latest fashion. Affluence, luxury, discrimination, confidence . . . they have all of these and more besides.

2. Berlei (plate 10a)

The advertisement is a little disjointed, with three pictures and four or more separate pieces of headline, but the size of the main illustration and the headline help to restrain the diffusion of attention. The two torso close-ups beneath the main picture echo the figures above and reinforce the underclothes as the product and the focus of attention.

Description. The scene is an archaeological site, barren and ruinous but for a single preserved colonnade. At the back, across a chasm, a woman stands in a niche holding a flag with the word 'freedom' written white on blue. Another woman stands vigorously on a boulder in the foreground. They are both clad in shape-suits, have long free hair, their arms and legs spread wide. They do not look at each other but rather into far-distance, and their expressions contain both neutrality and glory. Their poses are awkward and uncomfortable.

Interpretation. The women are dressed in such a way that they are incongruous in the setting. To resolve the incongruity the reader must resort to the text, though this in fact explains little. The clue to the picture is contained in the banner held by one of the women–they, and their surroundings are concerned with feeedom, with getting away from restrictions. The existence of the banner and the slogan harks back to marches and protests, though the demeanour of the actors is in no way militant. They are not involved with each other, but only with themselves, with making a public demonstration of themselves, and most specifically, their bodies. The reification of the body is emphasized by the headless torsos pictured below. The freedom of the banner and the ruins is not maintained by the actors themselves, who are static, artificial and insensitive. They are cut off from the natural setting, only connected to it in the most superficial way. In fact, it seems highly probable that the pictures of the actors have been taken in a studio and stuck on to a previously photographed background. This is a clear example of the woman as object, tending to the exhibitionistic, linked to the natural world but nevertheless cut off from her companions and her surroundings, which has been noted above with great frequency.

3. Enkasheer (plate 11b)

A very streamlined illustration, embracing both the headline and the copy within it and bled to all the edges. It has an 'all-over' tone and makes special use of colour, focus and lighting.

Description. A woman, unclothed, sits on a fur rug. There is no background and the only other item is a white, angular cup and saucer on the rug. Her knees are drawn up to her face and her long hair flows on to her shoulders and touches her legs. One hand rests on her thigh and the other on her foot.

Interpretation. The woman is completely immersed in herself–her pose is narcissistic and the tactile qualities of hands, hair and fur rug are accentuated by her nakedness. In her foetal position her face is indistinguishable from her legs, as if the mind and faculties were being absorbed by the body. She is cut off from everything–there is no back-

APPENDIX I 185

ground, just tactile sensations. The style of the illustration—the brown muted colours, muzzy focus and subdued lighting—adds to the heavy, sensual mood, to the smoothness, the softness, the gentleness.

4. Polyherb (plate 14)

While there are several competing elements in the advertisement, the approach is clear and not at all confusing. Colour, focus and close-up are all used to advantage, and the unusual position of the girl gives the illustration immediate impact.

Description. A girl is lying down in the grass, staring out of the picture but not connecting with the reader, partly because of the angle of her eyes, partly because she is not focusing on anything. Her long fair hair curves around her face and on to the grass. From the sight of a blue cuff we see that she is resting on her arm. Her lips are red and she has some make-up on her eyes. In the background the grass merges into some indistinct brown and green which gives the impression of woodland.

Interpretation. The girl is dreamy and introverted, lost in reverie within herself. It is not the inwardness of the girl that is the most vital aspect of the picture, however, but her relationship to nature. Her hair is free and natural and is in direct contact with the grass. The grass surrounds the girl's face, merging with her hair and the mistiness of the focus assists the intermingling of grass and hair—she could get no closer to the earth save by burying her head. She is involved in a real and direct connexion with nature, in contrast to the women in the Berlei riverbank. She is nature's child, earth goddess, wood-nymph—while remaining seductive and fashionably beautiful.

5. Dr White's (plate 15)

The large photograph, simple lettering and short copy make this a streamlined advertisement which ostensibly shuns the special use of any techniques, but which gives the impression of a documentary shot 'from life'.

Description. The scene is a street outside a large glass-fronted shop. The pavement is wide and paved with patterns of tiles. The central actor is a woman who holds a pushchair in one hand and a little girl in the other. The pushchair is loaded with three large carrier-bags. The woman and the little girl are dressed in raincoats and boots and both have long free hair. The woman is speaking to the child, who looks obstinate. The pavement is wet and another woman is passing in the background.

Interpretation. It is a wet dreary day; the mother is about to set off home from the shops with the pushchair laden with shopping and the little girl walking along holding hands. The child is not co-operative. The woman however is not particularly harassed though the illustration is ambiguous as to what the next development will be. The setting, the weather and the situation of the woman are all recognizably everyday and familiar. It is a situation with which a woman would find it easy to identify: rain, heavy shopping, recalcitrant child (and though the illustration does not indicate it) the monthly period to contend with. This is woman's burden exemplified. The emphasis is familiar and it is also functional: as the shop, the pushchair and the bags, the concentration on things and people all serve to indicate.

6. Norvic (plate 16)

A streamlined advertisement, in which the illustration, copy and headline are integrated and homogenous. The picture is a piece of precise still-life close-up photography which shows the details of each part of the deliberate arrangement of objects.

Description. The objects in the picture are three shoes of different styles and colours, some nuts (hazel, brazil, almond and walnut), a piece of winter jasmine and four old and leather-bound tomes. Two of the shoes rest on the pile of three books and the fourth is open to reveal what seem to be verses of a long poem, the title of which can just be discerned as Troilus and Cressida.

Interpretation. This is an illustration where much of the communication rests on the metaphoric function of the objects. The nuts and the jasmine stand for the country–but not any soft idyllic countryside, more a rugged and difficult countryside. The books stand for that which is traditionally thought to be good, that which the person of taste and discrimination (and education and culture) chooses. They are made of leather like the shoes, are solid and long-lasting. The whole arrangement is that of a tasteful still-life composition, and this adds to the qualities already described. These then, can be quickly seen to be shoes for the lover of the English countryside, tough and long-lasting, yet tasteful and the choice of every discriminating buyer, even before the copy is read, or without it being read at all.

7. Bread (plate 3b) and 8. Phensic (colour plate 2)

These two advertisements show the sheer visual power that an illustration can possess. They are both streamlined advertisements and make great use of visual techniques. In the former focus, colour, angle and close-up are all employed; in the latter the same techniques are used to a very different effect. The Phensic example is the reinterpretation of the old before and after, invested with much more dramatic impact.

Description. In the Bread advertisement there is a white plate on a white cloth. Resting on the plate is a knife and fork with their handles toward the reader, lettuce, and an enormous toasted sandwich including cheese, tomatoes, bacon and water-cress. The larger Phensic illustration consists of a close-up of a woman's face, her hands held to her brow, photographed through a filter which gives everything a blue tone. She is wearing a jumper. The woman's expression indicates that she is in pain. In the inset the woman is seen smiling, beside her an electric iron, her hand on a pile of completed ironing. She is made-up and wears a fashionable high collar jacket (which could be a dress). This time a different filter gives everything an orange/brown tinge.

Interpretation. The power of the supervisual derives in part from the fact that it needs little or no interpretation. The bread illustration says simply 'Here you are—doesn't it look delicious?'. The food looks real, appetizing, wholesome. The whole emphasis is on bringing out the taste through the visual appearance—no attention is paid to distractions of sophistication: the plate and the knife and fork are plain and solid like the food. The overall impression can be termed seductive.

The Phensic illustration depends equally on the excellence of the photography, although the subject suffers from the tendency of the supervisual to make everything look delicious. In other words the woman, who clearly has a dreadful headache, the whole world is concentrated in her head, looks rather beautiful in spite of her condition. Nevertheless, the overwhelming blue-ness and the simple pose bring home immediately the grinding tediousness of headaches. Next moment (in fact, simultaneously) the woman is bright and smiling—cured, coping and cock-a-hoop. The transition is marked by a simple change from the blue of pain and depression to the orange light of health and vitality. It is also marked by a change of attire and, of course, expression. The burden of the message is conveyed by simple visual techniques skilfully applied.

APPENDIX II. The Survey: Numerical Breakdown

Products

The following table shows the proportion which each of the product types comprise of the total, by percentage.

cosmetics	12·0		
hair preparations	7·5		
sanitary towels and tampons	1·3		
slimming preparations	1·8	all 'feminine':	22·6
clothes	8·8		
underclothes	4·7		
tights	2·5		
shoes	4·0		
wool	3·5	all clothing:	23·5
food	14·8		14·8
kitchen equipment	3·5		
floor coverings	2·0		
decorating materials	2·3		
furniture	1·8		
household accessories	3·9		
soft furnishings	2·4	all household (excluding food):	15·8
offers	4·1		
cigarettes	1·7		
careers	2·4		
business	1·8		
medical	3·1		
baby products	2·0		
children's clothes	1·2		
miscellaneous	6·2	all remainder:	22·5

Elements

The table is concerned with the way each illustration is made up of the four basic elements, and how many there are of each type of combination.

%	Product	Product + Actor	Actor
	A 9·5	E 13·9	I 11·3
+ props	B 18·2	F 8·5	J 10·5
+ setting	C —	G 4·5	K 3·5
+ props + setting	D 1·5	H 12·5	L 4·3

(M) solely props 1·5   (N) solely setting 0·1

Illustrations with *settings* make up only 26·3 per cent of the total, of which a half are of category H. This strikes one as a significantly small proportion. On the other hand 54·5 per cent contain *props*, 69 per cent contain *actors* and 68·6 per cent contain the *product*. Nearly 28 per cent of the illustrations are of category A or B, and therefore one supposes of fairly simple construction.

Note: A distinction should be drawn between cosmetics and the other products liable to product transformation, wool, food and decorating materials. In terms of constituent elements should the product be deemed to be there when it is in fact transformed? It is maintained that in the case of cosmetics the link between the product pre- and post-transformation is too tenuous to enable us to say that the product is, in any meaningful sense, there in the picture. The opposite is the case with food, wool and decorating materials, depending of course on specific instances. An advertisement illustration for paint which showed a room which was not clearly newly painted might be deemed to not contain the product.

Style

The distribution into the three categories was as follows:

	%
streamlined	41·6
basic	44·8
crowded	13·6

The classifications based on style are, of course, only a relative distinction—but there is a distinct emphasis at the streamlined end of the scale. A comparison over time might reveal further lines of interest in this area.

Techniques

The table shows the distribution by percentage to one decimal point, but the total will not be 100 as any number of techniques could be noted for each illustration. Blanks, i.e. those illustrations for which no special uses of techniques were noted, make up 26·2 per cent of the total. The table is concerned only with the remaining 73·8 per cent.

	%
close-up	38·3
lighting	8·7
colour	9·9
angle	13·8
focus	5·7
cropping	15·1
special effects	2·1
drawing	4·1
multiple pictures	2·1

Rhetorical Devices

The following figures show the percentage of advertisement illustrations making use of each of the devices; the total will again be over 100 as each illustration could (theoretically) make use of all four main types.

	%
association	45·0
the supervisual	18·7
product presentation/transformation	64·6
typification/testament	63·4
(testament accounting for 3·8)	

It seems that the advertisements are relying on the content of the illustration rather than the style and force of the visual image itself to communicate their message. The use of pictures is a step towards visual communication and away from reliance on words, but the tendency still is to turn *verbal* messages into corresponding visual ones, rather than to use visual ones in their own right.

Props

Of all advertisements 26·4 per cent have functional props
Of all advertisements 20·8 per cent have functional-metaphorical props
Of all advertisements 14·1 per cent have metaphorical props

As can be seen in the table above (Elements) 57 per cent of the advertisements use props in one form or another.

Little can be deduced from the relative incidence of the different types of props. One would suspect that the functional-metaphorical prop is the more subtle in relaying messages in that it is part of the furniture as well (i.e. it is camouflaged), while the metaphorical prop has no function other than to convey a particular, relatively manifest, message.

Settings

The staged/documentary dichotomy revealed the following breakdown:

	%
staged	38·4
documentary	61·6

but was subsequently felt to be of only limited use, as in most cases the staged settings coincide with domestic settings, and the documentary ones with outdoor or indoor non-domestic settings.

Familiarity:

	%
familiar	43
wishful	42
fantasy	15

Mood:

	%
everyday	41·0
romantic	26·0
bizarre	11·2
exotic	10·2
extravagant	11·6

Place of setting:

	%
indoor	54
outdoor	46

(a) INDOOR settings sub-divide thus:

	%
domestic	68·7
non-domestic	31·3

and the domestic settings as follows:

	%
ritzy	24·0
camp	8·4
traditional	9·7
mod	26·6
conventional	24·7
unclear/too faint	6·5

(b) OUTDOOR settings sub-divide thus:

	Country %	Greenbelt %	Urban %	Other %
local/familiar	27·5	18·5	17·0	—
exotic	14·0	5·0	15·0	2·4

There are about equal proportions of outdoor and domestic settings, with indoor non-domestic settings constituting a third area.

Actors

General: number and sex:
Of those illustrations including actors:
     59% featured one actor
     25·5% featured two actors
     15·5% featured three or more actors
     Illustrations featuring men only: 5·5%
     Illustrations featuring men and women: 24·2%
     Illustrations featuring women only: 70·3%

Children:
Children feature in 12½ per cent of the advertisements and in one-third of those illustrations children are unaccompanied by adults. Children are usually featured singly (66 per cent), but in *twos* in 24½ per cent and *threes and more* in 9½ per cent of cases.

Relationships:
Divide fairly evenly between the categories:

	%
reciprocal	25
semi-reciprocal	20
divergent	26
object	28

(including relationships, via the camera, with the reader).

Attention:
  (i) inward-directed: 65 per cent; outward-directed (i.e. to the reader) 35 per cent.
  (ii) of all inward-directed female attention:

	%
object	19·5
middle-distance	29·2
person	19·5
self	17·7
invisible	13·8

and in the case of males:

	%
object	19·6
middle-distance	4·7
person	59·2
self	1·2
invisible	15·3

Tactility:

Female:	%	Male:	%
nil	32·3	nil	23·4
object	29·0	object	37·4
person	7·4	person	27·2
self	32·3	self	12·0

APPENDIX II

Appearance:

		%			%
Female:	superior	3·0	Male:	sophisticated	35·5
	sophisticated	44·0		naïve	7·0
	naïve	11·5		plain	56·5
	plain	32·0		detached	1·0
	detached	9·5		superior	—

Expression:

		%			%
Female:	cool	13·5	Male:	carefree	19·0
	narcissistic	1·5		thoughtful	21·0
	soft	13·5		paternal	6·3
	kitten	3·5		practical	9·5
	carefree	11·2		comic	12·0
	catalogue	29·1		catalogue	10·5
	seductive	3·0		glad-eye	7·9
	practical	6·6		self-reliant	5·2
	comic	3·0		others	8·5
	maternal	4·5			
	others	10·6			

Pose:

		%			%
Female:	composed	9·2	Male:	composed	8·3
	narcissistic	9·0		dramatic	6·0
	seductive	2·8		carefree	4·8
	dramatic	6·3		dummy	12·0
	carefree	6·0		functional	36·0
	dummy	30·3		relaxed	27·0
	functional	24·0		others	5·9
	relaxed	8·4		(of which over ½=comic)	
	others	4·1			

Clothes:

		%			%
Female:	product	36·0	Male:	product	17·5
	exotic	13·2		conventional	37·2
	snazzy	3·6		casual	20·2
	office-wear	14·0		mod	3·5
	informal	15·5		uniform	4·7
	dirty-wear	1·1		working	2·4
	uniform	2·5		none	—
	none, or few	12·4		others	14·5
	others	5·2		(formal	4·5)

Hair:

		%			%
Female:	freeflowing	51·0	Male:	short-tidy	78·0
	shaped	27·0		medium/	
	moulded	22·0		slightly unruly	22·0
(about 25 % of the female actors have blonde hair)				long/untidy	—

Age:

The following breakdown was arrived at by noting the (estimated) upper age limit of the actor in each case:

		%		%
under 25	Female:	61·0	Male:	15·7
26–30		25·5		44·0
31–35		8·5		18·0
36–45		4·0		15·7
46–60		1·0		4·4
over 60		—		2·2

Bibliography

Abrams, M. 'Statistics of Advertising' from *Journal of the Royal Statistical Society*; Vol. 115, Part 2; 1952

Adams, C. F. *Common Sense in Advertising*; McGraw-Hill, New York, 1966

Alderson, C. *Magazines Teenagers Read*; Pergamon Press, Oxford, 1968.

Alloway, L. 'Iconography of the Movies' from *Movie*: No. 7; February 1963

Arnheim, R. *Art and Visual Perception*; University of California Press, 1954; Faber and Faber, London, 1967
—— *Toward a Psychology of Art*; University of California Press, 1966. *Towards a Psychology of Art*; Faber & Faber, London, 1967

Baker, Samuel S. *The Permissible Lie : The Inside Truth About Advertising*; Peter Owen, 1969; Beacon Press, 1971

Baker, Stephen. *Visual Persuasion, Marketing : The Effect of Pictures on The Subconscious*; McGraw-Hill, New York, 1961

Barthes, R. *Elements of Semiology*; Jonathan Cape, 1967
—— 'Rhetorique de l'Image' from *Communications* 4, 1964, translated in Working Papers in Cultural Studies, No. 1; Centre for Contemporary Cultural Studies, University of Birmingham
—— *Systéme de la Mode*; Editions du Seuil; Paris, 1967

Baster, A. S. J. *Advertising Reconsidered*; P. S. King & Son, 1935.

Beauvoir, S. de *Brigitte Bardot and the Lolita Syndrome*; André Deutsch, 1960; Arnos Press Cinema Program, 1972
—— *The Second Sex*; Knopf, 1953; Jonathan Cape, 1968

Berelson, B. and M. Janowitz (eds.). *Reader in Public Opinion and Communication*, Free Press, New York, 1966

Berg, C. *The Unconscious Significance of Hair*; Allen & Unwin, 1957; Guild Press Ltd, 1964
—— 'The Unconscious Significance of Hair' from *International Journal of Psycho-analysis*, Vol. 17; 1936

Berger, N. and J. Maizels. *Woman–Fancy or Free?* Mills & Boon, 1962

Berger, P. L. and T. Luckman. *The Social Construction of Reality : Treatise in the Sociology of Knowledge*; Allen Lane, The Penguin Press; Doubleday, 1967

Berger, P. *The Social Reality of Religion*; Faber & Faber, 1969

Biggs, F. *Colour in Advertising*; Studio Publications, 1956

Birdwhistell, R. L. 'Kinesics and Communication' from *Explorations in Communication*, ed. E. Carpenter and M. McLuhan; Beacon Press, 1960

Bishop, F. R. *Economics of Advertising*; Robert Hale, 1934
—— *Ethics of Advertising*; Robert Hale, 1949

Bonsiepe, G. 'Persuasive Communication–Towards a Visual Rhetoric' from *Uppercase*, ed. Theo Crosby, No. 5; 1961

Brandon, R. *The Truth About Advertising*; Chapman and Hall, 1948

Brophy, J. *The Face in Western Art*; Harrap, 1963

Brown, A. C. *Techniques of Persuasion*; Penguin, 1969

Burton, P. W. *Advertising and Copywriting*; Nicholas Kaye, 1950

Caplin, R. *Advertising–A General Introduction*; Business Publications, 1967

Caton, D. *Advertising Explained*; Allen & Unwin, 1949

Clayton, L. *The World of Modelling*; Tandem, 1969; International Publications Services, 1971

Copland, B. D. *Study of Attention Value*; Business Publications, 1958

Cudlipp, H. *Publish and Be Damned*; Dakers, 1953

Davis, M. *Handbook for Media Representatives*; Business Publications, 1967

Deutsch, H. *The Psychology of Women*; Volume 1, Girlhood (1944); Volume 2, Motherhood (1945); Research Books Ltd., International Universities Press, 1947

Devereux, G. 'A Note of the Feminine Significance of the Eyes' from *Bulletin of the Philadelphia Association of Psycho-analysis*, Vol. 6; 1956

Dexter, L. A. and Whaite, D. M. *People, Society and Mass Communication*; Free Press, New York, 1964

Dichter, E. *Handbook of Consumer Motivations*; McGraw-Hill, New York, 1964

—— *The Strategy of Desire*; McGraw-Hill, New York, 1960

Dixon, J. *Advertising*; Institute of Practitioners in Advertising, 1935

Eco, U. 'Articulations of the Cinematic Code', *Cinematics* No. 1; January 1970

Eisenstein, S. *The Film Sense*; Harcourt Brace, 1942

Ekman, P. *The Recognition and Display of Facial Behaviour in Literate and Non-Literate Cultures*; University of California Medical Center, 1968

Ekman, P. and Friesen, W. V. 'The Repertoire of Non-Verbal Behaviour: Categories, Origins, Usage and Coding' from *Semiotica* I, 1; 1969

Ellis, H. *Studies in the Psychology of Sex*, 2 volumes; Random House, 1936

Feldman, S. *Mannerisms of Speech and Gestures in Everyday Life*; International Universities Press, New York, 1969

Fenwick, J. 'Periodicals and Adolescent Girls' from *Studies in Education*, Vol. II, No. 1; University of Hull, 1953

Fletcher, A., Forbes, G., and Gill, B. *Graphic Design : Visual Comparisons*; Studio Vista, 1964; Reinhold, 1964

Flügel, S. *The Psychology of Clothes*; The Hogarth Press, London, 1950; International Universities Press, 1969

Friedan, B. *The Feminine Mystique*; Norton, 1963; Gollancz, 1971

Freud, S. 'Female Sexuality' in Volume 21 of *The Standard Edition of the Complete Psychological Works of Sigmund Freud*; The Hogarth Press, London

—— *New Introductory Lectures* in Volume 22 of *The Standard Edition of the Complete Psychological Works of Sigmund Freud*; The Hogarth Press, London

—— 'On Narcissism' in Volume 14 of *The Standard Edition of the Complete Psychological Works of Sigmund Freud*; The Hogarth Press, London

Gage, N. L. 'Judging Interests from Expressive Behaviour' from *Psychological Monographs: General and Applied*, Vol. 66, No. 18; 1952

Gail, S. 'The Housewife', from *Work: Twenty Personal Accounts*, Vol. 1, ed. K. Fraser; Penguin, 1968

Galbraith, J. K. *The Affluent Society*; Hamish Hamilton, 1958; New American Library, 1970

Gill, L. E. *Advertising and Psychology*; Hutchinson, 1954

Gloag, J. *Advertising in Modern Life*; Heinemann, 1959

Goffman, E. *Presentation of Self in Everyday Life*; Alan Lane, 1969; Doubleday

—— *Behaviour in Public Places*; Free Press, New York, 1963

Gombrich, E. *Art and Illusion*; Phaidon, 1962

—— *Meditations on a Hobby Horse and Other Essays on The Theory of Art*; Phaidon, 1963

Gregory, R. L. *Eye and Brain*; Weidenfeld & Nicolson, 1966; McGraw-Hill, 1966

—— *The Intelligent Eye*; Weidenfeld & Nicolson, 1970; McGraw-Hill, 1970

Griff, M. 'Advertising–the Central Institution of Mass Society', from *Diogenes*, No. 68; 1969

Hall, E. T. *The Silent Language*; Doubleday, 1959

Hall, S. 'Cultural Analysis', from *Cambridge Review*; January 1967

Hall, S. and Whannel, P. *The Popular Arts*; Hutchinson Educational, 1964; Pantheon, 1965

Harnik, J. 'The Various Developments Undergone by Narcissism in Men and Women', *International Journal of Psycho-analysis*, Vol. 5; 1925

Henry, H. *Motivation Research*; Crosby Lockwood & Son, 1958

Hobson, J. W. *The Influence and Techniques of Modern Advertising;* Institute of Practitioners in Advertising, 1965

Hogg, J. (ed.). *Psychology and the Visual Arts*; Modern Psychology Series, Penguin, 1969

Hoggart, R. 'The Case Against Advertising' from *Speaking to Each Other*; Chatto & Windus, 1970; Oxford University Press, New York, 1970

—— 'Contemporary Cultural Studies'; Centre for Contemporary Cultural Studies Occasional Paper No. 6

—— 'Literary Imagination and the Study of Society'; Centre for Contemporary Cultural Studies Occasional Paper No. 3

—— *The Uses of Literacy*; Chatto & Windus, London; Oxford University Press, New York, 1957

Horney, K. *Feminine Psychology*; Routledge & Kegan Paul, London; Norton, New York, 1967

Institute of Practitioners in Advertising (IPA)
British Code of Advertising Practice, 1964
Education, Social Class, and the Reading of Newspapers and Magazines, 1964
The Importance of Circulation Figures, 1956
Motivation Research, 1957

Jacobson, E. (ed.) *Modern Art in Advertising*; Paul Theobald, Chicago, 1946

Kaldor, N., and R. Silverman. *Statistical Analysis of Advertising Expenditure*; Cambridge University Press, 1948

Kelvin, R. P. *Advertising and Human Memory*; Business Publications, 1962

Kepes, G. *The Language of Vision*; Paul Theobald, Chicago, 1945

Klapp, O. *Heroes, Villains and Fools*; Spectrum, New York, 1962

Klein, V. *The Feminine Character : History of an Ideology*; Routledge & Kegan Paul, 1971; University of Illinois Press, 1972

Knights, C. C. *Layout and Commercial Art*; Butterworth, 1932

Langer, S. *Philosophy in a New Key: Art, Reason, Rite*; Harvard University Press, 1957

—— *Problems of Art*; Routledge & Kegan Paul, 1957

Leach, E. 'Magical Hair' from *Myth and Cosmos* (ed.) Middleton; Natural History Press, 1967

Leech, G. N. *English in Advertising : A Linguistic Study of Advertisement in Great Britain*; Longman; Humanities Press, 1966

Lewis, J. N. C. *Typography : Basic Principles*; Studio Vista, 1965

McEwan, J. *Advertising as a Service to Society*; MacDonald & Evans, 1956

McLuhan, M. *The Mechanical Bride*; Vanguard Press, New York, 1951; Routledge & Kegan Paul, 1967

—— *Understanding Media*; Routledge & Kegan Paul, 1964; McGraw-Hill, 1971

McMurtrie, D. *Modern Typography and Layout*; Library Press, 1930

Mailer, N. *Advertisements for Myself*; André Deutsch, 1961; Berkeley Publications, Panther Books, 1970

Marmori, G. *Senso e Anagramma*; Feltrinelli, Milan, 1968

Mead, M. *Male and Female*; Gollancz, Morrow, 1949; Penguin, 1970

—— *Sex and Temperament in Three Primitive Societies*; Routledge, 1935

Meyersohn, and Katz, 'Fashion and Fads', from *American Journal of Sociology*, Vol. 62, No. 6; 1957

Meynell, F. *Typography of Advertising*; Institute of Practitioners in Advertising, 1960

Millar, R. *The Affluent Sheep*; Longman, 1963

Myrdal, A. and Klein, V. *Woman's Two Roles*; Routledge & Kegan Paul (revised edition), 1968; Humanities Press, 1968

Oakley, A. 'The Myth of Motherhood' from *New Society*, 28 February 1970

Ogilvy, D. *Confessions of an Advertising Man*; Longman, 1964

Orwell, G. *Keep the Aspidistra Flying*; Gollancz, 1936; Secker & Warburg, 1954; Harcourt Brace Jovanovich, 1969; Penguin, 1970

Packard, V. *The Hidden Persuaders*; Longman; McKay 1957

Panofsky, E. *Studies in Iconology*; Harper Torchbooks, New York, 1933
—— *Meaning in the Visual Arts*; Penguin, 1970

Pearson, J., and Turner, G. *The Persuasion Industry*; Eyre & Spottiswoode, 1965

Peterson, T. *Magazines in the Twentieth Century*; University of Illinois Press, 1964

Priestley, J. B. *They Walk in the City: The Lovers in the Stone Forest*; Heinemann, Greenwood, 1936

Pye, D. *The Nature of Design*; Studio Vista; Reinhold, 1964

Reeves, R. *Reality in Advertising*; MacGibbon & Kee; Knopf, 1961

Rickman, H. *Understanding and the Human Studies*; Heinemann Educational, 1967

Roheim, G. from *International Journal of Psycho-Analysis*, Vol. 13

Rosenberg, B. and White, D. M. (eds.). *Mass Culture*; Free Press, New York, 1965

Sausmarez, M. de *Basic Design: Dynamics of Visual Form;* Reinhold, 1964; Studio Vista, 1965

Seldin, J. *The Golden Fleece*; Macmillan, New York, 1963

Simmel, G. *Das Relative und das Absolute im Geschlechterproblem*; 1911

Spottiswoode, R. *A Grammar of the Film: An Analysis of Film Technique*; Faber & Faber, 1935; University of California Press, 1950

Stone, G. P. 'Appearance and the Self', from *Human Behaviour and Social Processes*, ed. E. Rose: Routledge & Kegan Paul, 1962

Taplin, W. *Advertising–A New Approach*; Hutchinson, 1960
—— 'Facts and Figures on the National Outlay', from *Advertising Appraisal*; Times Review of Industry, 1960

Terman, L. M. and Miles, C. C. *Sex and Personality: Studies in Masculinity and Femininity*; McGraw-Hill, 1936

Thompson, C. 'Cultural Pressures on the Psychology of Women', from *Psychiatry*, Vol. V, No. 3; 1942

Thompson, D. *The Voice of Civilization*; Muller, 1943
—— (ed.) *Discrimination and Popular Culture*; Penguin, 1964
Thompson, D. and Leavis, F. R. *Culture and Environment*; Chatto & Windus, 1933
Trenchard, and Crissy, 'Trends in the Use of Certain Attention Getting Devices in Newsweekly Advertising', *Journal of Applied Psychology*, Vol. 35; 1951
Tunstall, J. *The Advertising Man*; Chapman & Hall, 1964
Wax, M. 'Themes in Cosmetics and Grooming'; *American Journal of Sociology*, Vol. 62, No. 6; 1956–57
Wertham, F. *The Seduction of the Innocent*; Museum Press, 1955; Kennikat reprint, 1971
Williams, R. *Communications*; Chatto & Windus, 1966
—— *Culture and Society*; Chatto & Windus; Harper & Row, 1958
—— *The Long Revolution*; Chatto & Windus, 1961
—— 'The Magic System' from *New Left Review*, No. 4; 1960
Wolf, H. 'A Designer's Dilemma in Mass Communication', from *Modern Publicity*; Studio Vista, 1968
Wollen, P. *Signs and Meanings in the Cinema*, Cinema One/Secker & Warburg; Indiana University Press, 1969
Young, F. H. *Techniques of Advertising Layout*; Partridge, 1947

Index of Authors Cited

Subject Index

Woman – *cont.*
  in popular imagination, 53, 63,
    71, 104, 148–82
  see also Actors; Expressions;
    Femininity; Hair; Psychol-
    ogy, female; Sexuality, female;
    Woman, images of
Woman and Home, see Magazines
Woman, images of
  career woman, 157–9
  hostess, 153, 156, 160, 172, 177

  mannequin, 153, 159, 160, 161,
    177
  narcissist, 60, 63, 64, 65, 69–71,
    137, 153–5, 160, 167, 177
  wife and mother, 72, 156–7, 175
Woman's Own, see Magazines
Women's liberation, 9, 72, 78–9,
    104, 108, 151, 157–8, 175, 177,
    179, 180–81
Wool, as product, 85, 89, 117, 126,
    171